DATE DUE

Demco, Inc. 38-293

LOCAL GOVERNMENT INNOVATION

LOCAL GOVERNMENT INNOVATION

ISSUES AND TRENDS IN PRIVATIZATION AND MANAGED COMPETITION

Edited by ROBIN A. JOHNSON
NORMAN WALZER

Q

QUORUM BOOKS
Westport, Connecticut • London

Library of Congress Cataloging-in-Publication Data

Local government innovation : issues and trends in privatization and managed
competition / edited by Robin A. Johnson and Norman Walzer.

    p. cm.

Includes bibliographical references and index.

ISBN 1–56720–382–5 (alk. paper)

    1. Public contracts—United States. 2. Municipal services—United States.
3. Public works—United States. 4. Privatization—United States. I. Johnson,
Robin A. II. Walzer, Norman.

HD3861.U6 C65 2000

352.5'38214'0973—dc21   00-028001

British Library Cataloguing in Publication Data is available.

Library of Congress Catalog Card Number: 00-028001

ISBN: 1–56720–382–5

First published in 2000

Quorum Books, 88 Post Road West, Westport, CT 06881
An imprint of Greenwood Publishing Group, Inc.
www.quorumbooks.com

Printed in the United States of America

Copyright Acknowledgment

Chapter 3 is adapted from E. S. Savas, *Privatization and Public-Private Partnerships*. New York, Seven Bridges Press, LLC, 2000. Used with permission from the
author.

Contents

Illustrations   vii
Preface   ix

1. Introduction and Overview   1
   Norman Walzer and Robin A. Johnson

PART I   Issues and Trends   15
2. The Evolution of Privatization Practices and Strategies   17
   Adrian Moore and Wade Hudson
3. Opportunities in Privatization and Outsourcing   37
   E. S. Savas

PART II   Operational Aspects   57
4. Selecting Services for Outsourcing   59
   John O'Looney
5. Structuring the Market for Service Delivery: A New Role
   for Local Government   85
   Mildred Warner
6. Providing Public Services through Long-Term
   Service Agreements   105
   Douglas Herbst and David Seader

7. The Role of Information Management in Making
   Competition Work   123
   Bridget M. Anderson
8. Impacts of Social Mandates in Contracting   141
   Margaret M. "Peg" Swanton

PART III   Results and Future Prospects   **167**

   9. Privatization and Managed Competition: Management Fad
      or Long-Term Systematic Change for Cities?   169
      Robin A. Johnson and Norman Walzer
10. Impact of Privatization and Managed Competition
    on Public Employees   191
    Christi Clark, Robin A. Johnson, and James L. Mercer
11. Impact on Public Organizational Structure and Behavior:
    Managed Competition and Privatization   211
    Ed Sizer
12. A Bold, Innovative Approach to Privatization: Lessons Learned
    from Atlanta   237
    Bill Campbell
13. How Far Can Privatization Go?   253
    John D. Donahue

Index   267
About the Editors and Contributors   273

Illustrations

TABLES

Table 2.1	Pitfalls of Performance Contracting and Strategies to Overcome Them	23
Table 2.2	Standard Performance Indicators	24
Table 2.3	Common Elements of Contract Monitoring Systems	31
Table 3.1	Local Government Services Contracted Out to Private Firms	39
Table 3.2	Summary of Before-and-After Studies of Contracting	43
Table 3.3	Twelve Steps in Contracting for Services	45
Table 3.4	Partial List of U.S. Government Corporations	48
Table 4.1	Key Technical Factors in Outsourcing Decisions	68
Table 5.1	Restructuring Cases by Form and Service Area	89
Table 5.2	Restructuring Complexity: Percent of Places Restructuring by Form and Service Area	99
Table 6.1	Long-Term Water/Wastewater Contracts Signed in 1997	113
Table 7.1	Iowa Department of Transportation, Pavement Markings ABC Results	127
Table 7.2	The Competition Cycle and Competition Tools Matrix	131
Table 7.3	Sample of Savings by Indianapolis	131
Table 7.4	Proposal Evaluation Criteria	135
Table 7.5	Sample: Savings Calculation	136

Table 7.6	Documents and Analysis Required throughout Competition Cycle	139
Table 9.1	Municipal Services with Largest Increase in Privatization, 1988–1997	172
Table 9.2	New Services Contracted, 1988–1997	173
Table 9.3	Municipal Services Most Likely to be Contracted, 1997	174
Table 9.4	Cities Studying the Feasibility of Adopting Privatization	176
Table 9.5	Trends in Involvement in Evaluation of Privatization	178
Table 12.1	Comparing the Bids for Atlanta's Water System	245

FIGURES

Figure 2.1	Success of Contracts with Varying Firm Autonomy	27
Figure 2.2	Jersey City Water Collections Incentives	28
Figure 5.1	Restructuring Factors, Average Level of Importance	91
Figure 7.1	ABC/M Implementation: Organization-Wide Approach	130
Figure 7.2	Preparation and Solicitation Cycle	134
Figure 8.1	The Feedback Loop	153
Figure 11.1	Organizational Chart Prior to September 1993	214
Figure 11.2	Organizational Chart Today	215
Figure 11.3	Impact of Competition on Number of Employees	220
Figure 11.4	Impact of Competition on Budget	221
Figure 11.5	Impact of Support/Service Employees	222
Figure 11.6	Competition Process Overview	228
Figure 11.7	Solid Waste Positions, FY94-FY99	231
Figure 12.1	Analytical Approach Frames Evaluation	242
Figure 12.2	Step Three: Best and Final Proposal Selection	244
Figure 13.1	Trends Since 1962 in Government Workers as Share of Population and Public Spending as Share of Gross Domestic Product	255

Preface

Privatization of public services has existed in many forms for decades. The fiscal austerity during the 1980s, however, caused city officials to find additional ways to provide services at a lower cost. Interest in privatization and contracting grew among city officials and private businesses that were interested in providing these services. Privatization was viewed as one of several management tools available to local governments.

With greater accountability being demanded and pressures on local public officials to maintain or reduce taxes, efforts to find innovative service delivery methods will probably increase. Cities such as Atlanta, Indianapolis, and Charlotte are examples showing that contracts with private businesses can work to benefit all parties concerned. Certainly, local officials must move ahead cautiously, and not all attempts at privatization or contracting have succeeded. Some cities, after an evaluation, have decided to provide services with municipal employees.

This book examines numerous issues related to privatization, managed competition, and contracting in cities. It is designed to objectively explore options available to local public officials in providing services. Many people have contributed to this project in various ways. Ms. Loleta Didrickson, former Comptroller, State of Illinois, sponsored much of the research on experiences in Illinois cities; Ken Alderson, Illinois Municipal League, sponsored several conferences at which the ideas were presented; and Lori Sutton and Nancy Baird, Illinois Institute for Rural Affairs, analyzed survey data and managed the manuscript preparation. Numerous local public officials shared experiences and answered questions about privatization efforts, and our appreciation is expressed to each of them. This book is dedicated to our families including Harlan, Delores, Frank, and Dawn Johnson and Dona, Steve, and Mark Walzer, for their love and support.

Introduction and Overview

Norman Walzer and Robin A. Johnson

For over twenty years, the public sector has come under increasingly close scrutiny as taxpayers have demanded greater accountability for public spending. Numerous examples of local and state initiatives or programs aimed at limiting tax or spending increases have been enacted. Some of these initiatives have resulted in adverse effects on service levels with critical services either not provided or underfunded because tax revenues were not available. In other cases, local and state agencies have found new ways to provide services with fewer revenues.

Local officials have responded to the imposition of tax caps, spending limits, and many other restrictions on public spending decisions in many ways—sometimes out of financial exigency but also in attempts to find better financing or management methods for delivering services. The search for efficiency in the public sector continues and has been brought about in many governments by continued efforts to introduce management practices and procedures used successfully in the private sector.

Numerous methods and approaches have been tried by public agencies over the years—some effective and others distant memories. Program Planning Budgeting Systems, Zero-Based Budgeting, Total Quality Management, and Activity-Based-Costing approaches, to just name a few, are all familiar to most local and state public officials. While different in specific format and approach, all were intended to find ways to deliver services in a more cost-effective manner and/or install more accountability with a product, namely public services, that is very difficult to quantify let alone measure.

In this way, government has some similarities with private companies. While some would argue that the two groups are completely different, both have gone through a variety of phases in which new management practices were tried. Some succeeded, some failed, and others were adapted to fit specific needs. In fact, some of the pressures on public agencies to try new budgeting and management approaches have come from successes in the private sector. Corporate executives and taxpayers alike expected public officials to keep pace with private businesses as they struggled to stay competitive.

Public agencies traditionally have felt less pressure for accountability because they enjoyed a sense of monopoly power and had the taxing power to generate required revenues. Many of the services provided are considered critical to the well-being of residents. For example, there is only one police or fire department to provide services in a city. As long as the service seemed effective, relatively little pressure was mounted to reduce costs or implement better management practices.

Most businesses, on the other hand, continually face new competitors trying to find new markets. They offer improved products, lower prices, better services, and expanded features to attract customers. Businesses have had to find ways to reduce costs in order to compete effectively with new firms. Improved management practices have been an important part of increasing the competitiveness of these companies.

The experiences of businesses in "tightening their belts" and becoming more efficient to meet competitive pressures have caused business leaders and taxpayers alike to demand similar actions by governments. Nationally, a major thrust arose in the early 1990s, under the title of Reinventing Government, to help public agencies adopt innovative approaches to determining markets, implement new management techniques, and otherwise become more efficient. Much of this initiative was created by the work of Osborne and Gaebler (1992). The national attention paid to these issues by Vice President Al Gore in the National Performance Review stimulated interest in many approaches, including privatization alternatives. In fact, the increased attention cemented interest in the issues by both Republicans, who are usually associated with private sector interests, and Democrats, who are traditionally seen as representing a labor constituency.

Governments have always bought services from companies and, for a long time, have hired private businesses to manage or deliver services through a contract. The pony express was one prominent, visible example of privatization from the nineteenth century, although it was not labeled as such at the time. Street and road construction and maintenance have often involved contracting with private builders. Because of the complexity and technical knowledge needed, water treatment has involved contractual arrangements between cities and private companies that can achieve significant economies of scale by providing this service. While these arrangements have existed for decades, and even centuries, the term privatization was not coined until the late 1960s by management expert Peter Drucker. Since that time, it has been seen as an integral part of the management toolbox used by local, state, and federal public officials.

PURPOSE OF THE BOOK

The growing importance of finding ways to control costs while maintaining high-quality public services has caused many cities to turn to various forms of privatization. Managed competition, in which public agencies compete with private agencies for an opportunity to provide services, has gained major attention because of successes in cities such as Indianapolis (Goldsmith 1997). Contracting with a private business to manage agencies that were formerly considered exclusively public responsibilities, such as airports, prisons, and schools, is now becoming a more common practice. It is even possible to find cities in which only a skeleton crew of public management employees exists with the vast majority of "public services" provided through contractual arrangements. For many years, city departments have served as profit centers by providing services to other cities (St. Paul, Fort Worth).

The collection of management practices used by cities and counties across the United States includes many different approaches, each aimed at addressing a specific concern. These approaches usually have a unique stamp, based on the management styles and attitudes of local public officials, city employees, and potential contractors. While it may be difficult for a local public official to replicate a process that has worked elsewhere, even in a city with similar characteristics, the general approach and principles that have been learned can be quite useful.

This book is intended to provide information on recent innovations in privatization and to address issues that have arisen as a result of these efforts. Leading scholars and practitioners who are familiar with contracting, privatization, managed competition, and other approaches describe the issues faced and the kinds of innovative approaches that have worked in cities. The contributors represent public and private agencies, academia, and think tanks. The result is a fairly comprehensive picture of current management practices used in privatization, spin-off strategies such as managed competition, and the important issues faced by officials that are crucial to long-term success.

A strength of subsequent discussions is the amount of in-depth information provided regarding recent innovative practices. Writers refer to specific practices and case studies that will help readers evaluate the practical experiences which local public officials and administrators have had with privatization approaches. While there is a large amount of literature dealing with the theory of privatization, this book provides readers with information on the practice of privatization, specifically detailing how it has evolved into an accepted management practice over the past twenty years.

Because of the large amount of experimentation with privatization efforts, many definitions of privatization can be found. In the simplest terms, *privatization* invariably means transferring responsibility for public services from government to the private sector in some fashion. The private sector can include nonprofit organizations, volunteers, and other public groups. It can also mean removing responsibility for a service entirely through the sale of a public asset to a private company. Alternatively, it can mean contracting for the provision of a service for a specific period of time while the public entity retains ultimate responsibility. This latter definition has come to symbolize privatization with the terms privatization and *contracting,* often used interchangeably. Subsequent discussions will adopt this definition.

Lack of a detailed understanding of privatization experiences has somewhat polarized various groups in discussions of the merits of specific privatization endeavors. Public employees, for instance, may express dismay at any mention of proposed privatization efforts, even when evidence suggests that they may come out ahead under private management or through managed competition. It is not uncommon for these groups to support certain types of private initiatives once they clearly see the potential benefits for them and feel comfortable that the proposed approaches will not be used to harm their positions.

At the same time, private agencies have argued that the "playing field" is not level—namely, that public agencies with which they must compete for the privilege of providing a service do not have to make a profit, receive favorable treatment in the evaluation process, pay taxes, or deal with a host of other factors. These groups may be reluctant to get involved in working for public agencies when a privatization or managed competition initiative is discussed.

In short, both groups need more and better information about privatization efforts and, in fact, that finding was one of the outcomes of a survey of municipal officials in Illinois which was given in 1995 (Johnson and Walzer 1996). Due to the experiences of the past decade, we now understand what works, what doesn't, and the long-term effects of these efforts on city management practices and services.

This book is intended to be of interest to three main audiences. Local and state public officials and administrators can learn some of the conceptual issues that must be addressed in implementing a privatization initiative and the approaches that seem to have worked elsewhere from their peers. No attempt in subsequent discussions is made to build a case for privatization. The experiences reported are described objectively, and potential users can decide whether the approach would work in their communities.

Because privatization approaches, in general, have gained such widespread interest in public administration circles, subsequent discussions should be of major interest in public administration classes and related forums. Students entering professional careers will, without question, engage in discussions about whether a public service should be provided by an in-house staff or whether a private agency should be asked to provide all, or part, of the service. Later discussions address many of the important issues involved in these decisions. Along the same lines, academics interested in conducting research into privatization as a management tool will find the discussions helpful in formulating and testing hypotheses.

In addition to public officials and students, informed voters, taxpayers, and those involved in evaluating public policies will find many of the discussions enlightening. Without question, privatization approaches will evolve as much or more in the future as they have in the past, and if they are effective they will continue to be used by local governments across the United States in new and innovative ways. Residents involved in local decisions must keep abreast of recent developments along these lines, and the discussions in this book can help.

OVERVIEW OF THE BOOK

The latest wave of privatization practices began in the late 1970s. While local officials experienced financial and administrative pressures arising from several sources, the main impetus leading officials to consider privatization was political. Prime Minister Margaret Thatcher's privatization efforts across the Atlantic created momentum in the United States to consider private sector alternatives to providing services. The election of Ronald Reagan as president in 1980 and the conservative movement to reduce the size of government also created a major impetus for putting privatization theory into practice.

Like most management reforms, privatization has some great success stories but also some significant failures. Without proper controls and oversight, privatization can create a monopoly condition, increase costs, and result in worse services than those that previously existed. With effective monitoring and oversight processes, however, privatization can achieve what its proponents say it can do—provide high-quality services at less cost to taxpayers.

While most of the focus on privatization has been at the federal level, local governments in specific cities have been at the forefront of innovative public-private partnerships during the past two decades. Because of the large number of cities involved and the diversity of approaches or techniques implemented, it is hard to quantify the number of services privatized, let alone the approaches used. City leaders—regardless of political party, ideology, or race—have fine-tuned privatization to meet their specific needs.

Privatization in cities has grown in recent years mainly through the latest wave of contracting with the private sector. Cities have shown a significant interest in contractual arrangements for solid waste collection and disposal during the past two decades, partly because of the financial problems faced in the 1980s and also because of the growing complexities involved in providing services.

Cities have always contracted for certain services. For example, cities outsource tree trimming because such services are not needed year-round. Contracting eliminates the need for full-time employees and increases efficiency by using such services only when needed. Avoiding the costs associated with fixed capital used relatively infrequently has encouraged city officials to contract with the private sector or cooperate with other governmental units to share equipment.

The latest trend has been long-term contracts for water and wastewater services. This trend has arisen mainly because of changes in federal regulations. Industry analysts, as well as some public officials, see water services as the next big growth area for privatization. These services must be provided on a regional basis in many cases, and high fixed costs for water facilities can foster cooperative efforts by neighboring governments or purchase of the services through a private firm that can incorporate economies of scale by serving several cities.

Cities are also increasing the scope of services for which they contract. Traditionally, cities have contracted "hard" services such as public works and some support services. Recent trends reveal that cities are privatizing more "soft" services such as those for health and human services. Often, these contracts are with nonprofit organizations, but there is some for-profit involvement. For example, cities now contract more for ambulance services because many private firms have been created to meet market demand. The advantages for the city are the abilities to transfer the personnel costs, especially employee benefits, to the private sector and to avoid the downtime costs associated with personnel and equipment. A private agency that serves a large regional area can spread these costs more effectively than a single city. The trend toward contracting a larger variety of services has also occurred at the state and federal levels, most likely reflecting greater experience with contracting practices and procedures.

Privatization in specific cities has been examined in recent years (Bissinger 1997; Goldsmith 1997; Norquist 1998), and much has been written about practices and principles (Donahue 1989; Savas 2000), but less has been written about how recent innovations in privatization approaches have changed the way that cities function and where privatization efforts may lead in the future. In fact, little may even be known about some of the recent innovations themselves.

Indeed, readers may be surprised to see how privatization has evolved over the years. In the past, proponents and opponents of privatization often resorted to tired phrases regarding the proper role of government and the private sector in providing services. Discussions in this book show how innovative local public officials have changed the nature of privatization and partnerships to fit local needs.

Officials from the private sector cheer the growth of contracting but usually express hesitation at some of the changes and requirements used in the bidding process. Public sector officials have overcome many of their fears of losing control by including performance standards in contracts but still declare contracting off-limits for certain services such as police protection. Academics will be interested in the way that public and private sector officials are merging their interests to create new opportunities for partnerships.

It appears safe to say that privatization has lost some of its ideological zeal in the past ten years. Pragmatic officials from the Democratic Party, such as Mayors Ed Rendell of Philadelphia, Richard Daley of Chicago, and Bill Campbell of Atlanta, have adapted contracting to meet the specific needs of their constituencies. Each city has contracted for certain services and each went about the process differently, but all three emerged with successful stories to tell.

On the flip side of the political coin, Mayor Stephen Goldsmith of Indianapolis showed how a Republican big-city mayor can change the service delivery paradigm. Goldsmith led the charge to allow unionized public employees to compete for contracts. The results have been impressive, with public employees winning many contracts, better quality of services, and hundreds of millions of dollars in savings. Some cities have put these savings into priorities such as police protection.

This book is divided into three main sections. The first section examines the most recent research on competition and privatization at the local level and traces the evolution of these management approaches. In "The Evolution of Privatization Practices and Strategies," Adrian Moore and Wade Hudson trace the evolving definition of privatization and show how the approaches developed by cities vary according to specific issues to be addressed in a public-private partnership. Even a few years ago, many of these ventures would not have been considered. City governments are sometimes involved in joint ventures with private agencies such as through the Build-Operate-Transfer or Build-Own-Operate models used in infrastructure programs.

As different approaches to privatization have brought governments more and more into managing operations, a need has grown for more sophisticated management systems. Performance-based strategies have been adopted by public agencies as they seek to make sure that a high level of performance is provided by the private business with which they are involved. Including performance measures as part of the negotiating process increases the likelihood that city residents will receive high-quality output from the contracting agency.

Moore and Hudson explore some of the reasons why private agencies have been able to perform well under the contracts and provide other

examples of ways in which city government involvement may enhance successful performance. They also explore the role of incentives in contract
management.

In "Opportunities in Privatization and Outsourcing," E. S. Savas provides specific examples of privatization efforts in cities around the world
and describes the overall effects that have been achieved. Changing attitudes toward the appropriate role(s) of government have created opportunities for new and expanded interactions with private agencies, not only in
the United States, but worldwide. Many innovative approaches have been
attempted with significant successes. According to Savas, the corner has
been turned with little, if any, likelihood that contracting will be reduced in
the future.

Savas argues that the next major services to be addressed include government-
owned enterprises, infrastructure, and social insurance. Many components
of these operations, such as the postal service, have begun privatization
efforts in various regions of the United States. If these ventures succeed, it
only makes sense that they will expand to other operations. Savas further
contends that the changing political climate will provide a setting to propel
privatization efforts further into the future, not only in terms of the current
types of activities but also into new service delivery arrangements.

The second major section of the book includes discussions of various
operational aspects of contracting arrangements. Not all public services are
suitable for contracting, and it is important that city officials understand the
key characteristics of the services that can be successfully contracted. A conservative attitude toward government's role in providing services combined
with efforts by taxpayers to contain tax increases can pressure local officials
to privatize services that, for many reasons, may not be appropriate.

In "Selecting Services for Outsourcing," John O'Looney provides a list of
important factors that should be considered by public officials in identifying services that can be outsourced to the private sector. In particular, he
argues that privatization decisions involve three types of issues: political,
economic, and managerial or organizational questions. He emphasizes that
the selection process is more than ideology; rather, it should be a decision
based on sound business practices for both the city government and the private contractor. Cost-benefit studies should be undertaken, for example.

O'Looney also argues that the timing of decisions is important. Local
public managers must analyze the phase of development or cycle of the service delivery. At some phases, outsourcing might be suitable, while it may
not be appropriate at other phases. The amount and type of contract management by city officials that is needed to make the outsourcing arrangement functional are important aspects of the service selection procedure.

A reading of the literature on privatization might cause one to think that
governments are mainly shedding services, either by selling private assets or
by long-term contracts with private companies. Actually, the situation is

much more complex, with the role of governments in the overall service delivery system being restructured and, in some cases, being redefined as public agencies actually compete with private companies in delivering certain services.

In "Structuring the Market for Service Delivery: A New Role for Local Government," Mildred Warner examines the restructuring process and shows how many governments have become entrepreneurial in nature and are, in some instances, generating revenues to support other city services through this process. Likewise, some governments, after experience with outsourcing and careful examination, have decided to provide the service with public employees. Either a decision to outsource or a decision to bring the service back into government represents an effort by the government to find an arrangement that provides a high-quality service at the lowest cost.

Using data from a recent survey of local governments in New York state, Warner examines ways in which governments have restructured the service delivery system, including interagency agreements, privatization or outsourcing, reverse privatization, governmental entrepreneurship, and discontinuing services. She proceeds to identify major factors underlying the decisions to deliver the services under a specific arrangement. A key factor identified is the opportunity to achieve economies of scale through interagency cooperation or through contracts with private businesses serving multiple governments. There are instances, however, when a need to gain greater control over the service delivery or to enhance the quality of services has caused governments to "deprivatize" specific services.

Many discussions of privatization alternatives focus on the short-term and involve a limited part of the overall service. At the same time, one must realize that some services, such as water provision, have been provided by private agencies (usually regulated) for decades. The question then arises, "Could long-term agreements with private agencies be used to provide city services?"

In "Providing Public Services through Long-Term Service Agreements," Douglas Herbst and David Seader examine recent experiences that cities have had with hiring companies to operate and manage water systems using long-term contracts and the issues that have arisen. One stimulus for greater interest in these long-term arrangements was that, in 1997, the Internal Revenue Service (IRS Revenue Procedure 97-13) lengthened the amount of time that management contracts for public utility property could be in effect and changed allowable methods of contract remuneration. Since the public utility definition includes water and wastewater treatment systems, the door was opened for long-term arrangements with private companies to manage these systems for cities. This approach has been adopted by some cities already and is under consideration by many others.

Under the new arrangements, cities can shift a significant portion of expensive service delivery to private agencies with appropriate levels of expertise and management capacity. The private company, on the other hand, by working with multiple governments, can capture economies of scale and thereby bid the service at a lower cost to taxpayers. Using a Design-Build-Operate approach adds a new dimension to the privatization process that, under the right circumstances, can be attractive to public officials and residents.

As city officials become more involved in the privatization process, especially in contract management, they face more complex management decisions. These decisions require more sophisticated data systems, which are oftentimes not currently available in cities. Traditional line-item budgets were not especially suited to cost-accounting principles; yet when a contract is being bid for a service, local officials must know what the service currently costs to provide.

Bridget M. Anderson, in "The Role of Information Management in Making Competition Work," examines the increasing role of information management in making privatization or managed competition work. In particular, she argues that Activity-Based-Costing/Management programs and the ability to conduct performance audits are key to successfully managing contracts with private agencies. These approaches will represent new efforts in many cities, especially those with limited capacities in terms of staff expertise. Fortunately, opportunities exist for cities to access software programs and training to introduce many of these concepts into their management operations. In fact, the time may come when a city will contract with a consulting-management firm to manage contracts with businesses for service delivery.

Anderson shows the potential cost-savings that can result from contracts for specific services and also illustrates the steps in the process that can lead to effective management of these efforts. She points out that providing services through contracts with companies may also involve changes in the organizational operation or administrative rules of the city. The bottom line, however, is that cities must have detailed and accurate information about the quantity and quality of services delivered by contractors and must know how these costs compare with in-house costs to provide similar services. This information has not always been available to local officials in the past.

Certainly, one of the reasons for a city to engage in privatization is to simplify operations by contracting for services that city employees find difficult to provide or cannot provide at a competitive cost. At the same time, however, cities try to remedy social problems through service delivery. Making sure that low-income residents live in healthy surroundings, have adequate housing, and have access to affordable education are issues that many cities consider in designing service delivery.

Conflicts can arise, however, when cities impose social mandates on service providers who also are being asked to deliver services at a competitive cost. While these conflicting objectives—low cost and social mandates—are valid, they make the privatization management process more difficult and raise important issues for local officials to consider.

In "Impacts of Social Mandates in Contracting," Margaret M. "Peg" Swanton examines the role of the social mandates and how they have been used in contracting for city services. Specifically, she raises the question of the effectiveness of social mandates when used in the privatization setting. A case can be made that additional reporting requirements, delays in processing, and other factors can add substantially to the costs experienced by contractors. Measuring the effectiveness of social mandates is always difficult but becomes even more important in a contracting environment in which bids submitted must be performance-based.

While there is little question that social issues must be addressed by city governments, Swanton raises the issue of whether addressing these concerns explicitly through the contracting process represents the best approach. In effect, the same rigor used to evaluate bids by private companies to provide public services should be used to evaluate the effectiveness of the procedure for delivering social mandates.

The third section of the book examines the overall effects of privatization approaches on local governments of different sizes. The discussions in this section are more empirically based with a focus on specific groups of cities that have been relatively innovative in their approaches. Managed competition and privatization are the main issues covered in the cities studied.

In "Privatization and Managed Competition: Management Fad or Long-Term Systematic Change for Cities?," Robin A. Johnson and Norman Walzer explore trends in privatization and managed competition in United States cities based on data from a 1997 survey conducted by the International City/County Management Association (ICMA). Trends in service delivery approaches are examined in an attempt to determine how privatization efforts in cities changed during the 1990s. They also discuss the management approaches used by local public officials in monitoring managed competition and/or contracts with businesses and changes in decision-making strategies.

Respondents to the ICMA survey reported the types of challenges they see arising as they become more involved in privatization activities. Certainly, gaining and retaining the support of public employees is key to the success of privatization activities. Finally, Johnson and Walzer examine how city officials have evaluated the success, or lack thereof, of privatization efforts. Citizen surveys, on-site inspections, and a variety of other activities were reported in the survey.

Concerns by public employees remain the most explosive and sensitive issue for local officials to address when considering privatization. A natural apprehension exists for municipal employees when they hear that substantial changes in service delivery procedures are coming and that these changes could dramatically affect their working conditions. Horror stories circulate and resentment builds in this type of environment when, in fact, there are probably as many or more situations in which employees have worked in cooperation with the privatization initiative and were better off in the new environment.

In "Impact of Privatization and Managed Competition on Public Employees," Christi Clark, Robin A. Johnson, and James L. Mercer show that many public officials involved in a privatization endeavor have worked with employees impacted by privatization to make sure that they are treated fairly. Some cities empower employees by helping them compete for contracts while others include employee protections in the Request for Proposals (RFPs). In some instances, employees have found that by working for a private company, they have access to better employment advancement opportunities within a larger organization. Perhaps the most direct evidence is when employees support continuation of the privatization initiative in a city or when a public unit of a city government competes successfully with a private company.

While employee opposition remains the leading hurdle to privatization in most cases, Clark, Johnson, and Mercer demonstrate that, increasingly, city officials are attempting to overcome this opposition through progressive policies towards employees. In fact, for privatization efforts to succeed, the hurdle posed by employee acceptance must be resolved satisfactorily by both parties. The increased attention paid to employee concerns could be one of the most significant differences in how cities approach privatization now as compared with twenty years ago. The authors suggest that involving employees early in the process is key as is providing opportunities for employees to make suggestions about ways to improve the overall service delivery process. City governments can play a major role in preparing employees to effectively participate in, and benefit from, privatization efforts.

The fact that privatization, as one of a variety of approaches, has moved ahead and is likely to be a permanent service delivery alternative used by cities leads to the question of what has been the effect of these approaches on cities. The answer to this question depends on the privatization approach used as well as the institutional or organizational structure of the city affected. Most likely, the impacts on the city are determined by the capacity of the city to accept these changes and its ability to respond by making the privatization efforts succeed.

Ed Sizer, in "Impact on Public Organizational Structure and Behavior: Managed Competition and Privatization," examines the impact of managed competition and privatization in the city of Charlotte, North Carolina, a leader in managed competition during the 1990s. He describes the process used by city officials to evaluate the appropriate roles for city government in providing services, how services should be financed, and what the most efficient delivery mechanism is for service delivery. The managed competition in Charlotte is a model site because it saved $5.1 million by reducing 272 positions with no layoffs. Through innovations, employees were able to save an additional $2.8 million. The administrative complexity of the city government was reduced substantially, and a customer service center was created.

Sizer illustrates the implementation of management practices described in earlier chapters. Having employees see their roles as asset managers with a responsibility to deliver essential services is an important consideration. Understanding competition for service delivery and knowing the internal costs of providing these services are key considerations. Focusing on customer (taxpayer) interests is an important management consideration in Charlotte and in virtually any successful operation.

The city of Atlanta is an excellent example of the changes that have occurred in privatization practices during the past twenty years. Last year, Atlanta became the largest city in the nation to privatize its water services. The agreement included many innovative practices during the proposal, competition, and awarding stages that are outlined by Atlanta Mayor Bill Campbell in "A Bold, Innovative Approach to Privatization: Lessons Learned from Atlanta." Campbell describes several lessons that the city has learned from water privatization efforts. He stresses that a businesslike approach, with integrity throughout, is crucial in organizational efforts and in making the privatization project run smoothly. The public interest must be protected and the process itself must be trusted. The fate of all groups involved in the negotiations must be addressed. Campbell frankly and directly examines the issues involved in privatization and the reasons why more cities will emulate Atlanta's example in the future.

The book concludes with a look into the future of privatization and where innovative service delivery practices may lead. As reported in the third chapter of the book by Savas, privatization is so well-established that it will remain an accepted system for delivering public services. Probably few would deny the truth of that statement. Privatization approaches have broadened into new areas, and new strategies have been implemented. One might expect these trends to continue.

In "How Far Can Privatization Go?," John Donahue takes an interesting and insightful look into some directions that privatization is likely to take in the future. Readers will find many of these insights provocative as well as informational. Among the trends identified are continued public sector reform that will make governments leaner and more customer-driven. Because much of the early stimulus for privatization efforts came from fiscal austerity, it follows that more prosperous economic times may bring reduced pressure for similar efforts in the future. At the same time, however, successful experiences with privatization attempts may reinforce these approaches in the minds of public officials.

Positive attitudes and confidence in the ability of governments to provide services efficiently are also important considerations. If the confidence in government grows more rapidly than that in business, one might see privatization efforts slow. Of course, the converse could also be true, and this confidence can be related to many factors unrelated to the success of privatization.

Advances in technology, especially information technology, may provide new opportunities for public–private partnerships and should allow public agencies to manage existing contracts better. It is difficult to predict the overall effect of telecommunications, computerization, and the host of other technological advances currently underway. Donahue suggests that these advances will open new opportunities for privatization.

CONCLUSION

Privatization, like many management trends before it, is not a panacea for all governmental problems. It can work in some cases but may not in others. Interested public officials must be aware that management policies are needed to ensure a successful privatization effort. These policies are changing and adapting to different circumstances in jurisdictions across the nation and even the world.

Privatization as a service delivery approach has evolved during this latest phase since the 1970s to something different from what original proponents developed. It will continue to change in the future to meet ever-growing and changing needs. Critics from both the pro-privatization and pro-government sides disagree with different aspects of the latest trends. The bottom line, however, remains that whatever form privatization takes, either in its purest sense or as managed competition, the ultimate test is whether citizens receive quality services at a cost-effective price. In that sense, at least, privatization, in many cases and in its recent forms, seems to have succeeded.

REFERENCES

Bissinger, Buzz. 1997. *A prayer for the city.* New York: Random House.
Donahue, John D. 1989. *The privatization decision: Public ends, private means.* New York: Basic Books.
Goldsmith, Stephen. 1997. *The twenty-first century city: Resurrecting urban America.* Washington, DC: Regnery Publishing.
Johnson, Robin A., and Norman Walzer. 1996. *Competition for city services: Has the time arrived? Privatization in Illinois municipalities.* Springfield: Illinois Office of the Comptroller.
Norquist, John O. 1998. *The wealth of cities: Revitalizing the centers of American life.* Reading, MA: Addison-Wesley.
Osborne, David, and Ted Gaebler. 1992. *Reinventing government: How the entrepreneurial spirit is transforming the public sector.* Reading, MA: Addison-Wesley.
Savas, E. S. 2000. *Privatization and public-private partnerships.* New York: Chatham House.

PART I

Issues and Trends

The Evolution
of Privatization Practices
and Strategies

Adrian Moore and Wade Hudson

Current trends in the field of privatization denote not only widespread acceptance but a maturation as well. As governments have gained experience and experimented with a variety of privatization techniques, ranging from public-private partnerships to asset sales, they have become more sophisticated in their use of complex strategies and techniques. The experiments expanded the bounds of what we consider to be privatization, and the experience has lent itself to greater use of performance contracts, public-private competitions, and similar practices often considered to be "best practices."

Getting a firm handle on municipal government's use of complex strategies and techniques is an exercise in frustration. As with other privatization issues, the data are sparse. Most government surveys of privatization focus on what is being privatized and why.[1] Data on complex implementation and strategic practices continue to lag behind due to the sheer number of municipal government agencies and an absence of any formal reporting system. Most of the data collections have not been systematic and were collected by various organizations focusing on a range of issues. We are left to piece together what we can from continuous observation of case studies and interviews with municipal officials.

This chapter focuses on the evolution of complex and cutting-edge techniques and practices that are shaping the future of privatization. We begin by exploring how the definition of privatization, or rather the collection of actions that fall under a broad definition of privatization, has evolved in recent years as new structures have been fit into the continuum between pure private and pure public provision. We proceed to examine how contracting practices are evolving, with particular focus on performance-based contracting, how it works or does not, and an initial assessment of best practices by city governments. Finally, we explore the evolving art and science of contract management—monitoring and evaluating contract performance.

THE EVOLVING DEFINITION OF PRIVATIZATION

The definition of privatization has become an indicator of evolution in techniques and practices. Privatization in its most traditional form referred solely to public sector divestiture of assets and service responsibilities, allowing the private sector to take over all aspects of service and service delivery. Early categorizations of privatization techniques, such as Savas (1987), still capture most of the privatization techniques practiced by municipal governments.

Time brings even more frequent examples that don't fit the traditional mold. For example, the joint-venture structure used in privatizing some county and state hospitals (Tradewell 1998) and some federal historic buildings (USGAO 1999a). Two forces seem to be driving experimentation with new privatization techniques and, hence, the evolutionary process of sustaining those that work:

1. In some cities, private contractors and municipal agencies have grown more comfortable with privatization and more certain of their abilities over the years. Confidence in their understanding of the bidding and award process, and their ability to work with private partners to achieve common goals, while maintaining policy control, makes municipal officials more willing to experiment.

2. A broadening scope of services are being privatized. When contracting for child adoption services, environmental remediation, or other complex or technical services, private contractors and municipal officials are more likely to build complex project structures to ensure control and results. Similarly, greater private involvement in providing infrastructure has entailed the mixing of public and private capital and concomitant financial complexity.

Experimentation and increasing complexity have helped create new forms of privatization that fit into the continuum between pure private and pure public provision. Privatization in its modern usage has come to embrace a wider range of practices from traditional asset sales and contracting for services to emerging forms of public-private partnerships and corporatization. A revised categorization, which is only complete until another innovation evolves, includes the following:

- *Asset Sale or Long-Term Lease.* The government sells or enters into long-term leases for assets such as airports, gas utilities, or real estate to private firms, thus turning physical capital into financial capital. In a sale-leaseback arrangement, a government agency sells the asset to a private sector entity and then leases it back. Another asset sale technique is an employee buyout. Existing public managers and employees take the public unit private, typically purchasing the company through an Employee Stock Ownership Plan (ESOP) (Gibbon 1996).

- *Contracting Out (Also Called "Outsourcing")*. The government competitively contracts with a private organization—for-profit or nonprofit—to provide a service or part of a service.

- *Corporatization*. Government organizations are reorganized along business lines. They are required to pay taxes, raise capital on the market (with no government backing—explicit or implicit), and operate according to commercial principles. Government corporations focus on maximizing profits and achieving a favorable return on investment. They are freed from government procurement, personnel, and budget systems (Bale and Dale 1998; Chang and Jones 1992; Spicer, Emanuel, and Powell 1996; USGAO 1998).

- *Franchise*. A private firm is given an exclusive right to provide a service within a specified geographical area.

- *Internal Markets*. Departments are allowed to purchase support services such as printing, maintenance, computer repair, and training from in-house providers or outside suppliers. In-house providers of support services are required to operate as independent business units competing against outside contractors for each department's business. Under such a system, market forces are brought to bear within an organization. Internal customers can reject the offerings of internal service providers if they don't like their quality or if they cost too much (Eggers 1997a, 29–30).

- *Joint Venture*. Government and private sector agencies form a joint board of directors to control asset management and service delivery and share responsibility for policy and management decisions. Assets may be owned by the government or by a new private firm. Operations and service delivery may be contracted to the private partner or jointly provided (Tradewell 1998, 25–29).

- *Management Contracts*. The operation of a facility is contracted out to a private company. Facilities in which the management is frequently contracted out include airports, wastewater plants, arenas, and convention centers.

- *Private Infrastructure Development and Operation*. The private sector builds, finances, and operates public infrastructure such as roads and airports, recovering costs through user charges. Several techniques are commonly used for privately building and operating infrastructure:

  - *Build-Operate-Transfer (BOT)*. The private sector designs, finances, builds, and operates the facility over the life of the contract. At the end of this period, ownership reverts to the government. A variation of this is the Build-Transfer-Operate (BTO) model, under which the title transfers to the government when construction is completed.

  - *Build-Own-Operate (BOO)*. The private sector retains permanent ownership and operates the facility on contract.

- *Public-Private Partnerships.* The public sector works along with the private and nonprofit sectors to provide services to a community. By teaming with the private and nonprofit sectors, agencies can benefit from each sector's special strengths, share risk, and minimize weaknesses.

- *Self-Help.* Community groups and neighborhood organizations take over a service or government asset such as a local park. The new providers of the service also directly benefit from the service. Frequently, the mechanism for self-help is a transfer of service delivery to a nonprofit organization. Governments increasingly are discovering that by turning some noncore services (e.g., zoos, museums, fairs, remote parks, and some recreational programs) over to nonprofit organizations, they can ensure that these institutions don't drain the budget.[2]

- *Volunteers.* Volunteers are used to provide all or part of a government service. Volunteer activities are conducted through a government volunteer program or through a nonprofit organization (Kessler and Wartell 1996).

- *Vouchers.* Government pays for the service; however, individuals are given redeemable certificates to purchase the service on the open market. These payments subsidize the consumer of the service, yet services are provided by the private sector. In addition to providing greater freedom of choice, vouchers bring consumer pressure to bear, creating incentives for consumers to shop around for services and for service providers to supply high-quality, low-cost services (Hall and Eggers 1995).

EVOLVING APPROACHES TO PRIVATIZATION AS A POLICY TOOL

As municipal governments gained experience and familiarity with privatization, they began to reevaluate their role and the nature of contracting. Often, they have come to view their role as one of ensuring that services are provided rather than that of actually providing services. This philosophical or attitudinal change has had many names, but we prefer to call it the purchaser-provider split. When the purchaser and provider are split, policy and regulatory functions are separated from service delivery and compliance functions and transformed into separate and distinct organizations.

The purchaser-provider split is central to government reforms in Australia, Great Britain, and New Zealand (Great Britain has uncoupled three-fourths of its civil service, while in New Zealand the percentage is more than 90%) and is becoming more prevalent in U.S. government management.[3] The goal is to free policy advisors to advance policy options that are in the public's best interest but may be contrary to the self-interests of the department. For example, a central problem with government organizations is "agency capture." This refers to the tendency of service departments to capture the policy advice process from policymakers and top managers, using this power to recommend themselves as service providers and to bias policy advice towards increasing the size of their budgets.[4]

Splitting policy functions from service delivery creates incentives for governments to become more discriminating consumers by also looking beyond government monopoly providers to a wide range of public and private providers. Uncoupling is also designed to reduce the conflicting objectives that arise when the same agency is involved in service delivery, regulation, and compliance. Both facets are a central foundation of the approach used by the city of Indianapolis in privatization and public-private partnerships.[5] For example, one department regulates businesses and residential dwellings while another is charged with eliminating unnecessary regulations. Similarly, the sole mission of an Enterprise Development group is to inject competition into government wherever possible and monitor public and private providers on an arm's-length basis.

By revising their role as a purchaser instead of a provider of services, municipal officials strive to refocus on their primary objective of providing the highest quality service at the lowest possible cost. In pursuit of these goals, agencies have begun to shift their attention away from input oriented contracts that emphasize methods of operation, number of employees, and hours of operation and concentrate instead on output/outcome-based contracts, more commonly known as performance-based contracting.

EVOLVING CONTRACTS—FEE FOR SERVICE TO PERFORMANCE-BASED CONTRACTING

Many municipal governments are fundamentally rethinking the way they contract out services. Previously, contracts tended to emphasize inputs: procedures, processes, wages to be paid, amount or type of equipment, or time and labor used. Performance-based contracting, on the other hand, is an output/outcome-based approach to contracting (Behn and Kant 1999; Eggers 1997a). Performance contracts clearly spell out the desired result expected of the contractor, but the manner in which the work is to be performed is left to the contractor's discretion. Contractors are given as much freedom as possible in finding ways to best meet the government's performance objective: "A performance contract is one that focuses on the outputs, quality and outcomes of service provision and may tie at least a portion of a contractor's payment as well as any contract extension or renewal to their achievement" (Martin 1999, 8).

Behn and Kant (1999) point out that performance contracting is ". . . one of the latest trends in public management" (471). While Smith and Lipsky (1993) argue that performance-based contracts have proliferated ". . . as the contracting regime has evolved" (91). As municipal governments expand their use of privatization, pressure increases to ensure results, control outcomes, and avoid problems. Performance-based contracts have emerged as a state-of-the-art contracting tool to give government managers better control over contractors and greater assurances of accountability.

Along with the increased autonomy that performance-based contracts give to contractors comes greater accountability for delivering the predetermined sets of outputs and/or outcomes. For example, several cities and states (Indianapolis, New York, Connecticut) contract with a private company called America Works to place welfare recipients in jobs. America Works is paid approximately $5,000 for each person placed in a private-sector job; however, it receives no payment for the time it puts into training, counseling, and job searching for clients unless they are placed in a job for at least six months.

By measuring a contractor's performance against a clear standard, performance contracting shifts the emphasis from a focus on process to a focus on product. Government's management role changes from prescribing and monitoring inputs to collecting and generating the results-based data needed to measure the impact of the work performed.

Unfortunately, using performance-based contracts does not create a trouble free paradise. Pitfalls remain both in the transition to performance-based service delivery and in implementation. Developing performance measures and ways to quantify them are works in progress for most municipal governments.[6] Siegal (1999, 370) reports that the ICMA data show that less than half of municipal governments even evaluate their service delivery. Performance-based contracting only works when based on relevant and quantifiable performance measures; therefore, a first step is evaluating the objectives of a given service and figuring out how to assess success and failure. Most cities are at best still reaching that first step.

Even after municipal officials have performance measures in hand, implementing performance-based contracts can be challenging. Officials must choose services which are suitable to performance-based contracts and must devise ways to tie payment to performance. As Behn and Kant (1999) argue, and indeed document, performance contracting is not a magic wand—it can be done well or poorly. They provide a nicely illustrated set of ten pitfalls that can, and do, befall officials who implement performance-based contracts without caution. More useful, they also provide a series of strategies for avoiding or overcoming those pitfalls (Table 2.1).

If performance-based contracts are no panacea, they still represent the cutting-edge of contracting best practices. Examining the practices and policies of governments who successfully use performance-based contracts gives us a sense of where the trends are going. This is a field of government management in which borrowing and imitation are rampant—everyone wants to copy performance measures and incentive schemes from someone who has already gone through the painful process of analysis and, sometimes, trial and error.

Table 2.1
Pitfalls of Performance Contracting and Strategies to Overcome Them

Ten Pitfalls
 1. Performance contracting may inhibit experimentation.
 2. Performance contracting may encourage innovation in cost cutting but not inservice delivery.
 3. Performance contracting may stifle overachievement.
 4. Performance contracting may not provide for start-up costs.
 5. Performance contracting may inhibit symbiotic relationships.
 6. Performance contracting may reward promises not performance.
 7. Performance contracting must rely on outputs not outcomes.
 8. Performance contracting uses measures that can distort behavior.
 9. Performance contracting may encourage creaming [cream-skimming].
10. Performance contracting may undermine equity and fairness.

Eight Strategies to Avoid Them
 1. Understand the relationship and difference between the mission and the message.
 2. Create contracts based on outputs that are (a) linked to the mission; (b) easy to measure, understand, and reproduce; and (c) facilitate benchmarking.
 3. Start simple and ratchet up.
 4. Monitor frequently lots of indicators of performance.
 5. Be prepared to learn, change, improve, and learn some more.
 6. Work collaboratively—not adversarially—with contractors.
 7. Pay vendors not just for the final output but for significant, well-defined progress.
 8. Favor contractors with a track record.

Source: Behn and Kant 1999.

When Are Municipal Governments Using Performance-Based Contracts?

In some sense, the answer is all over the map. Municipal governments use performance-based standards in contracts for a broad range of services from the more mundane such as trash collection and vehicle towing, to the more challenging such as social services.

In particular, the answer often depends on the process of developing performance measures. Some services are easier to measure than others. For example, with a water or wastewater treatment utility, drinking water and discharge standards imposed by state and federal environmental regulators provide a useful set of outcome measures. The city of Milwaukee tied performance payments to discharge standards when it privatized the operation of its water utility in 1998. If the private operator fails to meet standards, it is out of compliance with the contract and pays a penalty, but if the operator exceeds standards, it earns a bonus payment. In the first year of operation, the operator exceeded standards and earned a $50,000 bonus (Moore 1999).

Performance measures can go beyond water-quality standards. In 1996, Jersey City privatized operations in its water utility, and one goal was to improve bill collections. By letting the firm keep an escalating percentage of increases in collections, the city increased collections performance from 66 percent to 83 percent in two years (Eggers 1997a, 13).

The challenge is much greater with other services such as running the city jail or providing drug treatment programs. With a jail, it is easy enough to measure some policy and procedure compliance, but the main performance concern is preventing negative events such as escapes, riots, or assaults. It is hard to tie performance payments to preventing something that is already (hopefully) rare, and there are few positive events with which to tie per-formance measures in jails. That doesn't make it impossible, however. The American Correctional Association and the Federal Bureau of Prisons are working to develop performance measures for correctional operations. Some examples exist. For example, Australia uses performance contracts for its privatized prisons, and Connecticut bid out contracts to provide juvenile corrections services using performance-based contracts in 1999.

How Are Municipal Governments Developing Performance Measures?

From these and other examples, we can begin to assess typical prac-tices and some trends in how municipal governments are devising per-formance standards for privatizing services. Table 2.2 gives the general types of performance measures observed in practice. The following are typical techniques:

- *Borrowing.* The easiest way to develop performance measures is to copy them from some other city, county, or state government that has already worked through the details. Indianapolis, a pioneer in performance-based contracts, is a

Table 2.2
Standard Performance Indicators

- Quality Measures
- Customer Satisfaction
- Productivity
- Costs
- Continuous Improvement

---

frequent source of imitation. Borrowing has the advantage of capitalizing on success and avoiding repeated errors; it is a natural outcome of the evolutionary nature of performance-based contracting.

- *Benchmarking.* Even when performance measures are at hand, if there is no history of levels of services nor data to construct it from, municipal officials may have a difficult time deciding where the bar ought to be for each performance measure. One way around this is to use benchmarks. Municipal transit systems often use this method (Foote 1999). With even more challenging services—the city jail, for example—officials might follow the lead of Australia and Connecticut and select a set of other city jails to benchmark the private operator against. Part of the payment can be tied to meeting or exceeding a set of performance measures derived from averages of the benchmarked jails (Moore 1998).

- *Collective Creation.* Rather than going it alone, many municipal governments tap professional associations representing government officials. On a macro level, that is what the ICMA project is about, and its web site includes performance measures for a few services. Other efforts are underway as well; the American Correctional Association project was mentioned earlier, and similar programs are aimed at road maintenance and information technology (IT).

- *Tapping the Private Sector.* Often private service providers have experience with performance-based contracts or even performance measurement programs in the governments that hire them. Municipal officials can take advantage of that experience and have the bidders help them develop performance measures. For example, the request for proposals can stipulate that the contract will be performance-based and ask the bidders to propose a set of measures. If the measures are given points in the quality or best value evaluation of the bids, bidders will compete to provide the most attractive set of measures. Best of all, in the negotiation phase, the city can integrate the best of all the proposed performance measures; however, this method is limited by the bidders' incentive to make performance measures as easy on them as possible.

An example that combines realization of the purchaser-provider split and the process of defining service goals and performance measures occurred in Indianapolis during a restructuring of transit services. The city wanted to lower costs and increase service in its mass transit agency, and originally it had planned to simply contract out existing bus services. However, city officials soon discovered that, despite three decades of providing bus service, no one had ever really asked what public interest the transit agency was supposed to satisfy.

After asking this question, it became apparent that the real goal of the agency was to manage mobility in the regional marketplace, especially for low-income and physically dependent residents. In response, the city put out a bid for a firm to act as a "mobility manager," whose task it was to expand services to the transit dependent, with responsibilities including redesigning and rebidding various government-subsidized forms of transportation. The winning firm helped the city cut costs by one-third, saving $3 million while expanding service by 500,000 rides (Eggers 1997b, 110).

Given a means for developing performance measures, another consideration that municipal governments apply to determining which services are
appropriate for performance-based contracts is their comfort with granting
the contractor considerable autonomy. Surveys of privatization decisions
consistently show that loss of control is a leading reason for *not* privatizing. Moving from a standard contract services arrangement to a performance basis with increased contractor autonomy would likely encounter similar resistance. Sufficient comfort with the performance measures and
incentive structure in hand may help balance that resistance.

Comfort level is crucial because contractor autonomy is central to the
success and evolution of performance-based contracting. One reason that
governments do not operate as efficiently and effectively as the private sector is the public sector's myriad of hiring and firing procedures. If they are
to achieve cost-savings and productivity gains, contractors must be free to
operate outside this restrictive framework. Consider a principal finding of
a World Bank (1995) study of privatization and management contracts:
"[T]he more successful contracts enabled contract managers to pursue contract objectives independent of government policy, while the less successful
contracts made returns to the contractors dependent on government decisions outside their control" (143).

According to the study, governments interfere with personnel policies
more than any other area of contractor decision making, almost always
with a negative effect on performance. All but one of the unsuccessful or
borderline management contracts studied by the World Bank (1995) limited
the contractor's freedom and authority over labor. In contrast, nearly all the
successful contracts gave the contractor maximum autonomy to hire and
fire personnel and to set wages (Figure 2.1).

How Do Municipal Governments Create Incentive Structures to Support Performance-Based Contracts?

Performance measures do a city little good if it cannot use rewards and
penalties to induce performance results. As with devising the performance
measures in the first place, incentive structures can be tricky. For one thing,
finding the right balance of risk is not always easy. Contract incentives usually shift much of the risk to the contractor, who is rewarded for productivity improvement and penalized for poor performance or rising costs. This
system may require some tolerance for trial and error to determine what
incentives give the results really desired. An official with the state of Oklahoma describes the balance of risks well: "[Y]ou have to put enough risk in
a contract to get the vendor to pay attention and meet outcomes. We also
take some of the risk because there are perverse incentives if we take none.
But we don't want to take all the risk ourselves" (Kittower 1999, 48).

Figure 2.1
Success of Contracts with Varying Firm Autonomy

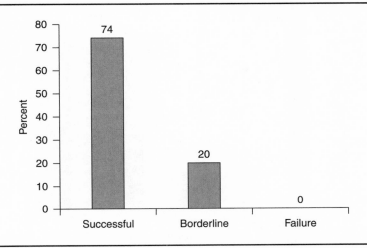

Source: World Bank 1995.

Behn and Kant (1999) describe three pitfalls that may await an exploratory incentive structure:

1. Incentives can inhibit experimentation if they encourage vendors to take the safest route to earn performance payments, rather than reward experiments as long as they do not decrease performance.
2. It is easy for incentives to focus vendors on innovative ways to cut costs rather than innovative ways to improve services.
3. Incentives encourage meeting baseline goals but often don't reward overachievement. That discourages innovations to push performance to new levels. (476ff)

Behn and Kant (1999) go on to describe strategies to help avoid these pitfalls, and the plethora of case studies of successful performance contracts and incentive schemes shows that it can be done (Eggers 1997a; Kittower 1999). Repeated observations of certain techniques and structures indicate they may be developing a track record of success. The four most common incentive structures follow.

Scaled Rewards The more a vendor achieves, the more he or she is paid. Often, the goal is to create an incentive for continuous improvement. Recall the Jersey City water utility contract with bill collection incentives. Figure 2.2 shows the incentive structure. It establishes a scale of rewards that encourages vendors to continue to improve performance—the more they collect, the more money they keep for themselves.

Local Government Innovation

Figure 2.2
Jersey City Water Collections Incentives

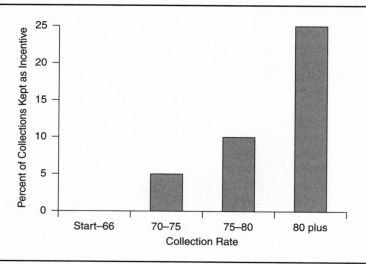

Source: Used with permission of Reason Policy Institute.

Shared Savings When the primary goal of privatization is to reduce costs and improve efficiency, letting the vendor retain some of the savings he or she generates is a popular incentive structure. Such arrangements are used frequently when outsourcing many process-oriented support functions such as IT, billing, and payroll. This concept is also creatively applied to nonsupport services. In 1995, the Indianapolis airport became the largest privately managed airport in the United States. The private operator guaranteed the city a minimum of $32 million in savings over a ten-year period, but hopes to achieve savings of $105 million. All savings over the $32 million baseline are shared by the operator and the Indianapolis Airport Authority, whose share ranges from 60 to 70 percent during the life of the contract (Eggers 1997a, 13).

Performance Penalties Financial penalties imposed on private providers usually take the form of reduced charges for the period in which the poor performance occurred or a credit against future charges. For example, in 1994, the Minneapolis Public Schools hired a private firm to act as superintendent. A maximum payment was set for achieving all performance measures, but the firm lost some of its payment for every measure that did not reach the performance goal. The first payment assessment came after 18 months, and the firm earned only 66 percent of the total performance payment (Eggers 1997a, 14).

Of course, vendors are concerned about incentives for the city to seek penalties to reduce their payments, while municipalities want to punish poor performance. Several approaches have been developed to reconcile these interests, including "earn back" provisions and "positive performance" credits. Earn back provisions allow a vendor to offset penalty assessments by exceeding performance in the next time period. Positive performance credits let vendors who exceed performance standards by a certain level bank those credits to offset potential future underperformance.

Capitated Payments   Most common in contracts for social services, capitated payment schemes require a vendor to agree to deliver the services in bundles for a fixed price per case. By providing a fixed payment in advance for a certain outcome, capitation shifts much of the burden of performance— and risk—to providers. A typical example might be a drug treatment program in which the service provider is paid a flat fee per person treated, subject to meeting established performance goals such as program completion.

THE EVOLVING ART AND SCIENCE OF CONTRACT MANAGEMENT

Privatization as a policy tool requires a new set of skills for government managers: understanding competitive markets, knowing how to value assets, making cost comparisons, managing a competitive bid, and managing contracts in place—this list only scratches the surface. All issues deserve considerable study, but the discussion here is confined to managing contracts in place.

Managing contracts is an art and a science. A firm grasp of contract law, an ability to measure performance compliance, and good accounting skills are valuable, but just as important are skills at negotiations, conflict management, and communications. Perhaps most important is a mental flexibility and adaptation that helps one to separate the unique features of a specific contract or issue from general principles and policies and to recognize and deal with unanticipated and changing circumstances. Many things change in the world of privatization, sometimes in a short period of time. The service provider industry can change dramatically in just a few years— new performance standards develop, new contract law emerges, and the people involved come and go (and personalities do matter).

It is no surprise that cities using privatization have begun to develop skills and practices at managing contracts. They recognize that the long-term value and sustainability of privatization as a policy tool depends on contract management, and contract management itself changes. Shifting from basic fee-for-service cost-plus types of contracts to performance-based contracts means a change in contract management practices. Unfortunately, it doesn't always go that way. Sometimes governments get bogged down in developing performance measures and contracts, and never get around to

revising their contract management practices (USGAO 1999b, 14); however, some governments have begun to refine the art of contract management and devised flexible, adaptable systems that grow and change with
their increased use of privatization.

MONITORING AND EVALUATING CONTRACTOR PERFORMANCE

The first and most important part of contract management is a system for
monitoring and evaluating performance. It can be complex or simple, but it
is always vital:

Public sector decision-makers have yet to learn from the private sector the signifi-
cance of managing outsourcing. Efficient monitoring, though costly, pays for itself
by preventing overcharges and poor quality performance in the first place by
recouping inappropriate outlays, and by disallowing payment for inadequate performance. (Prager 1994, 182)

Cities with well-developed contract monitoring systems have learned
to answer some basic questions: How many people are needed to monitor contracts? What should they be doing? and What kinds of internal
structures are needed as governments shift from service provider to service facilitator and purchaser? The bottom line is thinking about how to
monitor the service/contract before issuing the RFP or signing the contract. The monitoring plan, sometimes called a Quality Assurance Plan
(QAP), defines precisely what a government must do to guarantee that
the contractor's performance is in accordance with contract performance
standards.

Consequently, the better the performance standards, the easier it will be
to monitor the contract effectively. The design of the deal can make an
enormous difference in the future success of monitoring the contractor.
Such interdependence leads many cities to write the performance standards
and the monitoring plan simultaneously.[7]

Most monitoring plans focus on quantifiable measures as much as possible, including reporting requirements, regular meetings with minutes, complaint procedures, and access to contractor's records (if necessary). One
principle that seems to evolve often from long-running contracts is focusing
on monitoring and evaluating the major outputs of the contract so monitors don't have to waste too much time and resources monitoring mundane
and routine tasks that are not central to the contract. Including the individuals who will monitor the contract helps both with starting up the monitoring process and familiarizing the monitors and the vendors as early on
as possible.

Tailoring the Monitoring Plan to the Particulars of the Contract

Every contract is a little bit unique, and one-size-fits-all monitoring plans are rare. Cities that do a lot of contract monitoring emphasize the need to apply the general principles of monitoring plans in a fashion tailored to the needs of the specific contract. Different services require different types and levels of monitoring. Monitoring strategies that would be very effective for street resurfacing may be inappropriate for data processing.

Some services require less overt monitoring than others. For highly visible services that directly affect citizens, such as snow removal and garbage pickup, poor service will be exposed through citizen complaints. For complex or technical services, some cities hire a third party to monitor the contractor. Consequently, we see monitoring programs that emphasize on-site supervision, others that emphasize audits, and others that rely on customer surveys and other collected data (Kittower 1998).

Several factors seem to direct cities in determining the appropriate technique and level of monitoring for a given service, one of the most important being the level of acceptable risk for nonperformance. Where there exists a high level of risk for even minor problems—hazardous waste management, for example—monitoring techniques are often higher cost and higher control (Table 2.3).

Monitoring plans often change during the course of a contract. Some cities perform intensive monitoring for the first few months of a contract. For example, Indianapolis uses heavy monitoring for the first three to six months of a new contract, with 100 percent inspections and frequent meetings. They also usually waive liquidated damage assessments for the first three months. Kim Dershak, the city's director of enterprise development, in an interview with the authors in May 1999, argues that this shows the

Table 2.3
Common Elements of Contract Monitoring Systems

1. Requiring the contractor to present periodic reports.
2. Reviewing those reports carefully for adherence to the written contract.
3. Comparing wage rates and equipment charges for materials or rentals with the contract.
4. Verifying that all services, material, labor and equipment were actually received, used or consumed.
5. Using on-site inspections.
6. Tracking user satisfaction.
7. Tracking and following up on all complaints.
8. Citizen and user surveys.

contractor that monitoring is serious and also provides ample opportunity to iron out ambiguities in contracts; the frequent contact helps establish a relationship between the monitor and the contractor.

Developing relationships that ease communication and conflict resolution is a recurring theme in contract monitoring practices. Many cities emphasize that the contractor should be considered a strategic partner and given incentives to innovate, improve, and deliver better customer service. This is especially true with privatization activities that take public-private partnership of joint venture forms.

Municipal officials seem to rely more on regular communications and periodic meetings with an emphasis on consensus. When Las Vegas privatized provision of municipal bus services, it developed performance measures but left incentives and punishments flexible, and the city retained policy control of transit services. Since the vendor and the city work together on an almost daily basis, they formed a joint working group that reviews all performance data and jointly develops solutions to problems that arise (Kittower 1998, 73).

Parallel to striving for working partnerships with contractors, well-developed monitoring systems also emphasize the occasional necessity for contract terminations. Termination is the ultimate club in the hand of municipal officials and the final stage of accountability. Some monitoring plans use an escalating scale of punishment measures, reserving termination as a last resort. At the same time, many contract management practitioners emphasize the importance of documenting problems and attempts to solve them, as well as all communications and meetings with the vendor, creating a paper trail that supports the decision to terminate the contract.

Another tool used to manage conflicts or performance problems before they lead to termination, or even worse, to court, is a dispute resolution process. Frequently, this includes contract agreements to use Alternative Dispute Resolution (ADR) techniques—facilitation, mediation, and mini-trials—instead of resorting to litigation:

Outsourcing is a collaborative relationship that has to be worked on. The lawyers are very helpful in structuring a contract. Our job is to make sure we don't need them throughout the year. When the inevitable financial tensions arise, we have been able to have a "closed door" meeting of several financial people from both sides and share our mutual objectives. . . . Both sides feel a lot better when it is over. (McFarlane and Nolan 1995, 18)

Management Information Systems for Evaluating Contractor Performance
Monitoring systems that require data collection and analysis have driven cities to create new information management systems as contract monitor-

ing tools. Some use data inputs from performance audits; others link the evaluation system with a citizen complaint hotline.

Indianapolis, which has subjected more than 80 services to competition, found that keeping track of the performance of all those projects had become a daunting task. In essence, the city had a portfolio management problem. In order to get a better idea of actual contract performance and of the quality of the city's monitoring and evaluation systems, they launched a system of Initiative Management Reviews (IMRs).

One task of an IMR team is to determine the adequacy of current contract resources, personnel, procedures, and monitoring systems for any given service. The IMR team also takes a hard look at performance measures, comparing actual performance to the measures. When appropriate, the team will recommend changes in existing measures. A major element of the review process is determining the relative risk of each of the outsourcing projects. The higher the risk of nonperformance, the higher priority the initiative will be for an IMR.

Developing Contract Management Professionals   Governments at all levels are starting to recognize that greater use of privatization has broad human resource implications. Most civil service systems do not reward contract management experience and skills the same way they reward managing in-house service delivery and budgets. That is likely to change. At the same time, opportunities for professional training and education in contract management are proliferating, with state governments and federal agencies leading the way. Managing contracts can be more complex than managing in-house operations. It is a natural evolution of privatization as a policy tool to see professional contract management training and career tracks begin to emerge.

CONCLUSION

Privatization continues to grow dynamically, expanding its scope in services that have long been privatized and increasingly make inroads into new areas and services. Privatization techniques have also proven dynamic, with municipal governments adapting to changing circumstances and adopting proven techniques. The future promises to be equally dynamic. The use of privatization in social services, education, and public safety may increase dramatically in this decade. In those types of services, performance contracts will begin to migrate from output-based models to outcome systems, to focus contracts on ways of improving citizens' lives, and away from focusing on only what is to be produced. Shifting from monitoring park maintenance levels to evaluating community satisfaction with parks is a much more difficult task but one that focuses on the ultimate goal of service provision.

NOTES

1. Typical privatization surveys include International City/County Management Association (*Municipal Yearbooks,* 1988, 1992, 1997) and Chi and Jasper (1998).

2. Even as we write this, we find examples that don't fit neatly. Chang and Jones (1992) describe a type of privatization much like corporatization, but which creates a nonprofit rather than for-profit entity. It shares many characteristics with joint ventures and self-help modes of privatization.

3. Osborne and Gaebler (1992) described the emergence of this phenomena, describing it as government managers learning to steer rather than row.

4. See Laffont and Tirole (1991). For overviews of agency theory, see Eisenhardt (1989) and Grossman and Hart (1978).

5. The city's competition program web page (www.indygov.org/mayor/comp/pt1/chp1/ cfp.html) goes into considerable detail on both the philosophy and practice of "shopping" for services rather than simply providing them.

6. Witness the long-running efforts by ICMA and Government Accounting Standards Board (GASB) to move local governments to better use of performance measures. *Governing* magazine tracks this issue regularly; see, for example, Kittower (1998, 1999) and Walters (1998). The ICMA performance measurement project is at <www.icma.org/abouticma/programs/performance/>.

7. The Office of Management and Budget (OMB) (1996) recommends simultaneous development of performance measures and monitoring plans as a best practice.

REFERENCES

Bale, Malcolm, and Tony Dale. 1998. Public sector reform in New Zealand and its relevance to developing countries. *World Bank Research Observer* 13(1): 103–121.

Behn, Robert D., and Peter A. Kant. 1999. Strategies for avoiding the pitfalls of performance contracting. *Public Productivity and Management Review* 22(4): 470–489.

Chang, Stanley Y., and Roberta Ann Jones. 1992. Approaches to privatization: Established models and a U.S. innovation. *Government Finance Review* 8(4): 17–39.

Chi, Keon S., and Cindy Jasper. 1998. *Private practices: A review of privatization in state government.* Lexington, KY: Council of State Governments.

Eggers, William D. 1997a. *Performance-based contracting: Designing state-of-the-art contract administration and monitoring systems* (How-To Guide #17). Los Angeles: Reason Public Policy Institute.

Eggers, William D. 1997b. *Cutting local government costs through competition and privatization.* Sacramento: California Chamber of Commerce.

Eisenhardt, K. 1989. Agency theory: An assessment and review. *Academy of Management Review* 14: 57–74.

Foote, David. 1999. Measuring a transit agency's performance. In *Annual privatization report 1999,* ed. Wade Hudson, 17–20. Los Angeles: Reason Public Policy Institute.

Gibbon, Henry. 1996. *A guide for divesting government-owned enterprises* (How-To Guide #15). Los Angeles: Reason Public Policy Institute.

Grossman, Sandford J., and Oliver D. Hart. 1978. An analysis of the principal agent problem. *Econometrica* 51(1): 7–45.

Hall, John, and William D. Eggers. 1995. *Health and social services in the post-welfare state: Are vouchers the answer?* (Policy Study #192). Los Angeles: Reason Public Policy Institute.

Kessler, Kathy, and Julie Wartell. 1996. *Community law enforcement: The success of San Diego's volunteer policing program* (Policy Study #204). Los Angeles: Reason Public Policy Institute.

Kittower, Diane. 1998. Counting on competition. *Governing* (May): 63–74.

Kittower, Diane. 1999. Stepping up to performance measures. *Governing* (June): 46–54.

Laffont, Jean-Jacques, and Jean Tirole. 1991. Privatization and incentives. *Journal of Law, Economics & Organization* 7: 84ff.

Martin, Lawrence L. 1999. Performance contracting: Extending performance measurement to another level. *PA Times* (January): 1.

McFarlane, F. Warren, and Richard I. Nolan. 1995. Outsourcing at Kodak. *Sloan Management Review* (January): 9–23.

Moore, Adrian. 1998. Performance-based contracts: Getting more from private prisons. *Corrections Professional* 4(1) (September 4).

Moore, Adrian T. 1999. Water and wastewater. In *Annual privatization report 1999,* ed. Wade Hudson, 34–37. Los Angeles: Reason Public Policy Institute.

Office of Management and Budget (OMB). 1996. *A guide to best practices for performance-based service contracting.* Washington, DC: Office of Federal Procurement Policy, OMB.

Osborne, David, and Ted Gaebler. 1992. *Reinventing government: How the entrepreneurial spirit is transforming the public sector.* Reading, MA: Addison-Wesley.

Prager, Jonas. 1994. Contracting out government services: Lessons from the private sector. *Public Administration Review* 54(2): 182ff.

Savas, E. S. 1987. *Privatization: The key to better government.* New York: Chatham House.

Siegal, Gilbert B. 1999. Where are we on local government service contracting? *Public Productivity and Management Review,* 22(3): 365–388.

Smith, Steven R., and Michael Lipsky. 1993. *Nonprofits for hire: The welfare state in the age of contracting.* Cambridge, MA: Harvard University Press.

Spicer, Barry, David Emanuel, and Michael Powell. 1996. *Transforming government enterprises: Managing radical organisational change in deregulated environments.* St. Leonards, NSW, Australia: Centre for Independent Studies.

Tradewell, Richard L. 1998. *Privatizing public hospitals: Strategic options in an era of industry-wide consolidation* (Policy Study #242). Los Angeles: Reason Public Policy Institute.

U.S. General Accounting Office (USGAO). 1998. *Federal power: Options for selected power marketing administrations' role in a changing electricity industry* (GAO/RCED-98-43). Washington, DC: USGAO.

USGAO. 1999a. *Public-private partnerships: Key elements of federal building and facility partnerships* (GAO/GGD-99-23). Washington, DC: USGAO.

USGAO. 1999b. *Social service privatization: Ethics and accountability challenges in state contracting* (GAO/HEHS-99-41). Washington, DC: USGAO.

Walters, Jonathan. 1998. *Measuring up: Governing's guide to performance measurement for geniuses (and other public managers)*. Washington, DC: Congressional Quarterly Books.

World Bank. 1995. *Bureaucrats in business: The economics and politics of government ownership*. New York: Oxford Press.

Opportunities in Privatization and Outsourcing

E. S. Savas

Privatization is now commonplace throughout the world—in communist, socialist, and capitalist countries, in developed and developing countries, in democracies and dictatorships, and in what used to be called the East and the West. More than a hundred countries have officially endorsed privatization, and more are considering it (Rondinelli 1998). In the United States, it is being practiced by Democrats and Republicans; liberals and conservatives; blacks and whites; in big cities and in small towns; and at the local, state, and federal levels. It is no longer a partisan or ideological issue but a pragmatic and increasingly routine approach to governing and to managing public services (Daley 1996).

Privatization has been widely accepted and continues to advance, despite opposition, because of pressure to

- improve efficiency.
- reduce the role of government.
- allow private firms to perform commercial work that is not intrinsically governmental.
- expand the role of local, nongovernmental, and community-based organizations.

In addition, increasing affluence has reduced people's dependence on government, thereby reducing public resistance to greater reliance on market mechanisms (Savas 2000).

MASTERING THE JARGON

"Privatization" is a general term that encompasses the following methods:

- *Contracting out* services; called *outsourcing* when done by private firms
- *Managed competition*, in which the in-house unit competes against outside contractors
- *Issuing franchises* (e.g., for bus routes and for water supply systems)
- *Leasing government property*, as in New York State, where Governor George Pataki leased Stewart Airport to a British firm for 99 years
- *Issuing vouchers* (e.g., food stamps, housing vouchers, and vouchers for education so the public can obtain services in the marketplace)
- *Divesting government-owned enterprises and other assets* (e.g., the sale of Conrail)
- *Denationalization*, which is what divesting is also called when a national government does it, but local and state governments are divesting, too
- *Government withdrawal from activities, or load-shedding* (e.g., gradually cutting back on transportation services and letting the private sector fill the need) (Savas 2000)
- *Public-private partnerships* is a term used in three different ways: (1) referring loosely, and somewhat pretentiously, to any arrangement where the public and private sectors join together to produce and deliver goods or services such as contracts, franchises, and leases; (2) referring to complex, multipartner, privatized, infrastructure projects; and (3) referring to a formal collaboration between business and civic leaders and local government officials to improve the urban condition.

Privatization by contracting out conventional government services and selling off government-owned businesses and assets is going on at a brisk pace. More than 200 local government services, ranging from adoption services to zoo management, have been privatized (Table 3.1). The array of privatized activities is seemingly endless, limited only by the entrepreneurial instincts of business leaders and public officials. For example, private towing services rescue floundering pleasure boats for a fee, something the Coast Guard used to do at taxpayers' expense (Wadler 1998); state parks and resorts in New Hampshire and Georgia are leased to private firms (Hudson 1998); Riverside County, California, contracts with a private company to manage its 25-branch library system; and Jersey City in New Jersey is considering doing the same (Hanley and Strunsky 1998, B1).

Whereas contracting out specific services is by now standard practice, a private firm, appropriately named City Municipal Services, Inc., is serving as a public works department for several towns in Michigan, performing the entire array of traditional public works functions (Jordan 1997).

Municipal parking is also being privatized in interesting ways. The city of Richmond, Virginia, contracted with a company to manage its on-street

Table 3.1
Local Government Services Contracted Out to Private Firms

Addiction treatment, adoption, air-pollution abatement, airport operation, airport
    fire and crash response, airport services, alarm-system maintenance, alcohol
    treatment, ambulance, animal control, appraisals, architectural, auditorium
    management, auditing
Beach management, billing and collection, bridge (construction, inspection, and
    maintenance), building demolition, building rehabilitation, buildings and
    grounds (janitorial, maintenance, security), building and mechanical inspection,
    burial of indigents, bus system management and operation, bus-shelter
    maintenance
Cafeteria and restaurant operation, catch-basin cleaning, cemetery administration,
    child protection, securing child-support payments, civil defense communication,
    clerical, communication maintenance, community center operation, composting,
    computer operations, consultant services, convention center management, crime
    laboratory, crime prevention and patrol, custodial services
Data entry, data processing, day care, debt collection, document preparation, drug
    and alcohol treatment programs
Economic development, election administration, electrical inspection, electric
    power, elevator inspection, emergency maintenance, emergency medical services,
    environmental services
Family counseling, financial services, fire communication, fire-hydrant mainte-
    nance, fire prevention and suppression, flood-control planning, foster-home care
Golf-course management and operation, graphic arts, guard service
Health inspection, health services, home-aid service, homeless-shelter operation,
    hospital management, hospital services, housing inspection and code enforce-
    ment, housing management
Industrial development, insect and rodent control, institutional care, insurance
    administration, irrigation
Jail and detention, janitorial juvenile delinquency programs
Labor relations, laboratory, landscaping, laundry, lawn maintenance, leaf collec-
    tion, legal, legal aid, library operation, licensing, lottery operation
Management consulting, mapping, marina services, median-strip maintenance,
    mosquito control, moving and storage, museum and cultural
Noise abatement, nursing, nutrition
Office-machine maintenance, opinion polling
Paratransit system operation, park management and maintenance, parking
    enforcement, parking lot and garage operation, parking meter servicing, parking
    ticket processing, patrol, payroll processing, personal services, photographic
    services, physician services, planning, plumbing inspection, police communica-
    tion, port and harbor management, printing, prisoner transportation, probation,
    property acquisition, public administrator services, public health, public rela-
    tions and information, public works
Records maintenance, recreation services, recycling, rehabilitation, resource recov-
    ery, risk management

—continued

Table 3.1
Continued

School bus, secretarial, security, sewage treatment, sewer maintenance, sidewalk
    repair, snow (plowing, removal, sanding), social services, soil conservation, solid
    waste (collection, transfer, disposal), street services (construction, maintenance,
    resurfacing, sweeping), street lighting (construction and maintenance), surveying
Tax collection (assessing, bill processing, receipt), tennis-court maintenance, test
    scoring, towing, traffic control (markings, sign and signal installation and main-
    tenance), training (of government employees), transit management, transporta-
    tion of elderly and disabled, treasury functions, tree services (planting, pruning,
    removal)
Utility billing, utility meter reading
Vehicle fleet management, vehicle maintenance, vehicle towing and storage, voter
    registration
Wastewater treatment, water-meter reading and maintenance, water-pollution
    abatement, water supply and distribution, weed abatement, welfare administra-
    tion, worker compensation claims
Zoning and subdivision control, zoo management

Source: Savas 2000, Chapter 4.

parking program, including enforcement ("Central Parking Corporation
. . ." 1998). Parking tickets in New York City can be paid automatically
by credit card 24 hours a day via a toll-free number from any telephone in
the United States. A computer checks the validity of the card and the availability of funds during the transaction. This approach, provided by an innovative private contractor, is convenient for ticketed car owners and highly
cost-effective for the city, reducing handling and processing of about five
million checks a year. Similar responsive technology will be applied to collect many other kinds of fees and payments from the public ("24 x 7 Automated Parking Ticket Payment . . ." 1998).

Ending one of the most archaic arrangements imaginable, the U.S. Naval
Academy in Annapolis is selling its 865-acre dairy farm that has supplied
milk to midshipmen ever since 1911, after a typhoid fever epidemic in the
Academy was traced to tainted milk from a local distributor (Janofsky
1998). This absurd situation is rivaled by one in Pakistan, where the
national airline still owns a poultry farm in order to provide chicken din-
ners to its passengers.

The last state-owned vaccine laboratory in the United States, which
makes anthrax and rabies vaccines, was losing millions of dollars annually
and was finally sold by the state of Michigan (Miller 1998). American
embassies abroad are guarded not only by U.S. Marines, but also by private
firms under contract to the State Department ("The Wackenhut Corpora-

tion Wins Contract . . ." 1998). NASA turned to private contractors to manage its numerous unmanned satellites in space at a cost of $3 billion over ten years (Schneider 1998); the work includes data acquisition from spacecraft, data transmission to the end user, data processing and storage, ground and space communications, and operations at the mission-control center.

The U.S. Department of Defense (DoD) is teaming with the private sector to build, renovate, and manage military housing (Lobel and Brown 1998; Lobel and Marchand 1998). U.S. Army ammunition plants, managed by private contractors, are being used by various manufacturers for commercial purposes under the Armament Retooling and Manufacturing Support (ARMS) initiative enacted by Congress; 16 plants with 187 commercial tenants employing 2,882 workers were in the program by 1998 (Borgeson 1998). Surplus military material (equipment, building materials, and electrical supplies), which was worth more than $8 billion when initially acquired, is being sold for the DoD by one of the nation's largest disposition firms ("Arizona Firm Wins Contract . . ." 1998).

The St. Lawrence Seaway, owned by the Canadian government, is now being managed by a private group comprised of its major users, who hope to restore the Seaway's fortunes by making it more competitive with other forms of transportation ("St. Lawrence Seaway Goes Private" 1998). The U.S. government, however, continues to own the corporation that operates and maintains the part of the Seaway in U.S. waters.

In Britain, the first Labor government in almost twenty years stunned some of its supporters by abandoning its obsolete economic creed of nationalization and continuing the privatization policy initiated by the former Conservative prime minister, Margaret Thatcher. It announced plans to sell $4.9 billion of state assets over three years by divesting 51 percent of the air-traffic-control system and entering into public-private partnerships for the state-owned betting service and for the Royal Mint, which produces coins and banknotes (Bray 1998). It was also proceeding with plans to privatize the Underground, London's subway system. As a final striking example of the limitless opportunities for privatization, the British Defense Ministry is seeking proposals to privatize the Queen's airline (the Royal Air Force squadron) that transports the royal family, government ministers, and VIPs around the world ("Queen's Airline Might Go Private" 1998).

Outsourcing by the private sector is a growing phenomenon as companies subcontract with specialized firms to operate their computers; handle their logistics (such as warehousing and delivering); assemble parts; run their company cafeterias; process their mail; do their advertising, marketing, and public relations; staff their telephone order and help lines; administer their payrolls; manage employee benefits; and perform other mission-critical functions; and, thereby, turn themselves into virtual corporations.

They strip to the bare essentials, even leasing employees. When done properly, this does not "hollow out" the corporation; it reduces internal bureaucracies, flattens the organization, and affords greater strategic focus. In other words, outsourcing brings many of the same benefits to private corporations that privatization brings to governments.

Nonprofit organizations appear on both sides of the privatization equation. They outsource many of their internal support functions and provide services under contract to government agencies, principally in the social services field. Increasingly, however, private for-profit firms are entering that field successfully.

Privatization Works

Governments hire for-profit and nonprofit private organizations and pay them to provide services specified by the government. In the United States, governments at the local, state, and federal levels have contracted for services, usually under competitive conditions, for a wide range of activities. Contracting has been very successful, increasing efficiency and cutting costs without reducing the level or quality of services. Table 3.2 summarizes the results of the major studies of contracting for government services. These studies were conducted in several countries and at different levels of government by a variety of independent agents.

The Los Angeles County Auditor-Controller examined all 651 contracts entered into by the county over an eight-year period for data conversion; grounds maintenance; and custodial, food, laundry, and guard services. The contracts totaled $182 million and saved the county $86 million from its original in-house cost of $268 million; that is, the in-house cost was 47 percent greater than the contract price or, conversely, the contract savings were 32 percent. A total of 2,700 positions were eliminated—3.6 percent of the county's total (County of Los Angeles 1987, 40).

Los Angeles then expanded its privatization program even more aggressively, and a subsequent study two years later summarized the county's ten years of experience. A total of 812 contracts costing $508 million resulted in a savings of $193 million, or 28 percent; 4,700 positions were eliminated (6 percent of the total), yet this was accomplished with only a handful of layoffs (Goodman 1990). (No information is presented on the relative quality of the work or on the cost of contract administration and monitoring.) This study is especially compelling since the county official who conducted these studies is independently elected and is not part of the county administration that contracted for the services.

At the request of the U.S. Congress, the DoD reported before-and-after comparisons of its contracts for commercial services. The study covered all 285 contracts awarded during a two-year period for support activities such as data processing, food service, and audiovisual services, and revealed that the cost of this work when performed in-house prior to the competitions

Table 3.2
Summary of Before-and-After Studies of Contracting

Contracting Agency [Source of Study]	Number of Contracts	Cost before Contracting (Millions)	Savings (Percent)
Los Angeles County, 1979–1987 [Los Angeles County Auditor-Controller]	651	268	32
Los Angeles County, 1979–1989 [Los Angeles County Auditor-Controller]	812	701	28
U.S. Department of Defense, 1980–1982 [U.S. Department of Defense]	235	1,128	31
U.S. Department of Defense, 1983–1984 [U.S. Department of Defense]	131	132	33
U.S. Department of Defense, 1978–1986 [U.S. General Accounting Office]	1,661	2,270	27
U.S. Department of Defense, 1978–1994 [Center for Naval Analyses]	2,138	4,768	31
Wandsworth Borough, London, 1978–1987 [Centre for Policy Studies]	23	174	27
General Services Administration Public Buildings Service, FY92 [U.S. General Accounting Office]	576	NA	25
State of Western Australia, 1993–1994 [University of Sydney]	891	324	20

Source: Savas 2000.

had been 45 percent higher than the cost of the contract work, with a savings of 31 percent (Office of Federal Procurement Policy 1984). A similar study of all 131 contracts awarded the next year showed that the contracts cost $87.5 million but saved $43.9 million; therefore, in-house costs were 50 percent greater, and the savings were 33 percent (Wade 1986).

No data on comparative quality are offered, nor are the costs of contract administration and monitoring discussed. The studies cover only the cases in which contracts were awarded; presumably, there were many cases where no savings could have been realized and, therefore, no contracting took place. Thus, one cannot conclude from these Los Angeles and federal studies that *all* in-house services cost 28 to 50 percent more than comparable contract work.

The U.S. General Accounting Office (USGAO) (1988) examined 1,661 cost-comparison studies covering 25 major types of commercial functions performed by the DoD. This study encompassed the 416 studies (285 plus 131) previously discussed. The original cost of the in-house work was compared to the contractor bids and to lower-cost bids made by in-house units facing the threat of privatization. The USGAO found that the original cost had been 37 percent greater than the winning bid, and an estimated $614 million (27 percent) had been saved by this competitive process. This study was subsequently extended to cover eight more years—a total of 2,138 contracts. The updated data show that savings due to such competition increased to an average of 31 percent over the entire 16-year period (Kleinman 1996). As in the case of Los Angeles County, this study was carried out by an independent agency.

The other three studies shown in Table 3.2 reveal similar findings. The Borough of Wandsworth in London introduced competition for its municipal services. About one-third of the competitions were won by the in-house workforce and two-thirds by private contractors, leading to an overall savings of 27 percent (Beresford 1987). A USGAO (1994) study of the Public Buildings Service of the U.S. General Services Administration focused on custodial and maintenance contracts for buildings and found that savings averaged 25 percent for the services that were contracted out. The Competitive Tendering and Contracting Research Team at the University of Sydney studied contracting in the state of western Australia and found that savings averaged 20 percent of the precontract cost (Farago, Hall, and Domberger 1994).

What is most striking about Table 3.2 is how similar the results are in the United States, England, and Australia in that the savings in all three countries range from 20 to 33 percent. Although these before-and-after studies did not examine the quality of the contractors' work, other studies did and found no significant difference between the work performed by a government agency directly using its own employees and that of contractors selected by competitive bidding (Stevens 1984). Privatization by contracting for services clearly works. It works because it introduces competition among service providers and gives government agencies a choice among them.

The Process of Privatizing

Contractors and would-be contractors have to understand the privatization process from the perspective of the government that is contracting with private firms or engaging in managed competition, in which the contract may go to the inside unit or to a private firm. The idealized list of steps that governments follow is shown in Table 3.3.

Contractors often provide the impetus for the very first step in the sequence by calling on public officials and making them aware of the opportunities to contract for services. They can also participate in the feasibility study (step 3) to the extent of offering crude, ball-park estimates of

Table 3.3
Twelve Steps in Contracting for Services

1. Consider the idea of contracting out.
2. Select the service.
3. Conduct a feasibility study.
4. Foster competition.
5. Request expressions of interest or qualifications.
6. Plan the employee transition.
7. Prepare bid specifications.
8. Initiate a public relations campaign.
9. Engage in "managed competition."
10. Conduct a fair bidding process.
11. Evaluate the bids and award the contract.
12. Monitor, evaluate, and enforce contract performance.

Source: Savas 2000.

the potential contract cost if the public agency were to privatize. They can also work on step 6 by planning an attractive package for dealing with any redundant personnel and on step 8 by helping to gain public support for privatization.

If managed competition is employed by the government agency, step 9 requires an effort to assure that playing field is level. The following problems arise:

- *Public units don't include all of their costs.* Care must be taken to assure full pricing in the agency's bid; therefore, it is generally necessary to use an independent unit such as the management or budget office to validate the agency's bid and assure that all costs are included and no hidden subsidy exists.

- *A performance guarantee is required of the private provider but not the public provider.* What happens under managed competition if the contract is awarded to the in-house unit, which then fails to satisfy the terms of the contract? For instance, the unit submits a bid lower than its traditional cost because it says it will adopt more productive work practices, but it does not change its ways and its costs remain too high, or, perhaps, the quality of service is poor and fails to satisfy the performance standards called for in the contract. Private firms must post a performance bond; it would be fair but impractical to require the union to post one. "Loss sharing" has been suggested, that is, imposing a cost on the group of workers that won the bid, but this, too, is impractical; in-house employees cannot assume risk and cannot pay penalties for poor performance. The best way to handle this situation is to monitor the service closely, weekly or monthly, to see if the contractually promised results are being realized. If not, the arrangement should be aborted, and the contract should be awarded to the outside firm that submitted the best bid in the competition.

- *Risk is assumed by the private provider if it wins but no value is credited to it; whereas, if the public agency wins, the risk is borne by the jurisdiction, not the agency that submits the bid.* For example, for environmental services, the private sector bears the risk of compliance with environmental regulations and must pay any fines if they fail to comply. If a public agency fails to comply, the fine is paid by taxpayers, not the agency. If the risks are large and shifting them away from the public sector is important, the service may not be appropriate for managed competition but should be reserved for a private bidder. Alternatively, the cost of insurance can be added to the price of the public bid, as was done in San Diego in a managed competition to operate a wastewater treatment plant (Stevens 1984, 13).

- *Private firms must pay taxes and comply with regulations from which the public sector is exempt* (Eggers 1997). The value of taxes paid by the private firm should be subtracted from its bid price or added to the public bid.

- *In-house departments are sometimes allowed to delay their submission until the private bids are in, or to adjust their bids after seeing the private-sector bids.* Instead of managed competition, this is mismanaged competition.[1] Unless these biases are addressed, this approach will ultimately fail, in that no private bidders will respond and the jurisdiction will remain at the mercy of its in-house monopoly. The in-house bid must be submitted and opened at the same time as all other bids, and no adjustments after the fact should be allowed; any other practice is blatantly unfair. Public-employee unions complain, on the other hand, that it is unfair to expect them to engage in competitive bidding when they have never had the experience. They need training, but it should not be financed by taxpayers; it should be provided as a local service by the parent national unions such as the American Federation of State, County, and Municipal Employees and the American Federation of Government Employees. The cost of any consulting assistance to help the agency prepare its bid or proposal should be added to the agency's bid price.

New Opportunities

Privatization has advanced beyond the point of no return, and the examples given illustrate the continuing inventiveness of public officials in applying the concepts in new ways and saving substantial amounts of money. The next major areas to benefit from privatization are government-owned enterprises, infrastructure, and social insurance. The three are radically different and, therefore, so are the ways that their privatization is likely to evolve.

Government-Owned Enterprises

Government-owned enterprises (GOEs) throughout the world are being privatized and thrust into market environments. They go under many

names: government-sponsored enterprises, government corporations, public authorities, public-benefit corporations, state-owned enterprises (SOEs),
and parastatals—the last two terms are commonly used outside the United
States. In the United States, there are numerous government corporations,
generally described as state or federally chartered entities, created to serve
a public function of a predominantly business nature. The estimated number of federal corporations has ranged from 12 to 47, depending on the definition that is employed and who does the counting (USGAO 1995). It does
not require much imagination to predict that many of them should and will
be privatized.

A list of 31 United States government business enterprises is presented in
Table 3.4. One of these, the United States Postal Service (USPS), has already
started to privatize. In 1997, it awarded a five-year, $1.7 billion contract to
Emery Worldwide Airlines to create a network of ten Priority Mail processing centers along the East coast as the first step in contracting out the
processing of all such mail ("Postal Workers Rally . . ." 1998). Additional
entities engaged in business exist within government departments and are
not on this list; they may have to be corporatized prior to sale. Similar privatizations can be expected for government corporations at the local and
state levels. Some of the corporations might best be privatized by with-
drawing and allowing the private sector to handle the function, if it is
needed at all.

Infrastructure

Developing countries need more telecommunications, electric power, gas,
roads, railroads, and, in general, more of all kinds of physical infrastructure
to promote economic development, although this is a chicken-and-egg proposition. In the advanced industrialized nations, ever more stringent environmental controls on water, air, and land dictate new, more expensive efforts for
the prevention and treatment of pollution. In both cases, it means large capital investments in water supply and wastewater treatment systems, in power
generation systems that are less polluting, and so forth. It also means greater
emphasis on research and development and on applying advanced technology
in which there are economies of scale. This is a prescription for private-sector
involvement, for competition, and for the capital and in-house expertise that
are generally beyond the capacity of local governments. Public-private partnerships are ideal in these circumstances and are proliferating.

Transportation is another good target. Continued suburbanization is
straining the capacity of current transportation infrastructure and is calling
for more efficient use of that infrastructure as well as for new and improved
transportation modes. Privatized toll roads and the addition of toll lanes to
existing roads with automated toll collection and time-of-day pricing are of
proven value in reducing congestion.

Table 3.4
Partial List of U.S. Government Corporations

African Development Foundation
Bonneville Power Administration
Commodity Credit Corporation
Community Development Financial Institutions Fund
Corporation for National and Community Service
Corporation for Public Broadcasting
Export-Import Bank of the United States
Federal Crop Insurance Corporation
Federal Deposit Insurance Corporation
Federal Housing Administration
Federal Prison Industries, Inc.
Government National Mortgage Association ("Ginnie May")
Inter-American Foundation
Legal Services Corporation
National Credit Union Administration Central Liquidity Facility
National Railroad Passenger Corporation (Amtrak)
Neighborhood Reinvestment Corporation
Overseas Private Investment Corporation (OPIC)
Pennsylvania Avenue Development Corporation
Pension Benefit Guaranty Corporation
Power Marketing Administrations
Resolution Funding Corporation
Rural Electrification Corporation
Rural Telephone Bank
Southeastern Power Administration
Southwestern Power Administration
St. Lawrence Seaway Development Corporation
Tennessee Valley Authority
The Financing Corporation
United States Postal Service
Western Area Power Administration

Source: Derived in part from U.S. General Accounting Office 1995.

An added innovation is "congestion tolling," a system of dynamic pricing in which prices change every few minutes in response to changing traffic patterns and are flashed to drivers. This is being done in California, where it maximizes highway throughput because drivers can use a toll lane or a free lane depending on traffic conditions and on the value they place on their time (Poole 1998a). Private capital and public-private partnerships are fueling these capital-intensive improvements, and additional revenue is generated by sharing rights-of-way with fiber-optic communication lines (Poole 1998b). More private roads can be expected.

Burgeoning air travel throughout the world is crowding existing airports and endangering air-traffic control systems. It is no surprise that privatized airports are being built (Greece) and existing ones are being sold (Britain, Germany, Mexico, and New Zealand) or turned over to private management for operation and expansion (Indianapolis, New York, Puerto Rico, San Diego). Air-traffic control systems have been privatized in Canada, New Zealand, and Switzerland (Urquhart 1996); are being privatized in Britain (Bray 1998); and have been advocated (Gore 1993; Poole 1991; Savas 1995) and planned (Cole and Pasztor 1997; Franz 1994) in the United States.

Prisons are another kind of infrastructure, one in which privatization is growing through several different models (Chi 1998). First started in the United States, private prisons can also be found now in Australia, Canada, and Great Britain and are being introduced elsewhere. At the end of 1996, the 17 firms in this "business" housed 85,000 inmates in 132 secure adult facilities, including maximum-security and large prisons with more than 2,000 inmates. The number of inmates in private prisons had increased by one-third in that year, and continued rapid expansion in the number of such facilities was forecast (Thomas 1997); since only three percent of U.S. inmates were in privatized prisons, this is an area that offers great growth potential.

States accept out-of-state prisoners in such prisons, which are seen as economic salvation for declining communities because of the jobs they generate (Swope 1998). Given the success of incarceration in reducing crime, more private prisons are being constructed because the private sector can build them more rapidly and at lower cost through design-finance-build-leaseback arrangements. Real-estate investment trusts (REITs) that specialize in prison properties are being created, which make it easier to raise private capital for this purpose (Quinlan 1998).

Social Insurance

For more than a century, people have increasingly looked to government for retirement income, health care, and protection against poverty, which together can be called social insurance. The resulting system is the welfare state, which is widely perceived as being in crisis:

Twenty years ago, selling state-run businesses . . . to the private sector seemed politically impossible. Now governments everywhere are privatizing, whether they lean right or left. It is the commercial enterprises run by the state that seem to be out of place today, not the privatized one.

Will the next two decades bring a similar change in attitudes to the privatization of social insurance? There are at least three striking similarities between nationalized industries then and welfare states now: a widespread conviction that the old way has failed; plenty of good reasons to suppose that privatization could help solve at least some of the problems; and hostility to that apparently promising solution from a majority of the public. ("Social Insurance . . ." 1998, 22)

Policymakers in wealthy nations have avoided reconsidering the state's role in social insurance, but the time is right to do so since the system was designed for yesterday's world where poor health and poverty were the norm and life expectancy was 45 years ("Social Insurance . . ." 1998, 3):

The most sensible way to rethink social insurance . . . is to ask, what works? . . . Answering that question means being open-minded about the possibility that the private sector may replace much of what is now done by government, while admitting that there may be things that government can do better than private business, or even that only government can do . . . [The part played by private firms] should be large. Although they do not shout about it, governments are keen to shift more welfare provision into private hands to keep public spending under control and to avoid having to raise taxes or cut benefits. In many rich countries, the private share of social insurance has been edging up in recent years. (4)

The social area in the United States that is very likely to be partially privatized is social security, the government-run retirement system. A major policy debate has been triggered because this is a pay-as-you-go system in which payments from current workers go to retirees. Because the system operates on faith instead of actuarial soundness, it can be disparaged as a government-run chain letter. The looming problem is that there will not be enough workers in the future to pay similar benefits to today's workers when they retire. Individual retirement accounts (IRAs) in the United States and enforced private pension plans, as pioneered in Chile and copied in more and more countries, have the twin virtues of being actuarially sound and providing a much higher payoff to the worker upon retirement. The problems are how to manage the transition fairly, over several decades, for those who have contributed to the current system but are far from retirement; how to provide income transfers to those who could not save enough; whether and how to add income support for those who neglected to save enough; and what kind of government regulation is needed for privatized pension systems.

Privatization of other social insurance programs has proceeded in several ways. Social services have long been contracted out to nonprofit organizations in the private sector. This has been a "fatal embrace" because private, nonprofit organizations with distinguished histories have become, in effect, government surrogates subject to coercive regulations that sap their initiative and thwart their efforts to find better ways to help the needy (Berger and Neuhaus 1996); they lost their independence as they scrambled for government dollars.

Increasingly, however, for-profit firms have entered the field and are both providing services directly, such as child care and job training, and administering social programs under government contracts. Examples of the latter are determining eligibility for benefits, administering welfare-to-work programs, handling child welfare functions from foster care to adoption to family services, and tracking down "dead-beat dads" to collect support payments.

As the evidence mounts that for-profit firms can deliver equally high-quality services more cost-effectively than nonprofit governments, much more contracting will take place. This outcome should come as no surprise because for-profit firms generally provide quality services at a lower cost than nonprofit governments, as has been demonstrated. The ethos and the anti-market, antiprofit bias of the social services profession, however, combined with "holier-than-thou" attitudes, have blinded the nonprofit establishment just as government officials 30 years ago scoffed at the notion that for-profit private firms could undersell and outperform nonprofit government agencies.

Vouchers are emerging as the preferred privatization method for some social welfare services. This is happening for two reasons:

1. Social services have been monopolistic, and vouchers introduce competition which destroys monopolies and improves services (Pruger and Miller 1973; Reid 1972; Savas 1971); nonprofit organizations deplore vouchers as much as public sector unions deplore contracting out, and for the same reason.

2. It is difficult to specify quality standards in social services contracts, but vouchers offer a solution because standards do not have to be articulated; voucher recipients simply choose the program they like among the available suppliers. For example, child care has been "voucherized" in two ways: (1) with vouchers that permit parents to enroll their child in approved day-care facilities and (2) with cash allowances that allow parents to hire a relative or friend to care for their child.

Education vouchers work the same way: parents do not have to be professional educators, or even literate, to select the schools that they deem best for their children. Services for which vouchers can be used include food, housing, education, health care, child care, home care, elder care, job training, and family services.

Yet a third way for privatizing social welfare functions—beyond contracting with firms for direct service delivery and introducing vouchers—appears on the horizon. The family and voluntary groups—religious, charitable, neighborhood, civic, and so on—are two of the principal institutions of the private sector (the market is the third). These voluntary groups, also called nongovernmental organizations (NGOs), are playing a growing role.

The Alliance for National Renewal, which is active in promoting this approach, illustrates the philosophy this way:

[M]ore than 5 million at-risk children . . . are growing up in severely distressed neighborhoods, communities beset by . . . "family-crushing variables" like drugs and violence. Faced with mounting concern about the future these children face,

communities are focusing on integrated, multi-partner efforts to improve neighborhoods as the chief vehicle for stabilizing families and improving the chances that
today's children will survive tomorrow.

Increasingly, these initiatives are being supported by partnerships among government agencies, businesses, foundations, and nonprofit organizations that break down
old barriers. Where families and communities are concerned, these organizations
have concluded that innovation is required. And they are discovering that when they
forge strong working relationships with one another, they can help even the most
modest neighborhood uncover hidden assets and create hope ("Communities that
Strengthen Families" 1997, 3).

The interrelated social problems that plague America today—school tru-
ancy and dropping out, irresponsible insemination, teen pregnancy, out-of-
wedlock births, motherhood without marriage, child and spousal abuse,
drug and alcohol addiction, and crime and public disorder—with all their
attendant consequences, have resisted government solutions. School
dropouts can barely survive in an information age, and young men raised
without fathers dominate the ranks of violent criminals.

The re-creation of civil society is therefore of paramount importance
(Goldsmith 1997). This means encouraging families, promoting responsible
fatherhood, instilling moral values (Blankenhorn 1996), reversing the nor-
malization of teen pregnancy, sustaining mediating institutions without suf-
focating them, and supporting religion.

Family-based programs strengthened by community and neighborhood
efforts and faith-based programs guided by religious groups offer great
promise. For example, inner-city ministers have succeeded in increasing
marriage rates among their flock; sending forth more college-bound young-
sters from their communities; and reducing unemployment, addiction,
crime, and other antisocial pathologies (Freedman 1994; Levy 1998; Will
1998). There will be more efforts to marshal the power of mediating institutions, families, and communities, sometimes with government in supporting roles, in partnerships to achieve a higher level of social welfare.

A New Public Philosophy

Throughout the world, we are experiencing a reorientation of government, a redirection away from a top-down approach, an abandonment of
the reigning assumption that a powerful, active, and interventionist government, manned by a caring, intellectual elite and driven by good inten-
tions, is the basis for a good society. This change is most evident in the
United States, which is a forerunner of such trends. Between the over-
whelming rejection of Barry Goldwater, the Republican candidate for president in 1964, and the resounding re-election of President Reagan, the
Republican candidate a scant twenty years later in 1984, a dramatic change
had occurred in public attitudes. So profound was this change that when

President Clinton became only the third incumbent Democratic president to be re-elected in 160 years, he did so by dropping the pet programs of the left, shifting toward the right, adopting the more centrist programs of his Republican adversaries, and declaring an end to the era of big government. Everett Carll Ladd (1998) explains it this way:

From the beginnings of Franklin Roosevelt's presidency on through the Great Society, those advocating expanded governmental programs domestically often found the winds of public sentiment at their backs. "More government" was progress. Now, in contrast, while most Americans aren't antigovernment, a majority no longer believes that expanding the state is the answer. Those advocating big new government programs, especially ones centered in Washington, encounter resistance far greater than they did in the New Deal and Great Society years. The results of the health-care debate of 1993–94 are a case in point. Ideological fundamentals [such as] confidence in private initiatives and the importance of policies that encourage them are [not changing]. (A22)

Privatization is in the ascendancy, even in unlikely settings. A paean of victory is not needed, however, for those who have advocated prudent privatization for the last 30 years. Will this success continue? Will privatization be overtaken by other forces? Is it merely another management nostrum, having its day in the sun but doomed to be supplanted? I think not. Privatization is not merely a management tool but a basic strategy of societal governance. It is based on a fundamental philosophy of government and of government's role in relation to the other essential institutions of a free and healthy society. Privatization is a means, not an end. The end is better government and a better society.

NOTE

1. Ron Jensen deserves the credit for this wonderful phrase.

REFERENCES

Arizona firm wins contract to sell $8 billion in military surplus. 1998. *AOL News* (September 23).

Beresford, Paul. 1987. *Good council guide: Wandsworth 1978–1987*. London: Centre for Policy Studies.

Berger, Peter, and Richard John Neuhaus. 1996. Peter Berger and Richard John Neuhaus respond. In *To empower people: From state to civil society* ed. Michael Novak, 150. Washington, DC: AEI Press.

Blankenhorn, David. 1996. *Fatherless America: Confronting our most urgent social problem*. New York: HarperCollins.

Borgeson, Douglas. 1998, October 14-16. *The armament retooling and manufacturing support team*. Paper presented at the Annual Conference of the National Council for Public-Private Partnerships, Atlanta, Georgia.

Bray, Nicholas. 1998. Britain's Labor, miming Tories, unveils 3-year privatizing plan. *The Wall Street Journal* (June 12): A9.

Central Parking Corporation awarded contract to manage on-street parking in Richmond; Contract highlights. Continued growth in privatization of municipal parking programs. 1998. *AOL News* (July 13).

Chi, Keon S. 1998. Prison privatization. *State Government News* (March): 38.

Cole, Jeff, and Andy Pasztor. 1997. U.S. air system seen as threat to the economy; Partial privatization of FAA, greater self-regulation is urged in broad study. *The Wall Street Journal* (December 11): A4.

Communities that strengthen families. 1997. *Governing* (October): special section by the National Civic League.

County of Los Angeles. 1987. *Report on contracting policy in Los Angeles County government.* Los Angeles: County of Los Angeles.

Daley, Dennis. 1996. The politics and administration of privatization. *Policy Studies Journal* 24(4): 629–631.

Eggers, William D. 1997. *Competitive neutrality: Ensuring a level playing field in managed competition.* Los Angeles: Reason Public Policy Institute.

Farago, S., C. Hall, and S. Domberger. 1994. *Contracting of services in the Western Australian public sector.* Sydney: University of Sydney, Graduate School of Business.

Franz, Douglas. 1994. F.A.A. reorganizes with eye toward privatizing air control. *New York Times* (December 1): A16.

Freedman, Samuel G. 1994. *Upon this rock: The miracles of a black church.* New York: HarperCollins.

Goldsmith, Stephen M. 1997. Rebuilding civil society. In *The twenty first century city: Resurrecting urban America,* ed. S. M. Goldsmith, 171-192. Washington, DC: Regnery Publishing.

Goodman, John C. 1990, June 11. *Office of Chief Administrative Officer, County of Los Angeles.* Paper presented at The Third National Conference of the Privatization Council, Washington, DC.

Gore, Al. 1993. *Creating a government that works better & costs less: National performance review.* Washington, DC: U.S. Government Printing Office.

Hanley, Robert, and Steve Strunsky. 1998. Jersey City weighs private management of libraries. *New York Times* (June 29): B1.

Hudson, Wade. 1998. New Hampshire and Georgia lease state-owned resorts. *Privatization Watch* (October). Los Angeles: Reason Public Policy Institute.

Janofsky, Michael. 1998. Midshipmen to get milk through middleman. *New York Times* (July 19): A16.

Jordan, W. Stanley. 1997. The turnkey approach. *Public Works* (September).

Kleinman, Sam. 1996. *DoD commercial activities competition data.* Alexandria, VA: Center for Naval Analyses.

Ladd, Everett Carll. 1998. Why Clinton's scandals helped his party. *The Wall Street Journal* (November 5): A22.

Levy, Collin. 1998. Civil society's paramedics. *The Wall Street Journal* (November 20): W17.

Lobel, Ron, and Jay Brown. 1998. Privatization promises to build military family houses better, faster, cheaper. *Council Insights Newsletter* (May). Washington, DC: National Council for Public-Private Partnerships.

Lobel, Ron, and Kim Marchand. 1998. Military housing privatization—the nuts and bolts. *Council Insights Newsletter* (June). Washington, DC: National Council for Public-Private Partnerships.

Miller, Judith. 1998. Company led by top admiral buys Michigan vaccine lab. *New York Times* (July 8): A19.

Office of Federal Procurement Policy. 1984. *Enhancing governmental productivity through competition.* Washington, DC: Office of Management and Budget.

Poole, Jr., Robert W. 1991. Building a safer and more effective air traffic control system. *Reason Foundation Policy Insight* (126) (February).

Poole, Jr., Robert W. 1998a. Good news for hotlanes and tollways. *Privatization Watch* (September). Los Angeles: Reason Public Policy Institute.

Poole, Jr., Robert W. 1998b. Sharing rights of way a win-win deal for states, companies. *Privatization Watch* (September). Los Angeles: Reason Public Policy Institute.

Postal workers rally against priority mail giveaway. 1998. *AOL News* (May 26).

Pruger, Robert, and Leonard Miller. 1973. Competition and public social services. *Public Welfare* (Fall): 16–25.

Queen's airline might go private. *Associated Press* (AP-NY-11-15-98, 1143 EST).

Quinlan, J. Michael. 1998. Prison privatization moves to the next level. *Council Insights Newsletter* (July). Washington, DC: National Council for Public Private Partnerships.

Reid, P. Nelson. 1972. Reforming the social services monopoly. *Social Work* (November): 44–54.

Rondinelli, Dennis A. 1998. Privatization, governance, and public management: The challenges ahead. *Business & the Contemporary World* 10(2): 149–170.

Savas, E. S. 1971. Municipal monopoly. *Harper's Magazine* (December): 55–60.

Savas, E. S. 1995. Is air traffic out of control? *New York Newsday* (June 9): A36.

Savas, E. S. 2000. *Privatization and public-private partnerships.* New York: Chatham House.

Schneider, Greg. 1998. Lockheed gets NASA space pact. *Baltimore Sun* (September 26): 12C.

Social insurance: Privatizing peace of mind. 1998. *The Economist* (October 24): special section, 22.

St. Lawrence Seaway goes private. *Associated Press* (AP-NY-09-30-98, 1401 EDT).

Stevens, Barbara J. 1984. Comparing public and private-sector productivity efficiency: An analysis of eight activities. *National Productivity Review:* 395–406.

Swope, Christopher. 1998. The inmate bazaar. *Governing* (October): 18–22.

Thomas, Charles W. 1997, August 21. Testimony regarding correctional privatization given before the Little Hoover Commission, State of California, Sacramento.

24 × 7 automated parking ticket payment program introduced by Nextlink Interactive in NYC. 1998. *AOL News* (October 1).

U.S. General Accounting Office (USGAO). 1988. *Federal productivity: DoD functions with savings potential from private sector cost comparisons.* Washington, DC: USGAO.

USGAO. 1994. *Public-private mix: Extent of contracting out for real property management services in GSA* (Report, GAO/GGD-94-126BR). Washington, DC: USGAO. (Derived from Table I.5.)

USGAO. 1995. *Government corporations* (Report GAO/GGD-96-14). Washington, DC: USGAO.

Urquhart, John. 1996. Canada's House of Commons to approve bill on privatizing air-traffic control. *The Wall Street Journal* (June 3): C13.

The Wackenhut Corporation wins contract for embassy security. 1998. Available online: <www. prnewswire.com> (October 15).

Wade, Jr., J. P. 1986. *Report to Congress: The DoD Commercial Activities Program* (April 11).

Wadler, Joyce. 1998. Belying the legend of the crusty old salt. *New York Times* (July 1).

Will, George F. 1998. A man who makes his community grow. *New York Post* (November 15): 63.

PART II

Operational Aspects

4

Selecting Services for Outsourcing

John O'Looney

From the perspective of a public administrator, selecting a local government service for outsourcing is a primal act. Moving a service from public provision to the private sector substantially affects all three dimensions of public administration: the political, the economic, and the managerial. By definition, acts of this sort are risky. The costs and benefits of a specific outsourcing decision, moreover, will often affect all three of these dimensions and can occur together as a "mixed" result. Logically, one would assume that appropriate selection of services to be contracted out would result in maximum gains and minimal losses.

However, the literature on management fads suggests the possibility that the popularity of privatization as a management tool could lead public officials to contract services indiscriminately (Abrahamson 1996). In a worst case scenario, suggested by John Donahue (1989), political pressures would induce officials to privatize functions that are better left to government and to retain services that could be better performed by private firms (13). Systemic inefficiency of this sort could be fostered by a natural desire among private firms to carve out the most profitable function. More ominously, such inept service contracting could evolve from corrupt or inappropriate relationships between public and private sector actors or application of undesirable choice criteria.

This chapter provides public officials and managers with a list of factors to consider in any outsourcing decision and several tools for understanding how these factors might interact so as to provide a more or less favorable environment for private provision of a service or function.

POLITICS, IDEOLOGY, AND TIMING IN DEVELOPING CRITERIA
FOR SELECTION OF SERVICES

In an ideal world, selection of a service for potential outsourcing would be made based on objective and agreed-upon criteria that can be easily measured and applied. Since we do not live in such a world, selection criteria are themselves a subject of considerable debate. At a minimum, political, ideological, and timing concerns play a role.

Politics

Politics play a role in outsourcing decisions both in terms of electoral politics and with respect to the impact of political cycles. The influence of electoral politics occurs at both a parochial and a more universal level. At the parochial level, politics affect the overall tendency to contract services by satisfying constituencies that are ideologically in favor of or against outsourcing; and secondly, it can play a part in the choice of services for outsourcing since the selection is seen as a way to reward one's friends. While each factor is likely to be important in the selection process, they both tend to be idiosyncratic and jurisdiction-specific, rather than universal in their effect.

In contrast, there is a universal aspect to the potential for elected officials to use a fiscally successful privatization event to accumulate political points. That is, politicians are immediately better off if they can point to a large expenditure saving caused by a decision to outsource a specific service. In this instance, contracting services, such as those that will immediately require heavy capital expenditures, are likely to have a much higher political payoff than outsourcing services that do not provide for equally-rich bragging rights in the short term even though their outsourcing may have more substantial long-term benefits. The effect of the electoral cycle on the focus and agenda setting of decision makers is well-recognized, and there is no reason to believe that outsourcing decisions are exempt.

Often electoral politics will combine with public managers' desires to be seen as innovative or on the cutting edge to induce an outsourcing choice. The allure of outsourcing in this case is based on potential private sector providers having access to more sophisticated equipment or expertise than available in-house. Small cities are often in this situation since they cannot typically afford (or justify the expense of) equipment or expertise that will not be used sufficiently to warrant in-house purchase (Ammons and Hill 1995).

Ideology

The terms of the outsourcing debate range from the pragmatic to the ideological and can be roughly divided into several camps, each with a particular set of primary values and ways to assess the success or failure of an outsourcing effort. These camps include a Pragmatist/Managerial camp, a Government Reduction/Property Rights camp, a Public Choice camp, an Efficiency camp, an Equity/Accountability camp, a Moral Foundation camp, and a Core Competency camp. As the following list and discussion suggest, the motivations for outsourcing, or failing to outsource, a specific service can be complex and can be based on ideological or reform ideals as much as on simple economic calculations.

Pragmatist/Managerial. Follow the example of other local governments that appear to have been successful. Use criteria that appear to be most important to local stakeholders. Pragmatists would be the ones most likely to act on the basis of surveys of other managers and community leaders; hence, pragmatists might use different criteria in choosing to outsource different services. They would take note, for example, of the degree to which services had already been contracted out by other governments (Table 9.3), the level of satisfaction with these services, and frequently cited reasons for the outsourcing of specific services. For example, they would recognize that the "reduce cost" reason for outsourcing was cited by public managers of large city services at least twice as often as all other reasons combined for public works/transportation and support functions of government. They would also note, however, that the "reduce cost" rationale barely maintained its place as the leading reason with respect to health, human services, public safety, and parks and recreation services (Dilger, Moffett, and Struyk 1997). While flexibility is a strength of the Pragmatist/Managerial camp, a potential weakness is a "managerial fad" or "follow the leader" syndrome.

Government Reduction/Property Rights. Don't just outsource. Establish true private ownership of all assets that do not meet the strict criteria of being public goods (a good like national defense that a number of people can simultaneously consume and that the benefits of which are difficult or expensive to confine to a select group). Private ownership engages self-interest to heighten the level of responsible management of the asset.

Public Choice. Outsource in cases where it is likely to reduce the capacity of government to act as a monopolist and when it will increase competitiveness among providers (Niskanen 1968).

Efficiency. Outsource whenever the net dollar benefits of doing so are positive. Although a large number of studies do suggest that outsourcing is associated with net dollar benefits to government, George Boyne's (1998a) recent review of such studies argues that the case for outsourcing's superior efficiency has yet to be proven. Among the studies that Boyne considered to be most credible, the evidence for higher efficiency for contracted delivery was mixed. Additionally, the case for efficiency in specific functions often tends to be based on (1) only a single study per service or a single data point (one data point used to represent contracted services versus numerous government providers of the service) or (2) on comparing situations in which the unique circumstances of service delivery in the compared areas are not accounted for (not accounting for factors such as population density, type of collection, or capital resource differences among refuse collectors). Finally, Boyne argues that some of the lower level of expenditures associated with outsourcing may be due to a willingness to trade lower service levels for lower taxes.

Equity/Accountability. Only outsource services for which providers can be held strictly accountable for both delivery and equitable provision. Services in which "creaming" or "cherry picking" of clients or tasks takes place should be avoided as this leads to inequality. Similarly, service provision strategies where it becomes difficult for the public to identify who is responsible for performance and what the standards for accountability are should be avoided. Recently, school researchers have questioned the practice of outsourcing the services of school social workers because such practices implicitly endorse the work of these contractors—even though these external providers do not meet the same procedural standards for redress of grievances as do public schools (Osborne, Collison, Dykeman, and Birdsall 1998). On the other hand, in some cases, private providers of services such as water or criminal corrections may be held to higher standards of accountability than public providers who may have to meet less stringent liability standards (Clark, Heilman, and Johnson 1997; O'Looney 1998).

Moral Foundation. Because government is founded on a set of guardian values that are different from commercial values, we should avoid or be very careful about having government become heavily involved in activities that are traditionally part of the commercial moral syndrome (contracting, bargaining, etc.) and also avoid having private firms become heavily involved in activities (policing, planning, tax assessment and collection, water quality control) that have traditionally been provided by the public sector (Jacobs 1992). Using public-private associations such as public authorities to escape the bounds of traditional public ethics should also be suspect. Whenever one does attempt to reshape the traditional boundaries of commercial and governmental services, it is necessary to create new cultural and educational processes so as to prevent systemic corruption. For example, if a private firm were to assume land planning tasks that involve a great deal of discretion, the staff performing these tasks would probably need to be recruited and trained in a different manner than is customary among private firms so as to ensure this discretion. Also, policies normally associated with the public sector (e.g., whistle-blower rewards) may need to be instituted. In addition to the need to keep separate the respective roles of the public and private sectors, moral foundation theorists also make similar arguments regarding the interaction between the public sector and the

NGO, nonprofit, or civil society sectors. Outsourcing to such groups is suspect in part because of the potential for government to unduly influence the amounts and types of participation in these sectors (Nowland-Foreman 1998).

Core Competency. Maintain core services in-house. Only outsource ancillary services. This camp follows the business literature that suggests that businesses that maintain a core focus are more competitive than those that attempt to do all things. Governments may have more difficulty than your average business figuring out what makes a service a core service. Also, core functions can change over time. For example, data processing was once seen as an ancillary function; its successor, information technology, is now being viewed by many businesses as a core function (Gore 1993; Perlman 1999).

Timing and Phase of Development

The timing of an outsourcing (or in-sourcing) decision involves the time when the decision is made in relation to the phase in the cycle of institutional arrangements for the delivery of the service. Gomez-Ibanez and Meyer (1993) have identified a cycle of institutional arrangement for transit services, and Kraemer (1998) has extended this analysis to water supply services.

The cycle that these scholars identify is described as a vicious one since no single method of delivering services (public or private) remains superior for extended lengths of time. Instead, the actions and reactions in each sector generate incentives to change the sector that provides the services. Kraemer (1998) suggests that the cycle will often begin with a service, such as water supply, being delivered by a small private firm. Over time, market forces lead to mergers and acquisitions that ultimately lead to the concentration of market power by the firm providing the service. Such monopolistic or near-monopolistic power is then tamed through the establishment of a government-backed regulatory system that controls prices or otherwise constrains the ability of the firm to generate large profits.

In the history of the regulation of water supplies, providers were often required to install fire hydrants or to serve poor areas of the community despite the lack of opportunity for profit from such areas. The loss of profit potential in turn leads to a withdrawal of capital as investors turn elsewhere for wealth-generating opportunities. This undercapitalization ultimately leads to a decline in the quality or level of service, though for some services like water, the decline is not noticeable until the system is substantially stressed (by bad weather or excess demand). When the service deteriorates too much, the government will often step in and nationalize or in-source the service, provide new capital, and continue to subsidize the service. Through time, when a service is provided by a large public bureaucracy, the subsidies grow in order to overcome the built-in inefficiencies of such bureaucracies. At some point, the subsidies grow and make the inefficiency so obvious that a budget crisis results. Governments then decide to privatize or outsource the service. At this point, the cycle may start again.

Given enough time, public managers might be able to time their outsourcing choices. It is often the case that managers feel pressured to choose services to outsource at a specific moment in time. Consequently, public managers may not consciously think about phase of development as a factor in selecting services to outsource (or in-source). In addition, phase of development may or may not be a factor that affects all services alike. Theory would suggest that it affects highly capitalized services, yet services with low capital demand may go through similar cycles. For example, wherein welfare services were once the business of private charities and then the responsibility of government, in recent years, more of these services have been contracted with private firms. Many observers, however, are skeptical that these services would remain in the private sector if the economy deteriorated.

ECONOMIC CONSIDERATIONS

Repeatedly, surveys of public managers show that the primary goal in choosing a service for outsourcing is to achieve savings (Dilger, Moffett, and Struyk 1997). Assuming that a cycle of outsourcing as described earlier exists, we can conclude that savings from outsourcing can be achieved at certain phases in the cycle but are less attainable at other points. Such an understanding suggests that simply choosing to outsource a service because contracting led to savings in another community may be a mistake. Moreover, as the brief review of the theoretical literature on service contracting cited suggests, effectively selecting services for outsourcing may be more complex than a follow-the-leader strategy. This is the case even if one only attends to the literature focusing on efficiency issues.

The literature is replete with studies and critiques of the accounting methods used in determining whether to outsource particular services. There are two primary reasons for inadequate accounting of cost and benefits: (1) the failure to include the social, health, and human services costs of the part-time employment among private contractors that often replace the full-time employment of in-house workers (Hatry 1988; Shanker 1995) and (2) the failure to fully account for the overhead cost of in-house contract management and related services that must be provided before, during, and after outsourcing has occurred. Hidden costs of this type can include contracted personnel who must be trained by in-house staff, use of government-owned equipment, the need for additional public relations services, and the risk involved with an unexpected termination of a contract. Hidden, and therefore unaccounted, costs also exist with in-house services, including the cost of governments following more rigorous occupational safety and civil rights regulations (Hakim and Blackstone 1996).

Inadequate cost accounting is obviously not an insurmountable barrier in conducting an economic study to select services for outsourcing. In fact, cities are following the lead of Indianapolis, Indiana, and Charlotte, North Carolina, in using Activities-Based-Costing systems to account for costs that may otherwise be overlooked (O'Looney 1998).

Other local governments use the federal government's Circular A-76 methodology to evaluate the desirability of maintaining in-house versus external service provision, although this methodology has been criticized for taking the price submitted by a contractor as a given. Prager and Desai (1996) advise public managers to check to see whether a potential contractor is employing resources below competitive prices (or practicing initial low-ball bidding) and whether the contractor is alternatively using its monopolistic position to extract excess profits from the government.

Theory of Competition

Most economic analyses of contracting have been based on the idea of competition. According to outsourcing advocates, a public manager's threat to turn to another supplier (or to provide the service in-house again) will ensure that a contractor is efficient as well as responsive to the local government's needs. A periodic review of contracts should theoretically allow governments that use outsourcing to benefit from industry-wide advances in products, techniques, and quality- and cost-controls (Brown and Brudney 1998; Ferris and Graddy 1986).

Unfortunately, the theoretical benefits of outsourcing are based on the assumption of a competitive market or on what some scholars call the "contestability" factor. *Contestability* is the degree to which many contractors would be willing to bid for a service contract. Where there are many sellers, the market is by definition contestable. Contestability, however, can exist even when only one or two firms currently offer a service, if other firms currently provide a close substitute for the service or if there are a number of firms that could quickly switch to providing the service without substantial up-front investments.

Contestable markets are those in which new providers would arise if the government paid slightly more than current providers of a specific service charge. Unfortunately, for public managers seeking a quick rule of thumb to select services to outsource, contestability tends to be a local and dynamic factor. It is logical to assume, however, that contestability is much greater in large cities than in small communities, especially for specialized services.

The notion of competition (and its refined correlate "contestability") has a central place in the literature on economic criteria for outsourcing. In recent years, however, the development of transaction cost economics has contributed additional concepts that must be understood in developing a sound methodology for selecting services for outsourcing—*task complexity* and *asset specificity.*

Task complexity is important because complex tasks make it more difficult to specify with any precision the components of the service being provided and expected production costs. Such uncertainty increases the contract negotiation or bargaining costs as a government attempts to learn the actual production costs (by studying what other governments have paid for similar services, prototyping the service, and so on).

Moreover, if the contract is being let go because potential contractors know more about the task than the government, the bargaining environment is one in which vendors can potentially gouge the government without being caught. Finally, complex tasks that typically involve newer, more sophisticated technologies demanding training on the part of in-house staff and span multiple operational areas tend to raise the governance costs of contracts for complex tasks.

Asset specificity refers to the degree to which an input into a service or production process is only valuable for that specific service or process. That is, if the input (machinery, labor, and so on) is to be used in the delivery of another service, its value will be less. The asset's value is specific to a particular service or process. For example, machinery designed to sort recyclable materials may not have any other use and therefore becomes worthless if it is no longer performing that function. Asset specificity can apply to capital goods, labor, and locations.

The potential for one side in a contract to take advantage of the other side is increased in cases of high asset specificity. Asset specificity can become a factor in outsourcing costs, for example, when a contractor is forced to make a large investment in materials or training that will only be valuable for one specific government contract. In this case, the asset specificity works against the contractor.

On the other hand, if a government were to build a number of computer software applications on the foundation of a specific package of development software, the asset specificity would tend to work against the government whose new modules effectively tie it to the development software vendor. Asset specificity will increase the cost of a contract whether or not the asset specificity is on the side of the contractor or the government. The increased costs come from the ability of the party who is not holding specific assets to act self-interestedly. Asset specificity tends to increase costs directly, as the party holding the specific assets bargains for a premium. It also indirectly increases the cost of bargaining, as the party who looks ahead toward holding the high specificity assets will likely attempt to negotiate for protections against the potential for their "holding the specific assets bag."

Globerman and Vining (1996) have molded these concepts into an innovative framework for analyzing the desirability of service contracts in terms of the degree to which the costs of a contract for a specific service will be greater or less than might be expected were the bargaining and contract implementation to take place in a context-less world. Essentially, Globerman and Vining have created a typology based on the contestability, task complexity, and asset specificity concepts. The resulting matrix includes seven possible combinations of these three factors (Table 4.1).

While Globerman and Vining's (1996) framework was originally created to analyze contracting in the technology area, it has broader applicability. In addition to developing the framework, the authors also suggest several strategies for dealing with each. In general, governments can take steps to reduce task complexity (by breaking up complex tasks into component parts, by retaining in-house expertise, or re-engineering the task), to increase contestability (through active recruitment of vendors, better marketing of RFPs, aggregating or disaggregating contract components depending on the set of potential bidders), or to decrease asset specificity (through greater use of standardized materials and components).

In terms of selecting services for outsourcing, a public manager might give extra consideration to services whose complexity, contestability, and asset specificity can be affected by managerial choices or actions of this sort. More specifically, with the spread of the Internet worldwide, it is likely that services can be provided through a digital medium. For example, information, data analysis, map creation, consulting, legal services, financial, procurement, and accounting services will likely be more susceptible to strategic action on the part of public managers. That is, the Internet should increase opportunities for public managers to enhance contestability and to lower task complexity and asset specificity in selected service areas.

Provision of services whose unit costs tend to be high because of the lack of local economies of scale will be stronger candidates for outsourcing than may have originally been the case. For example, the cost per session of psychiatric services for a rural community that only needs ten or less sessions per month can be extraordinarily high due to transportation costs. Some such communities will employ an in-house psychiatrist whose services require less than full-time demand; however, if this service is provided via the Internet on a contracted basis, the per session cost could be substantially less, thereby making the outsourcing decision the economically correct one.

Scale Economies

The issue of scale economies is another important factor in selecting services for outsourcing. Optimum scale tends to differ from service to service. In general, scale economies are more prevalent in services with a large capital investment in equipment that may have substantial maintenance costs

Table 4.1
Key Technical Factors in Outsourcing Decisions

Case	Task Complexity	Contestability	Asset Specificity*	Dominant Problems
1	Low	High	Low	None. Without asset specificity or high task complexity, opportunism is unlikely to occur, and contestability is not likely to be undermined.
2	Low	High	High	This case turns on the high asset specificity. Because the service is highly contestable (i.e., a lot of firms have the needed skills), it is very likely that the asset specificity is related to physical assets that would have to be created to carry out the contract. Bidders will either require a premium on the contract or they will choose to use a production technique that involves less asset specificity but that is also less efficient.
3	Low	Low	High	This case involves both parties holding each other hostage. The government has a strong position because the assets that the contractor will purchase in fulfilling the contract will make that firm vulnerable. The contractor's strength comes from the low level of contestability.
4	High	High	Low	The key problem in this case is the government's uncertainty about what exactly it will receive in terms of performance. While contractors may have opportunities to exploit the contract, they will be careful in this regard because of the high contestability.

Table 4.1
Continued

Case	Task Complexity	Contestability	Asset Specificity*	Dominant Problems
5	High	Low	Low	This case is similar to Case 4 but involves the government being in a weaker position during the contract implementation phase. With low contestability, the contractor will have a strong temptation to act opportunistically. Moreover, this strong position can be leveraged during the bargaining phase to set higher prices.
6	Low	Low	Low	The key factor in this case is the low contestability as the other factors favor the government's position.
7	High	Low	High	This is the worst case scenario for governments since all three governance costs are present. Attempts to control one factor will typically backfire by increasing the costs of another factor (e.g., having multiple contractors will address the contestability issue, but will simultaneously multiply the costs associated with high asset specificity).

*Assumes that the asset specificity is borne by the contractor rather than the government.

Source: Globerman and Vining 1996.

but can serve a large number of consumers (Stein 1990). This may explain in part why cities have not abandoned mainframe computer technology. It may still be cheaper from a total system maintenance perspective (though not by processed bytes per dollar) for local governments to use mainframe technology rather than PC-based systems.

Scale costs can be substantially affected by the specific services included in an outsourced package. While economies of scale for police patrol services may not be sufficient to justify outsourcing these services in communities with more than 50 officers, including specialty crime labs as part of the service contract may make the choice to outsource economically appropriate.

Another factor affecting economies of scale is the need to provide flexible levels of service (Deacon 1979). If a resort community needs extra police services in the summer months, choosing to contract with an adjoining, nonresort community to provide these services could offer net benefits for the local government.

Ironically, a public manager who identifies contract opportunities based on an analysis of the government's ability to realize the benefits of increased economies of scale may end up working against the government's long-term interest in contestability and low asset specificity. By choosing a vendor with optimum scale economies, the government may unwittingly provide the vendor with increased market power directly and/or indirectly because the government now depends on the vendor's specific assets and technologies.

Economies of scale can also be affected by the ability of the government to monitor the quality of the contractor's services. A recent study of health care contracts in which the contract payments were based only on number of patients treated (and not on the quality, type, or costs of the treatment) found that such contracts are only efficient when it is feasible to serve all patients wanting treatment (Chalkley and Malcomson 1998). As this research suggests, economies of scale must be understood in light of the larger purposes of the services provided.

Finance and Start-Up Costs

Finance and start-up costs also must be considered in selecting services for outsourcing. Avoiding substantial finance costs as well as large overhead and start-up costs is cited as one of the major economic rationales for contracting with private firms (Ferris and Graddy 1986; Savas 1987; Williamson 1986). When there is great need for a quick start-up or when financing is impossible to obtain (e.g., voters fail to approve a bond referendum), this rationale has weight.

On the other hand, it has also been noted that local governments typically have a financing advantage over private firms (Giglio 1998). Cities and counties are often able to obtain below market loans through state or federal programs or through issuing their own bonds. This advantage is often cited as unfair by outsourcing proponents and is used as a reason not to contract for service delivery by those who oppose service contracting on general principles. The governmental financing advantage most often affects the choice to outsource services with high capital costs. Typically, the choice to contract for road, bridge, water supply and treatment, and construction projects might be skewed by the governmental advantage with financing.

Tolerable Level of Risk

The issue of financing, especially as it relates to public works projects, is related to another economic consideration—calculation of the cost of the tolerable level of risk. Proponents of service contracting appropriately note that risk does not *per se* present a barrier to outsourcing a service. One can always require that the contractor be bonded, insured, penalized, and otherwise required to take precautions to ensure delivery of the service. If these steps can be taken at a cost that still allows for the vendor to charge a competitive price for the service, outsourcing would be the reasonable choice (everything else being equal).

While appropriate contract terms can provide for assurance that the vendor will perform under the contract, additional risks may be beyond the control of the contractor. These risks—regulatory delay or change in governmental policies, permits, procedures, and fees—are not easily or cheaply insured against. As such, it has been recognized that contracting or privatization of some public works projects has been impeded by these types of risks. Typically, the dollar measure of such risks is reflected in the difference between the finance cost of a project to a government versus the finance cost for the same project for a private firm (Giglio 1998; Poole 1998).

Costs and Benefits of Ownership

The costs and benefits of ownership represent another economic consideration in selecting a service for outsourcing. Ownership is obviously a two-edge factor. On the plus side, it can lower long-term costs, make profitable sales of products such as maps or title abstracts possible, and provide a capital basis for efficient enterprise operations. On the negative side, ownership often involves ongoing maintenance costs, costs related to transforming capital assets into liquid assets, and a need for the extraordinary political will to provide for long-term capital replenishment when it would be politically more expedient to provide tax relief or new services to citizens.

Ownership issues typically come into play in three situations:

1. If a service is potentially profitable, this can possibly move the outsourcing choice in either direction. If the government has a product or service whose value cannot be realized due to factors such as freedom of information regulations, the government may choose to privatize or license the service/product and receive payment from the purchaser or licensee. On the other hand, if the government can capture the value, it may choose to keep the revenue production in-house.

2. Service entry costs may be incurred in a lumped fashion. Services such as refuse collection are often initiated at a single point in time which, in turn, means that all the equipment used to provide the service tends to wear out at approximately

the same time. Governments faced with such a cost will often choose to out-source the service to avoid large and politically undesirable finance costs.

3. A budget crisis may make the sale of assets a strong temptation. In this case, the consequences of a sale of assets can differ depending on the contestability of the service in question. For a city blessed with many potential service providers, the sale of capital assets used in the provision of the service may be without risk; however, for a small community with few potential providers, the sale of such capital assets can be ill-advised because of the high costs associated with reestablishing service delivery capabilities (Ammons and Hill 1995).

Scope of Economic Purposes and Contracted Services

A newly emerging economic consideration in the selection of services for contracting is related to the scope of economic purposes for service con-tracting. Traditionally, outsourcing has been guided by a laissez-faire, mass production economic model. This approach has focused on identifying low cost contracting opportunities.

Alternatively, new models of flexible, quality-focused production have led to some questioning of the traditional model. One way in which this questioning has arisen in the context of service contracting is through the puzzling results from a study of the relative cost of building public versus private wastewater treatment plants. Heilman and Johnson (1992) com-pared public and private wastewater treatment plants in terms of what the theory of privatization would suggest for such projects. As expected, they found that the private sector projects could get on-line much faster than those in the public sector; however, when these researchers conducted a regression analysis of the relative costs of private vis-à-vis public projects, they discovered that the privatized projects appeared to be considerably more expensive.

In a subsequent article, Clark, Heilman, and Johnson (1997) attempt to explain the puzzling results in terms of differences in incentive structures and the scope of interest of private and public managers involved in the projects. The public projects involved local governments contracting with construction firms to build a treatment plant that would ultimately be oper-ated by municipal employees. The private projects, on the other hand, would be both constructed and operated by the same private firm. The authors suggest that, in the former case, the construction contractors, "have a self-interest in building the project cheaply but no interest in how well or badly the facility operated after they receive payment" (144). While con-tractors are prevented from cheating on the contract through inspection and monitoring processes, little or no incentive exists to build in quality or to do more than the minimal level of work called for in the contract.

The private projects, on the other hand, differ both at the level of choos-ing the construction firms to do the work and at the level of design. That is, private firms tended to choose construction firms that combined strengths in both the low cost and quality areas, whereas the public projects were awarded based on low-cost bidding. With respect to the design phase, the private projects tended to include more redundancy and quality features. The purpose of these features, the authors argue, was to lower the overall operating costs of the plant. In one case, a feature that was not reimbursable under Environmental Protection Agency grants was included in the private project because it enabled the plant to provide services in more extreme situations and to potentially avoid court or EPA penalties that would hurt the long-term business prospects of the firm.

An implication of this research in selecting services to outsource is that public managers must consider the extent to which it is appropriate to contract the full range of associated service activities (design, building, operation, and maintenance) in order for the benefits of an integration effect to be obtained.

MANAGERIAL CONSIDERATIONS

While economic considerations have long held the most prominent position in selecting services to outsource, managerial considerations are now receiving more attention. This is in large measure due to the complexity of the political and economic decision criteria outlined so far in this chapter. One of the manager's roles in the context of outsourcing decisions is to attempt to weigh these factors; however, there are also specific considerations which are more administrative and organizational in character than economic or political.

Gaining Control of Costs

In general, contracting is often viewed as a plus in terms of overall public management goals. In addition to allowing managers to concentrate more fully on core governmental activities, outsourcing tends to provide managers with increased opportunities to restructure service delivery around performance measures and to gain greater control over the full cost of services. This benefit may be especially valuable in services such as information technology or geographic information systems in which cost overruns have historically been a major problem (Regan and O'Connor 1994; Sprague and McNurlin 1993).

In addition, because service costs and cost increases can be stipulated and insured through contract provisions, executive managers can often be more effective and appear more businesslike in their role as intermediary between elected officials and operations. Unfortunately, if the purpose of service contracting is to address deficiencies in local government operations, such managers are also likely to encounter the paradox of service contracting.

Namely, citizens lobby to contract for governmental services because, relatively speaking, they believe government is not competent to deliver these services, but, paradoxically, the same government must have the competence to develop, implement, and monitor effective service contracts.

Delivery Delays

Another managerial area of general concern that service contracting can often effectively address is the problem of service delivery delays. Because contracts can be written to specify delivery deadlines and to sanction contractors who cannot deliver on time, service contracting is an especially effective tool for this problem (Brown and Brudney 1998).

Operational Uncertainty

Operational uncertainty is another managerial problem that outsourcing is well-fitted to address. This concern exists whenever a manager cannot be sure how a new technology, organizational structure, or work process will actually work or what it can achieve. What outsourcing provides in this case is the potential for benchmarking how a system or process will perform when operational before actually implementing it throughout the entire government. Outsourced benchmarking can give managers a more realistic assessment of what to expect without getting emotionally involved in the benchmarking test itself.

Scale Factors in Using Outsourcing as a Means of Reform

Unfortunately, while service contracting can often be an effective tool for these persistent managerial problems, it is not a tool that can be used in a cost-effective manner at a microlevel if outsourcing is not otherwise warranted. That is, it may not make sense to privatize a department simply because departmental managers cannot deliver services on time and on budget. It may not make sense to outsource a function even if such outsourcing appeared to be warranted based on criteria such as basic efficiency, core competency, accountability, and so on. This is the case because the economies of scale of the outsourcing function itself may not have been considered. Outsourcing may not be efficient until a certain number of functions are outsourced.

CONSIDERATION OF POTENTIAL IMPACT OF OUTSOURCING AT FIVE LEVELS OF ORGANIZATION

In addition to specific management of the outsourcing process, managers and policymakers need to consider the potential impacts of outsourcing on the overall structure and organization of government. Potential impacts exist at five levels: (1) an interorganizational, (2) an organizational design, (3) an organizational relations, (4) a technical or functional, and (5) a contract management.

Interorganizational Level

At the interorganizational level, outsourcing can be seen as both a method of more loosely coupling or decoupling the central work of government from more ancillary functions, or it can be viewed as a means of coupling or decoupling the work of government with that of other organizations. To complicate matters further, each of these trajectories can be viewed as either good or bad. For example, believing that there is a need for greater integration of the work of human service providers and seeing a government possibly using a service contract to induce such behavior on the part of private service providers, one would see outsourcing as a good approach.

On the other hand, if the same action was taken in the context of the government outsourcing the pieces of a coordinated public service system to multiple private providers, a service integration advocate would see outsourcing as a net negative. In contrast, if one did not value more service integration, the same outsourcing actions would take on the opposite characteristics.

The effect of outsourcing on interorganizational relationships is substantially affected by the choice of service delivery design models. Elsewhere, it has been suggested that there exists certain archetypes of service delivery designs (vouchers, public sector choice, public bureaucracy, public and private managed competition, fragmented bureaucracy, monopoly, and whole system contracting) that possess certain strengths and weaknesses related to such factors as task or organization coupling and the ability of consumers to exercise "voice" and "exit" options (O'Looney 1993). The way in which managers shape the design of the delivery system can shape the type of relationships and paths of influence that will exist among governments, private firms, NGOs, and citizens or consumers.

Organizational Design Level

Selecting services for successful outsourcing should be guided in part by an understanding of organizational types. While there are numerous ways to categorize organizations, a typology proposed by Wilson (1989), and used by other scholars (Tang, Robertson, and Lane 1996), provides a good starting point for understanding how organizational type might influence the choice of services to outsource. Wilson suggests a categorization of organizations into four types: (1) production, (2) procedural, (3) craft, and

(4) coping. The key to defining these types is the degree to which outcomes and outputs can be measured.

In production organizations, both outcomes and outputs are easily measured, and therefore, managers can use fairly cut-and-dry incentives such as piecework rates to motivate workers. In a procedural organization, outputs are observable and measurable, but outcomes are not. An example of this type of organization would be a mental hospital or an agency that regulates occupational safety. In these organizations, it is fairly easy to measure the number of counseling sessions or safety inspections but rather difficult to measure long-term mental health improvements or avoidance of disasters. In such instance, Tang et al. (1996) suggest that managers create incentive systems based on outputs but allow for deviation from standard procedures when there is credible evidence that the standard procedures are leading to goal displacement. Managers may also need to promote professionalism and professional norms among employees whenever and wherever these are compatible with the organization's goals.

In craft organizations, outcomes, but not outputs, are observable. Research scientists who produce published articles or insurance adjusters who work off-site and produce finished claims represent examples of craft production workers. In this production model, it is relatively futile for managers to attempt to specify work procedures. While it may be possible to develop incentives based only on outcome measures, this approach can become problematic because of the potential for shirking whenever outcomes are the result of the contributions of several individuals. As such, in craft organizations, managers are advised to attempt to promote shared professional values and self-regulation of work activities. In addition, there is some evidence that the creation of autonomous, self-directed teams (Miller and Monge 1986), the use of carefully crafted hiring criteria (Chatman 1989), and the intensive socialization of new employees (Johnston and Snizek 1991) may be effective improvement strategies in craft organizations.

Neither outcomes nor outputs can be easily observed or measured in coping organizations. Elementary and secondary schools, human services, and police services are prime examples of coping organizations. Because of the measurement problem, managers' efforts to specify procedures or establish reward systems based on outcomes frequently meet with resistance or failure. Employees can easily shirk their duties without being observed, and incentive systems often result in workers focusing their efforts on what is most easily measured, rather than on what is important. Tang, Robertson, and Lang (1996) suggest that commitment in such circumstances has to do with the development of shared values, a strong psychological commitment to the organization itself, managers' ability to provide workers with adequate support when outsiders complain about a worker's actions, and highly visible and effective leadership.

While Tang, Robertson, and Lang (1996) were primarily concerned with the relationship between organizational type and organizational commitment, organizational type should also be a key criteria in the selection of services for outsourcing. Obviously, production services, everything else being equal, will be more easily and successfully outsourced than services organized along other lines. Procedurally organized services will be more or less easily outsourced, depending on factors such as the ability of government staff to develop adequate means of monitoring contractors' activities. Successful outsourcing of craft-based services, on the other hand, depends more on the ability of governments to identify outcomes that can be effectively monitored. In both cases, however, the literature suggests that selecting services to outsource must be guided by an assessment of the existence of more subtle and intangible capacities and skills (professionalism, leadership, mechanisms for socialization, psychological commitment and strong organizational values, teamwork, and so on) on the part of the vendor organization. Moreover, these factors become extremely important in decisions to contract services that are delivered via a coping organization.

Ironically, services delivered via coping organizations include those most frequently outsourced (human services) as well as services that governments least frequently outsource (police services). This anomaly probably has more to do with what governments see as their core competencies and with the history of these functions than with organizational types. For example, the federal government's intermittent bursts of grant funding and use of community involvement mandates has undermined the propensity of local governments to deliver human services in-house; however, instead of contracting with for-profit firms, which is typically the case in most local government contracts, human service contracts tend to be awarded to nonprofit organizations (Ferris and Graddy 1986). Such nonprofit organizations more closely resemble governments in their decision-making processes, customer relations, and management approaches than for-profit firms. Moreover, as outsourcing of this type expands and the government exerts more influence on nonprofit organizations, the resemblance is likely to increase (Smith and Lipsky 1993). Continued in-house delivery of police services, on the other hand, suggests that organizational type may be related to choice of services to outsource. Theoretical work that attempts to answer the question of why some work is produced in-house rather than through contracts or markets supports this notion (Ouchi 1980; Williamson 1985).

Organizational Relations Level

Organizational relations refers to the degree to which a service is provided by an organized or powerful group of employees. There are four potential situations in this regard: (1) service employees are not organized in the private sector, but are in the public; (2) are not in the public sector, but are in the private sector; (3) are organized in both sectors; or (4) are organized in neither the public nor the private sector. In general, academic research has focused on only the situation in which public sector employees are thought to exert excess compensation (or rent) due to their strategic position. In this regard, the power of local government employees has been measured in terms of level of unionization, level of wages, and ratio of staff to the local population, according to the structure of government. The findings have been mixed and the explanations contradictory. For example, unionization has led to a lower level of outsourcing because of political resistance or has led to higher level of service contracting because unionization is taken as an indicator of the presence of a high level of organizational slack which points to the potential for substantial savings through outsourcing. While the net effect of public employee power on outsourcing frequency is still unresolved (Boyne 1998b), managers should obviously consider both of these explanations in weighing services for possible outsourcing.

Technical or Functional Level

For many services, there is a strong technical aspect to contracting that must be managed. A difficulty created by outsourcing is the potential for what has been described as the "hollow organization" or an organization that has not retained enough technical expertise and resources to ensure wise outsourcing choices. This problem has often been observed in contracts for high technology services (USGAO 1997) and is compounded by shortages of skilled personnel and managers who do not know enough to be able to assemble the needed technical resources or who believe that it is sufficient to rely solely on contractors for technical advice (Crawford and Krahn 1998).

While contract management techniques can expand the range of technology-based services that can be successfully outsourced, recent research suggests that in some technology fields, governments would be well-advised to think and plan very carefully before fully outsourcing such services. The difficulty with outsourcing IT services, for example, is that such services will frequently affect other functions. As such, the IT managers must have sound relationships with those who will be affected by IT systems. Logically speaking, in-house IT managers will, in most cases, be better able to perform this boundary-spanning role and address the political and administrative demands that typically accompany the implementation of new technology (Ferris and Graddy 1986; Quinn and Hilmer 1994).

Implementing innovative IT projects is usually very risky even under the best circumstances. Removing in-house managers and employees from the implementation process may make it even more difficult to inspire and maintain the commitment and ancillary resources and leadership needed to make the project succeed (Regan and O'Connor 1994). In this regard, Brown and Brudney's (1998) study of implementing geographic information systems (GISs) under various levels of outsourcing is instructive. These scholars found that moderate levels of contracting for the implementation of GISs can yield benefits for organizations. With higher levels of outsourcing, however, not only did the positive effects not appear, but as governments moved toward delivering services exclusively through contractors, the result was that projects were less likely to be delivered on time and within budget. In addition, the contract-only projects tended to produce fewer benefits in terms of operational productivity and performance, organizational decision making, and improved customer service. Perhaps the most telling finding in this study was the identification of a break-even point that was much lower than outsourcing advocates might have predicted. Brown and Brudney report that local governments that contract 25 percent or less of a GIS project tend to receive benefits, while those that contract out more than 25 percent tend to suffer increased costs or declining performance benefits. Very high levels of outsourcing appear to erode internal management capacities, such as oversight and planning, as well as feelings of in-house ownership and involvement of staff in project activities and design. While one of the traditional rationales for outsourcing has been the need to gain access to expertise and technologies that one could otherwise not obtain, the lesson of Brudney and Brown's research tends to reverse this logic. That is, instead of contracting for services to supplement deficits in expertise, managers should consider restricting their outsourcing to those tasks that they understand well but that they may need extra help to fulfill. The fact that local governments vary in the degree to which they contract out services may explain how the literature can report a wide range of outsourcing experiences.

Outsourcing can also have unique effects in particular technical areas. For example, a review of Canadian experiences with contracting for science and technology services reported a mixed set of costs and benefits related to outsourcing. Increased budget flexibility was associated with outsourcing, but non-outsourced public laboratories appeared better equipped to provide continuity and accumulation of knowledge over time (Dalpe and Anderson 1997). Understanding the technical content of a service should lead to a more customized outsourcing strategy.

Contract Management Level

Selecting services to outsource should probably be most influenced by political, economic, and organizational factors; contract management skill also has a role to play in selecting services to outsource if we assume that specific styles of or approaches to contract management may be more suitable to the successful outsourcing of some services rather than others.

For example, classic contract management productivity tools such as performance-based contracting, centralized accounts management, standardized contract language, risk management and monitoring procedures, and low-bid contract awards can probably be effectively applied to contracts for services with clearly observable outcomes and outputs. On the other hand, if the contracting environment is more complex, other sets of tools and contract management skills may be needed. For example, if the proposed outsourcing is for a service that involves a high degree of technology, contract management techniques such as forcing vendors to stake their reputation on their work, close scrutiny of the personnel used and their training requirement, using a wide variety of contract payment methods, mandating periodic communications (Rickover 1979), and use of evaluation data from several sites can reduce the contractor advantage (Crawford and Krahn 1998).

In a similar fashion, successful outsourcing of services when the potential exists to disrupt delicate relations with government employees will likewise demand a special set of contract management skills and strategies. Jackson (1997) suggests that managers in these situations be ready to implement or manage such strategies as job enrichment for employees that remain, two-tiered salary schemes, preferential hiring/transfers/retraining for displaced employees, restricting contracting to expanded—not existing—services, matching the rate of outsourcing to the rate of attrition, and requiring contractors to offer right of first refusal to displaced workers. In addition, Becker, Silverstein, and Chaykin (1995) suggest that understanding and skill in reshaping employee benefit packages may be crucial in efforts to overcome employee resistance to outsourcing existing services when the public sector benefit package differs substantially from the private sector package for the same service.

The specific skills needed to successfully manage contract awards in different service areas can also vary. Gooden's (1998) study of the practices followed by successful and not-so-successful contract award managers suggests that the success in awarding human services contracts demands a much more subtle approach to contractor services, one that combines standardized contract management practices with a thorough understanding of social work goals and programs. That is, these contract managers needed to master both technical and relationship aspects of the awards process in order to succeed.

Similarly, other research (O'Looney 1998) makes a case for contract managers of specific service areas such as technology services to devote a much greater portion of their time than is traditionally the case in managing the contractual relationship. The implication for selecting services to outsource is that one should only consider contracting services for which one is prepared to provide high-quality contract award and management services.

CONCLUSION

This chapter has briefly outlined and explored a range of issues that managers should consider in selecting services to outsource. Broadly speaking, these issues can be arranged into three categories: political, economic, and managerial/organizational. Within each category, several subissues such as the analysis of the moral foundations, the transaction costs, and the interorganizational impacts of an outsourcing decision were explored.

While we can identify the stated reasons for local government managers deciding to contract out specific services, current knowledge does not allow us to accept these stated reasons as either empirically valid or normatively desirable. This is not to suggest that managers should either wait until science has caught up to practice or initiate overly expensive decision-making processes. Instead, what this review suggests is that public managers keep an open mind about outsourcing, consider the full range of issues and evidence that might affect their choices, and engage in sufficient dialogue to make good faith and defendable decisions regarding their selections.

The experience of the state of Massachusetts is instructive. Here the issue of what constitutes an accurate cost accounting became highly, but not overly, politicized. As a consequence of Republican Governor William Weld keeping an open line of communication with the Democratic legislature, politics actually worked the way it is supposed to work, according to Bruce Wallin's (1997) review of the process. The result was the state's becoming one of the first to outline a specific, well-thought-out, and bipartisan process for privatization/outsourcing. The process includes both moderately pro-outsourcing elements such as support for identifying potential for savings from outsourcing as well as elements that indicate a more cautious approach to selecting services for outsourcing such as being sure to include contract development and procurement costs in the estimates of the total cost of outsourcing.

While the process used will likely still need refinement, it does attempt to address the potential for partisan, institutional, or ideological predispositions that lead to over or underuse of outsourcing. As Wallin (1997) argues, when it becomes difficult to determine or agree on cost-savings, the process for decision making becomes all that more important. The Massachusetts effort in this regard represents a good beginning point.

REFERENCES

Abrahamson, E. 1996. Management fashion. *Academy of Management Review* 21: 254–285.

Ammons, David, and Debra J. Hill. 1995. The viability of public-private competition as a long-term service delivery strategy. *Public Productivity and Management Review* 19(1): 12–24.

Becker, Fred, Gail Silverstein, and Lee Chaykin. 1995. Public employee job security and benefits. *Public Productivity and Management Review* 19(1): 22–33.

Boyne, George A. 1998a. Bureaucratic theory meets reality: Public choice and service contracting in U.S. local government. *Public Administration Review* 58(6): 474–484.

Boyne, George A. 1998b. The determinants of variations in local service contracting: Garbage in, garbage out? *Urban Affairs Review* 34(1): 150–163.

Brown, Mary Maureen, and Jeffrey L. Brudney. 1998. A "smarter, better, faster, and cheaper" government: Contracting and geographic information systems. *Public Administration Review* 58(4): 335–345.

Chalkley, Martin, and James M. Malcomson. 1998. Contracting for health services with unmonitored quality. *Economic Journal: The Quarterly Journal of the Royal Economic Society* 108(449): 1093–1110.

Chatman, J. A. 1989. Improving interactional organizational research: A model of person-organization fit. *Academy of Management Review* 34: 339–347.

Clark, Cal, John G. Heilman, and Gerald W. Johnson. 1997. Privatization of wastewater treatment plants: Lessons from changing corporate strategies. *Public Works: Management and Policy* 2(2): 140–147.

Crawford, John W., and Steven Krahn. 1998. The demanding customer and the hollow organization. *Public Productivity and Management Review* 22(1): 107–118.

Dalpe, Robert, and Frances Anderson. 1997. Contracting out of science and technology services. *Administration and Society* 28(4): 489–510.

Deacon, R. 1979. The expenditure effects of alternative public supply institutions. *Public Choice* 34: 381–397.

Dilger, Robert J., Randolph R. Moffett, and Linda Struyk. 1997. Privatization of municipal services in America's largest cities. *Public Administration Review* 57(1): 21–26.

Donahue, John. 1989. *The privatization decision: Public ends, private means.* New York: Basic Books.

Ferris, J., and E. Graddy. 1986. Contracting out: For what? With whom? *Public Administration Review* 46(4): 332–344.

Giglio, Joseph. 1998. Private toll roads. *Public Works: Management and Policy* 2(4): 286–293.

Globerman, Steven, and Aidan Vining. 1996. A framework for evaluating government contracting-out decisions with and applications to information technology. *Public Administration Review* 56: 577–586.

Gomez-Ibanez, J. A., and J. R. Meyer. 1993. *Going private: The international experience with transport privatization.* Washington, DC: Brookings Institute.

Gooden, Vincent. 1998. Contracting and negotiation: Effective practices of successful human service contract managers. *Public Administration Review* 58(6): 499–509.

Gore, A. 1993. From red tape to results: Creating a government that works better. Washington, DC: U.S. Government Printing Office.

Hakim, Simon, and Erwin Blackstone. 1996. Privately managed prisons go before the review board. *American City & County* 111(4):40–47.

Hatry, Harry P. 1988. Privatization presents problems. *National Civic Review* (March/April): 112–117.

Heilman, John G., and Gerald W. Johnson. 1992. *The politics and economics of privatization: The case of wastewater treatment.* Tuscaloosa: University of Alabama.

Jackson, Cynthia. 1997. Strategies for managing tensions between public employment and private service delivery. *Public Productivity and Management Review* 21(2): 119–136.

Jacobs, Jane. 1992. *Systems of survival: A dialogue on the moral foundations of commerce and politics.* New York: Random House.

Johnston, G. P., and W. E. Snizek. 1991. Combining head and heart in complex organizations: A test of Etizioni's dual compliance structure hypothesis. *Human Relations* 44: 1255–1272.

Kraemer, R. A. 1998. Privatization in the water industry. *Public Works: Management and Policy* 3(2): 104–123.

Miller, K. I., and P. R. Monge. 1986. Participation, satisfaction, and productivity: A meta-analytic review. *Academy of Management Journal* 29: 727–753.

Niskanen, W. 1968. The peculiar economics of bureaucracy. *American Economic Review* 58: 293–305.

Nowland-Foreman, Garth. 1998. Purchase-of-service contracting, voluntary organizations, and civil society. *American Behavioral Scientist* 42(1): 108–123.

O'Looney, John A. 1993. Beyond privatization and service integration: Organizational models for service delivery. *Social Services Review* 67(4): 501–534.

O'Looney, John A. 1998. *Outsourcing state and local government services: Decision-making strategies and management methods.* Greenwood, CT: Quorum Press.

Osborne, Judith L., Brooke B. Collison, Cass Dykeman, and Bobbie A. Birdsall. 1998. External service providers in schools: A three-state study. *NASSP Bulletin* 82(594): 105–112.

Ouchi, William G. 1980. Markets, bureaucracies and clans. *Administrative Science Quarterly* 25: 129–141.

Perlman, Ellen. 1999. Billion-dollar outsourcings are taking root. *Governing* 12(5): 94.

Poole, Robert W. 1998. Private toll roads: Changing the highway program. *Public Works: Management and Policy* 3(1): 3–9.

Prager, Jonas, and Swati Desai. 1996. Privatizing local government operations. *Public Productivity and Management Review* 20(2): 185–203.

Quinn, J. B., and F. G. Hilmer. 1994. Strategic outsourcing. *Sloan Management Review* 37(4): 43–55.

Regan, E. A., and B. N. O'Connor. 1994. *End-user information systems.* New York: Macmillan.

Rickover, H. 1979. (August 16). *Principles of the naval nuclear propulsion program* (Naval Reactors Letter, Serial 082175).

Savas, E. S. 1987. *Privatization: The key to better government.* New York: Chatham House.

Shanker, Albert. 1995. Does privatization work? *State Legislatures* (May): 28.

Smith, S., and M. Lipsky. 1993. *Nonprofits for hire: The welfare state in the age of contracting.* Cambridge, MA: Harvard University Press.

Sprague, R. H., Jr., and B. C. McNurlin. 1993. *Information systems management in practice* (3rd ed.). Englewood Cliffs, NJ: Prentice-Hall.

Stein, R. M. 1990. *Urban alternatives: Public and private markets in the provision of local services.* Pittsburgh: University of Pittsburgh Press.

Tang, Shui-Yan, Peter J. Robertson, and Charles E. Lane. 1996. Organizational types, commitment and managerial actions. *Public Productivity and Management Review* 19(3): 289–312.

U.S. General Accounting Office (USGAO). 1997. *High-risk series: Defense contract management* (GAO/HR-97-4). Washington, DC: USGAO.

Wallin, Bruce A. 1997. The need for a privatization process: Lessons from development and implementation. *Public Administration Review* 57(1): 11–20.

Williamson, Oliver E. 1985. *The economic institutions of capitalism: Firms, markets, relational contracting.* New York: Free Press.

Williamson, Oliver E. 1986. The multidivisional structure. In *Organizational Economics,* eds. J. B. Barney and W. G. Ouchi, 163–187. San Francisco: Jossey-Bass.

Wilson, James Q. 1989. *Bureaucracy: What government agencies do and why they do it.* New York: Basic Books.

5

Structuring the Market for Service Delivery: A New Role for Local Government

Mildred Warner

INTRODUCTION

Local government efforts to restructure service delivery in order to increase efficiency and reduce costs are not new. What *is* new in the past twenty years is the increased emphasis given to privatization as a service delivery option. Privatization is but one restructuring option available to local governments. In reality, local governments employ a mix of restructuring forms which should be studied in combination. There is a long history of inter-municipal cooperation through which governments can create economies of scale by joining with other governments to provide a service.

Recently, we have seen evidence of governmental entrepreneurship—a system in which local governments expand services and raise revenues by competing for private sector clients. As privatization has become more important, so too has reverse privatizing (bringing previously contracted services back under direct public sector control). Government is not merely shedding its services to the market, it is actively structuring the market of local suppliers, creating competition where none would exist otherwise. When examined in this light, restructuring of service delivery should not be viewed as a dichotomy between public and private provision; rather, the full array of restructuring alternatives should be assessed.

To ensure the benefits of scale and competition, governments may engage the market as direct providers or seek to structure the market by creating competition. Since competition is key to efficiency, and adequate oversight and monitoring is key to quality control, it is reasonable to expect increased market behavior by local governments as a complement to privatization. Rather than relinguish service provision to private providers, governments are creating a wider market of service providers. In this new market for service provision, we can expect direct public sector service provision to continue to accompany privatization.

Using data from a 1997 survey of township and county governments in upstate New York, this chapter provides evidence that governments use a complex mix of restructuring alternatives to achieve multiple goals. The nature and relative importance of three alternatives to privatization— (1) intermunicipal cooperation, (2) reverse privatization, and (3) governmental entrepreneurship—are described. This chapter also provides insights into which factors local elected officials must consider in their decisions to restructure. Case studies of local governments in New York state show how governments balance service quality, economic efficiency, local control, and responsiveness to residents by using a mix of restructuring alternatives of which privatization is but one alternative.

BACKGROUND

Local governments are under pressure to create greater efficiencies while maintaining service quality and enhancing responsiveness to citizen concerns. Privatization, as an alternative to public service delivery, can help achieve these goals by encouraging competition, creating economies of scale, and allowing for greater consumer voice through the marketplace. Inefficiencies in the provision of public sector goods are attributed in part to the monopoly status of many public sector providers, bureaucratic insulation from citizen preferences, and inflated labor costs due to civil service provisions (Savas 2000).

There is much debate on the relative merits of privatization. While proponents argue that the free market is more efficient (Reason Foundation 1997; Savas 2000), moderates emphasize the role that government must play as regulator to prevent monopoly pricing and to ensure accountability to public values (Donahue 1989; Osborne and Gaebler 1992), and skeptics warn about corruption and loss of public sector jobs (Sclar 1997; Sclar, Schaeffer, and Brandwein 1989; Starr 1987).

Local public officials are aware of the important issues at stake in these debates and, thus, view their restructuring alternatives from a broad, pragmatic perspective. The importance of governmental leadership (e.g., knowledge, risk taking) in privatization and restructuring decisions has been well-documented (ICMA 1983; Osborne and Gaebler 1992).

The benefits of privatization—efficiency, economies of scale, and consumer voice—can be achieved through other means. Restructuring alternatives which expand the public sector role include intermunicipal cooperation, reverse privatization, and governmental entrepreneurship. Intermunicipal cooperation allows local governments to achieve economies of scale while keeping services within the public sector. In states where consolidation is possible, a few metropolitan governments are emerging as cities absorb their suburbs (Orfield 1997; Rusk 1993). In New York state, consolidation is politically infeasible, but intermunicipal cooperation for service delivery is widely encouraged and relatively easy (Office of the State Comptroller 1994).

Reverse privatization, through which governments bring previously contracted work back in house, complements privatization. Public-private competitive bidding has been used effectively in the United States and Great Britain to encourage public sector units to become more efficient or to create competition (Osborne and Plastrick 1997; Young 1992). Governments are also expanding services to areas traditionally provided by private contracts if they feel greater efficiencies can be secured through public provision.

Governmental entrepreneurship is another means to achieve economies of scale while maintaining services in the public sector. In this case, government units actively compete for private sector business to gain economies of scale (Osborne and Gaebler 1992).

Previous studies of privatization have failed to differentiate restructuring which shrinks the public sector role (privatization) from government expansion via intermunicipal cooperation, reverse privatization, or governmental entrepreneurship. Census of Government data on contracting do not differentiate intermunicipal cooperation from privatization. The ICMA surveys of alternative service delivery measure intermunicipal cooperation but do not measure reverse privatization or governmental entrepreneurship.

Beyond external restructuring lies another alternative—internal restructuring—which uses workplace innovation, greater labor management cooperation, and heightened attention to consumer feedback to increase efficiency (Applebaum and Batt 1994). Large centralized government bureaucracies are giving way to leaner, more flexible management and delivery systems (Osborne and Plastrick 1997). Rigid public sector management systems (civil service rules, procurement policies) designed to prevent corruption are now being criticized as inflexible, unresponsive, and inefficient (Bennett 1990; Osborne and Gaebler 1992; Savas 2000). To the extent that this *internal* decentralization of authority results in improved governmental performance, it may provide an effective alternative to privatization.

TQM is an important example of ways to achieve efficiency. While TQM is gaining popularity with local governments across the country (West, Berman, and Milakovich 1994), experience in New York has been uneven, with cost-savings hard to quantify (Blumner et al. 1998). Deficiencies in public management were cited as the major cause of cost differences between public and private sectors in New York (Lauder 1992). Thus, significant increases in efficiency could be obtained without resorting to external forms of restructuring (privatization, intermunicipal cooperation).

Recent studies of the scope of workplace restructuring in the public sector, however, emphasize the difficulties of workplace transformation (Blumner et al. 1998; Hebdon and Hyatt 1996). Public officials may be inclined to externalize services through privatization rather than face the internal challenges of workplace restructuring.

This chapter focuses only on external forms of restructuring. Primary emphasis is given to describing the nature of reverse privatization and the complex ways governments mix restructuring alternatives.

DATA

Data used in this chapter are drawn from a survey administered to all chief elected and appointed officials in townships and counties in New York state outside New York City (Warner and Hebdon 1997). The research was conducted in collaboration with the County Legislators and Supervisors Association (CLSA) of New York state. A preliminary survey of 552 chief elected town and county officials in April 1996 found little new privatization at the local level in New York state. Of 133 respondents, only 17 had privatized and five were considering privatization in the future. Many respondents described alternatives to privatization, such as internal restructuring and intermunicipal cooperation, which could be used to achieve similar goals.

To better understand the full range of restructuring alternatives, key informant interviews and focus groups were held with experienced local government officials and union representatives. Five types of restructuring were identified along with 14 factors that influence government decisions to restructure. In addition to privatization and intermunicipal cooperation, the focus groups stressed the importance of reverse privatization and governmental entrepreneurship. They claimed that local governments do not merely respond to market conditions, they play an active role in structuring the market by creating competition and economies of scale.

Based on these focus groups, a new survey was developed and administered during winter 1997 to assess the full range of restructuring activity by upstate township and county governments. The survey distinguished five forms of restructuring:

1. Intermunicipal cooperation (mutual aid, joint production, creation of a special district, or contracting with another governmental unit)

2. Privatization (contracting out, transfer of assets or program to the private for-profit or nonprofit sectors, or to a public benefit corporation)

3. Reverse privatization (bringing a program or assets back in house from the for-profit or nonprofit sectors or from another government or public authority)

4. Governmental entrepreneurship (government contracts its services to private or nonprofit sector clients)

5. Cessation of services

The survey measured new cases of restructuring (since 1990) across seven broad service areas. Respondents also ranked and described the factors important in their decision to restructure or not. In addition, respondents were invited to briefly profile individual cases of restructuring. Out of a total of 989 upstate towns and counties, 222 responded, and 108 of these reported restructuring activity since 1990.[1] Responding governments reported 556 individual cases of restructuring, and 155 of these were described in greater detail in the case study section of the survey. Intermunicipal cooperation was the most common restructuring option used by New York state local governments (55%). Privatization was next in importance (28%), but reverse privatization (7%) and governmental entrepreneurship (6%) provided a counterbalance. Cessation of service (4%) was rarely chosen as a restructuring method (Table 5.1).

Restructuring was highest in public works where intermunicipal cooperation was the most common form (due in large part to cooperation among town highway departments). Privatization, reverse privatization, governmental entrepreneurship, and cessation were highest in this service area as well. Public safety and support functions were the next most common service areas to be restructured.

Intermunicipal cooperation was the preferred restructuring form in all service areas except health and human services where privatization (to

Table 5.1
Restructuring Cases by Form and Service Area

Service Area	Intermu-nicipal Cooperation	Privatization	Reverse Privatization	Government Entrepre-neurship	Cessation	All Forms
Public Works	101	37	6	8	9	161
Transportation	21	19	5	1	1	47
Public Utilities	32	9	3	2	2	48
Public Safety	53	10	3	3	2	71
Health and Human Services	14	24	6	7	5	56
Parks and Recreation	26	14	5	3	2	50
Support Functions	34	24	5	7	1	71
Other	26	17	7	1	1	52
All Services	307	154	40	32	23	556

Of 222 responding governments, 108 governments restructured, accounting for 556 separate cases of restructuring activity.

Source: Warner and Hebdon Survey of New York State Townships and Counties 1997.

nonprofit organizations) was the most common. Reverse privatization and governmental entrepreneurship had the highest incidence in service areas where other forms of restructuring were also high.

FACTORS LEADING TO RESTRUCTURING

According to their ranking of the factors important in the decision to restructure service delivery, local public officials take a pragmatic approach to restructuring. Impact on local government budget, service quality, and economic efficiency were the top-ranked factors (Figure 5.1). The next most important factors were managerial concerns regarding service provision (management, labor, leadership, and monitoring). Community values, legal issues, and information concerns ranked next in importance. Political concerns, past experience, and local employment impact ranked even lower. Surprisingly, unionization was considered the least important factor, especially by those governments that had restructured.

In general, differences in factor rankings between restructuring and nonrestructuring governments were not large; however, Figure 5.1 shows that restructuring governments considered financial impacts, service quality, and managerial variables to be more important than nonrestructuring governments.

In contrast, nonrestructuring governments ranked community values, information, legal issues, past experience, and unionization as more important than governments that had restructured. While much of the restructuring literature gives primary importance to economic efficiency and unionization factors as benefits and barriers (respectively) to restructuring, these results suggest local governments actually give greater attention to service quality, community values, and technical aspects of service provision. The lack of emphasis given to unionization and political factors by governments that actually restructured suggests that these factors are not as serious a barrier to restructuring as popular wisdom would suggest.

In addition to ranking the importance of the factors, respondents were invited to provide descriptive comments. These comments reinforce the emphasis given to service quality and community values. As one respondent noted, "Budget is a prime consideration as long as service is not compromised." Most of the comments under the service quality category showed great concern for customer service and governmental responsiveness:

"Customer service and access is first priority."
"The goal of quality, responsiveness, and citizen access has been critically important in assessing every single restructuring possibility (critical)."
"They [citizens] need to know they are the customer, and we [government] need to provide the best."

Figure 5.1
Restructuring Factors, Average Level of Importance

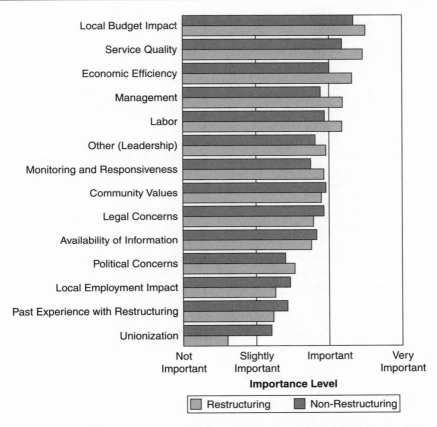

Note: Respondent rankings of the importance of each factor (0 [not important], 1 [slightly important], 2 [important], and 3 [very important]) were averaged over the 108 governments which restructured and the 114 which did not restructure.

Source: Warner and Hebdon Survey of New York State Townships and Counties 1997.

"Government should constantly look for responsiveness and quality of services."
"You have to answer to the public."
"Any attempt at being more responsive or more accessible is important."

Respondents indicated restructuring should result in quantifiable improvements in service quality:

"[We] would not privatize if the private sector was not able to maintain or surpass government quality level."

"[We] focus not only on quality of customer service, but also on measurable outcomes of those services."

"[It] must be of equal or better service quality."

Governmental oversight was deemed critical to ensuring quality and citizen access:

"We evaluate the restructuring changes as to the impact on residents/customers."

"Citizens' demands/needs require attention to how service will be delivered."

The need for local governmental control was echoed in the Other (Leadership) category as well. Of the descriptive comments used to describe this factor, 21 respondents indicated loss of local control and autonomy to be the primary concerns.

"Most residents of the town prefer local leadership. They do not want local control to slip away."

Descriptive comments under the community values category stressed the need for local control as well as the value citizens place on having the service provided locally:

"[We] do not want to lose control."

"Small community residents like to keep service delivery 'in house.'"

"Operation of county residential health care facility (infirmary) is a community tradition."

"[We] value local service delivery."

Other community values comments reflected citizen concerns about continued access to service after restructuring:

"Our mental health privatization raised considerable concern in the community to deal with the fear that our residents who need care will not be able to continue to receive such care under the new organization."

"In our effort to privatize our county-owned nursing home, we have encountered significant resistance due to our tradition of providing care throughout the county."

While one respondent stressed taxpayer concerns—"taxpayers are concerned more with quality and quantity of services than legacy and vested interests"—more respondents felt citizens were reluctant to see change and saw a need for government to make sure that change was consistent with community values. The need for governmental leadership in the restructuring decision was also stressed:

"It sometimes takes a lot of convincing to have people change the way they receive a service."

"Tradition and identity are difficult to change; we need to look at consolidating services, making sure to continue to provide services at the same levels."

"Community values should be looked at closely before changes are made."

"People have a difficult time, both internally and externally, with change."

Political values regarding the size of government did not rank highly among respondents. Only two respondents described a goal of shrinking local government's role:

"We are very concerned about public opinion; the size of government."

"Reduce bureaucracy; limit the levels of government (reduce the size)."

The rest stressed the need for a continuing government role:

"Local government should maintain control over local problems and issues."

"Providing high-quality services cost effectively was critical; public accepted [this] as a good idea—[taking] steps in the right direction; worked through procedural issues with loss in some cases, with resistance in others (turf)."

"[We] [d]etermined that change would be accepted as long as a local government contact person remained as a link—for accountability and responsiveness."

Local government leaders recognize the complexity of balancing economic efficiency with service quality, community values, and responsiveness to citizens. Change requires careful leadership. The close accountability of local government leaders to the citizens, and the direct impact and high visibility of local service restructuring decisions requires a broad pragmatic approach. It is no wonder that local officials pursue a mix of restructuring alternatives.

ALTERNATIVES TO PRIVATIZATION

Three alternatives to privatization are described here: (1) intermunicipal cooperation, (2) reverse privatization, and (3) governmental entrepreneurship. Using quantitative results as well as qualitative descriptions from the more detailed case studies, the nature of restructuring and rationale for each restructuring choice is illustrated.

Intermunicipal Cooperation

Intermunicipal cooperation is the most well-known and widely used alternative to privatization. In New York state, regulatory support for cooperation was widened in 1987 with the revision of Article 5-G to

General Municipal Law which allows any city, town, village, county, or special purpose district (school, fire, water, and so on) to enter into a cooperative or contractual agreement to provide a service (Office of the State Comptroller 1994).

Ninety-eight governments reported 307 separate cases of cooperation. Mutual aid agreements were most common (76 cases), especially in public works and public safety. Results show municipalities are moving toward more formal arrangements, however, as joint production and contracting are the next most common forms of cooperation. Contracting out to another government (53 cases) was more common than contracting in (39 cases)—a reflection of the consolidation inherent in intermunicipal cooperation. Formation of special districts (27 cases) or authorities was less common—a reflection in part of the desire to maintain more direct local control. The survey also measured cooperative investment of funds (24 cases). Cost-savings and better service coverage were the mostly commonly cited benefits of cooperation.

Turf and concerns about continued citizen access were the most commonly cited barriers. Thus, even though cooperation keeps the service public, residents still fear that loss of local control will reduce service responsiveness. Governments respect this need for local identification with the service provider.

Many respondents described efforts to achieve cost-savings in indirect services (equipment sharing, dispatching, joint purchasing, and bidding) which the customer does not directly see, while keeping the direct part of service delivery local. For example, several towns described linking volunteer ambulance services with the more professional staff of larger government- or hospital-run services to solve the shortage of adequately trained medical technicians, while maintaining local volunteer service identification. Similarly, there were no mergers among town highway departments, but many described significant savings in cooperative snowplowing agreements and joint purchasing, especially of large equipment.

The ability to exercise market power was clearly a motivation for intermunicipal cooperation. This was described by respondents in the town of Pendleton which joined six other towns to create a garbage consortium where they consolidated bidding on waste and recycling collection. In addition to lower collection costs and tipping fees, they were able to cut costs in half: "Being a consortium of seven towns, we get better bids."

The most frequently described cases of intermunicipal cooperation were in the area of public works (equipment sharing, joint plowing, garbage and recycling, and water), public safety (ambulance service and dispatching), and administrative support functions (bookkeeping, tax assessment, judges, and legal services).

Reverse Privatization

Reverse privatization refers to those services which had been contracted out but have now been returned to direct governmental provision. This could include services or assets taken back from the for-profit sector, the nonprofit sector, a public authority or public benefit corporation, or another government. The survey tracked services brought back in house (35 cases) as well as transfer of assets back to the municipality (5 cases). Twenty-seven governments reported a total of 40 cases of reverse privatization. Reverse privatization was largest from the for-profit sector (16 cases), less from the nonprofit sector (9 cases), and smallest from inter-municipal cooperation (5 cases), or a public authority (2 cases).

Like privatization, respondents pursue reverse privatization to reduce costs and improve service quality; however, the desire for greater accountability, coordination, and control over service provision were listed as benefits as often as cost-savings. In some cases, respondents acknowledged that reverse privatization did not save money, but their chief motivation was to improve service quality and control. Four broad types of reverse privatization were reported: (1) bringing services back in house from the for-profit sector, (2) bringing services back in house from the nonprofit sector, (3) bringing services back in house from intermunicipal cooperation, and (4) governmental expansion into services traditionally provided by the private sector.

For-Profit to In House. The most common form of reverse privatization was bringing services back in house that were previously provided by the for-profit sector. Cost controls, better service, more accountability, and more consistency in service delivery were the most commonly stated benefits:

- Genesee County ceased its contract with the private sector fixed based operator for airport operation and fuel service. Their goals were "better service, fewer complaints, cost controls." They cited "more accurate cost allocation, increased airport traffic, and T-hangar rentals" as benefits. Barriers to the reverse privatization were "previous f.b.o. litigation, FAA regulation, tenants' skepticism."

- The rural town of Schroon bought out its contract with the Environmental Facility Corporation for sewer service in 1991 and took on the service as part of town government. Estimated cost-savings from the program were $400,000.

- Ulster County brought its occupational therapy contract back in-house in order "to provide better coverage for residents." Despite the barrier of having to contract out "when the occupational therapy coordinator is on vacation, etc.," the county felt that providing the service with an in-house employee "provides continuity of care to residents, more hours of therapy." While this increased employment by one full-time equivalent, the county felt the move "probably saves money."

Support services are commonly thought to be excellent targets for contracting out because the service is discrete and quality is easy to measure; however, concerns with quality and consistency drove two towns to bring such work back in-house. The town of Rochester brought back in house its payroll and bookkeeping functions in order to achieve "cost savings, more accountability, and better monitoring of financial picture."

Another town brought back in house its contracts for code enforcement of fire, land-use, and buildings. Its goal was "to get better service, have a consistent officer, and not so many changes." Despite the higher cost, it "hopes to provide better, more efficient code enforcement." The decision to bring the work back in-house was primarily a management consideration. We "were able to get [a] highly qualified assessor at [a] reasonable cost. Had contractor do code enforcement—[there was a] continual change of inspectors—[so we] decided to do the job in-house."

A more unusual case was the town of Penfield which is in the process of purchasing streetlights and taking over their maintenance from Rochester Gas and Electric (RG&E). Although "RG&E does not want to sell" and the "town needs to find the capital to invest," the town feels that "capital investments will be offset by operating cost savings." Cost-savings are "minimal now, but could become substantial as the town becomes responsible for maintaining more lights." The town's goals are to be more "cost effective, save money, and provide quality service."

Nonprofit to In House. Bringing contracts back from the nonprofit sector was the next most common form of reverse privatization. The nonprofit sector is a frequent contractor for health and human services but is less stable than a government agency and often pays workers lower wages and benefits. The Office for the Aging in Livingston County was brought back in house under county control to "stabilize the funding and improve coordination and economies of scale in programming for the elderly." The Council of Churches remained a partner in the new county government-based initiative. The action allowed the county to provide "more services for the same dollars" and to "improve benefits" for workers in the agency. The county listed the following barriers to the activity: "legal, public support, the state, fiscal."

Intermunicipal Cooperation to In House. Bringing back services from intermunicipal cooperation was the least common form of reverse privatization. Regaining local control and increasing the ability to get the desired type and level of service were the most commonly mentioned goals. The town of Gardiner stopped using the county mainframe and began to use its personal computers to maintain its property information systems database. The goals of this action were to increase "control over data input and the ability to handle [their] own reporting." The town had been frustrated by the "county's extreme reluctance to deal with PCs." The project resulted in "improved access to data, reduced input time, better data control, [and the] ability to produce and sell [their] own reports."

Berlin, along with another town, took over its solid waste program from the Eastern Rensselaer Solid Waste Management Authority and cited large savings. The town of Hammond "withdrew from a cooperative group with five other municipalities due to poor service from the code enforcement officer," but noted that "other towns/villages did not experience our trouble."

Governmental Expansion. In addition to bringing services back in house which had previously been contracted out, governments reported new areas of activity where they had used outside contractors traditionally but now realized they could perform the work more efficiently themselves. Several counties reported the adoption of self-insurance schemes for health insurance. In addition to saving several million dollars per year over the costs of nonprofit or for-profit insurance providers, they also reported "local/internal control of costs, self-determination of benefit levels, and a more logical budgeting process" as benefits. The cases ranged from self-insurance for the entire health plan to just the prescription drug program. In some cases, governments joined with neighboring governments in the region to create a larger risk pool.

In Putnam County, contracts to rebuild low-span bridges were brought back in house. Previously, all bridge work had been contracted out, but officials realized they could use in-house staff to construct and repair low bridges. Not only did this save money, it also improved employee morale since department engineers enjoyed being able to design bridges, not just supervise work of outside contractors.

Governmental Entrepreneurship

This alternative was the least common, and most unexpected, given the current rhetoric about less government. Twenty places reported a total of 32 cases of governmental entrepreneurship; however, it may come as little surprise that when governments think about the market in terms of contracting for services, they also may think about how to use the market to generate revenues. Advertising on public buses and trains has been a long tradition. Shrink-wrapping buses to become a moving billboard is a newer phenomenon. Renting space in bus terminals, train stations, restaurants, and stores is now commonplace.

The use of public-private partnerships is becoming more common, as governments seek to capture more of the benefits of the market. There is growing interest in public-private partnerships for school construction in cities. For example, in New York City's financial district a new elementary school has been built in a mixed use building—commercial space on the ground floor, the school on the next five floors, and apartments on the floors above that. The government provides long-term leases to apartments and stores which help subsidize the school construction (KPMG Peat Marwick 1998).

In this survey, governmental entrepreneurship was most common in public works, health and human services, and support functions. Oswego County has a garbage burning steam plant which sells the excess steam to a local manufacturing plant. The county earns about $1 million each year from the program and has helped keep a large employer (over 150 employees) in the county.

The town of York considered building a manure-burning power plant and selling power to electric companies; however, the low price of electricity and lack of interest from local farmers caused the town to abandon the idea.

The town of Ossian has been entrepreneurial primarily with public sector clients. While this strategy would ordinarily be categorized under intermunicipal cooperation, this town sees itself as competing with private contractors for other towns' business. The supervisor believes the town wins the contracts over private bidders because "the towns in the area like to help each other out whenever they can." As a sparsely populated town with just 900 residents and 25,000 acres of land, they must keep their small highway department staff busy year-round. The town owns specialized equipment—a ditching machine—which other towns do not have.

Governmental entrepreneurship helps justify investment in new or specialized equipment by increasing utilization of equipment through an expanded customer base. Governments look first to other governments, as in the case of Ossian's ditching machine, but some are willing to directly serve private sector clients as well. For example, Chautauqua County allowed its print shop to market services to local businesses and nonprofit organizations as well as other municipalities to increase the scale of business and justify the capital investment in a new printing press.

UNDERSTANDING COMPLEX RESTRUCTURING

It is clear that restructuring cannot be seen as a simple shift from public to private production of services. Governments employ a range of restructuring alternatives to best meet local service needs and market conditions. To better understand the nature of restructuring, respondents were grouped into places that did simple, moderate, or more complex restructuring. Simple restructuring involved use of only one form of restructuring. In all cases, these places used either cooperation or privatization. Moderate restructuring involved use of two forms of restructuring, and the most common combination was cooperation with privatization. Complex restructuring occurred when three or more forms were used.

Governments which opt for complex restructuring provide an interesting profile. These governments appear to be more sophisticated than their peers and may provide a model for the range of restructuring activity which can be expected among local governments in the future. All of these places used intermunicipal cooperation and almost all used privatization. More than half used reverse privatization and governmental entrepreneurship, and over a third used cessation of service (Table 5.2). Not only was this group more likely to use each of the restructuring alternatives, they also had a higher level of restructuring activity overall. Of the cases of restructuring found across all municipalities in the survey, these complex places represented one-half of all cooperation, two-thirds of all privatization, and almost all of the reverse privatization and governmental entrepreneurship.

The governments that chose complex restructuring were more likely to restructure a broader range of services. Compared to the governments that chose simple restructuring, complex restructuring governments were at least twice as likely to restructure in any service area as their simple restructuring counterparts. While public works and public safety were still primary targets for restructuring activity, these complex restructuring governments were five times more likely to restructure in heath and human services and four times more likely to restructure support functions. Health

Table 5.2
Restructuring Complexity: Percent of Places Restructuring by Form and Service Area

Form	Simple	Moderate	Complex
Intermunicipal Cooperation	73.5	97.4	100.0
Privatization	26.5	69.2	94.3
Reverse Privatization	0.0	12.8	62.9
Government Entrepreneurship	0.0	7.7	48.6
Cessation	0.0	12.8	34.3

Service	Simple	Moderate	Complex
Public Works	47.1	79.5	88.2
Transportation	14.7	28.2	37.1
Public Utilities	8.8	35.9	37.1
Public Safety	20.6	51.3	51.4
Health and Human Services	8.8	20.5	48.6
Parks and Recreation	17.6	33.3	42.9
Support Functions	14.7	46.2	62.9
Other	20.6	41.0	48.6

Simple: Governments using only one form of restructuring, n=34
Moderate: Governments using two forms of restructuring, n=39
Complex: Governments using three or more forms of restructuring, n=35

Source: Warner and Hebdon Survey of New York State Townships and Counties 1997.

and human services are more difficult to restructure because the services are difficult to measure, and quality is hard to assess. Likewise, support functions require a sophistication and willingness to think of those aspects of the service production process which can lend themselves to contracting.

To gain a better understanding of how governments combine restructuring forms, two municipalities from this complex restructuring group are described.

Putnam County—Governmental Leadership Approach

Putnam County in the suburban fringe of New York City provides an excellent example of the entrepreneurial style of the complex restructuring governments. The county lists five cases of privatization, six cases of intermunicipal cooperation, six cases of reverse privatization, and two cases of government entrepreneurship. The county executive states, "It has been the trademark of the administration and the county legislature to make the county very responsive to the changing times and to bring the best ideas of restructuring and managerial efficiency to our government." While the executive sees clear benefits to privatization—in cost-savings, new technology, and managerial expertise—he is also attuned to citizen concerns and the need to maintain service quality: "We always feel that a microscope is focused on us with all these decisions. They are critically evaluated during the annual budget process; we monitor the private firms closely to evaluate their effectiveness and contract performance." Balancing citizen concerns with economic considerations makes the restructuring decision an important political test. "It can come down to counting votes on the county legislature. Some proposals have been approved by a single vote."

In Putnam County, privatization is one tool in the mix of restructuring options. For example, in data processing, they use a mix of privatization and intermunicipal cooperation. They have contracted out data processing to a private data processing company but have also joined with other municipalities to provide a county wide municipal record center with state-of-the-art retrieval and processing. They prepare tax bills for all schools, towns, and villages and do payroll for some municipalities using the private contractor. This effort enables them to gain scale efficiencies in the public sector and the private sector simultaneously while saving $250,000 per year.

While janitorial services have been privatized since 1990, more recently they contracted out mental health services to a nonprofit corporation which takes contracts from counties on both sides of the border (Connecticut and New York). They have been quite satisfied with the results. Recycling was less satisfactory, and that contract was brought back in house in 1997. They also starting rebuilding bridges with in-house staff rather than private contractors (as previously described).

The county has been especially creative in meeting its office space needs by purchasing preexisting office space from the private sector rather than building new and by renting excess space to nonprofit agencies.

The county executive describes his efforts as "top down" but "well-received." He describes union relations as "adversarial with significant respect and major cooperation." He explains, "We have been through two rounds of lay-offs, two major department privatizations, and overall significant employee downsizing. Overall, a difficult process due to civil service and union parameters."

Genesee County—A Cooperative Approach with Labor

Genesee County, outside Rochester, is also engaged in a broad range of restructuring activities. As part of a comprehensive plan, they are examining the possibilities for restructuring land-use, economic development, transportation, government administration, law enforcement/emergency management, parks/recreation/culture, health/social services, utilities, and housing. Overall, the county reported four cases of privatization, seven cases of intermunicipal cooperation, two cases of reverse privatization, and two cases of governmental entrepreneurship.

The county is examining a range of internal restructuring options as well: implementing technology to increase efficiency, right-sizing managerial staff, consolidating, reducing duplication of services, and instituting performance-based pay. To date, the county has pursued a more cooperative approach with employees and was recently profiled as one of three counties statewide which served as models for labor management cooperation (Blumner et al. 1998). As the county chair describes it, "Right-sizing government is our goal. Privatization has a negative impact on county employees; we must carefully educate throughout the process." The county recognizes "the importance of our workforce and appreciation of their vital contribution, the need for fair wages within limits, fair negotiations." The county uses labor management committees to interface with union personnel to improve interpersonal relations and to create two-way communication in order to educate and understand one another. These committees allow for ongoing conversation which enables "straightforward, intense periods of collective bargaining advocating a cooperative effort." Overall, the county chair is "committed to an environment of cooperation, integrity, and openness, with a desire to elicit active citizen participation, create a quality of life which values our county as a desirable place to work and live, [and] respect [the] county's heritage."

The county studied the possibility of nursing home privatization as part of the strategic planning process previously mentioned but also created a labor management committee within the home to identify areas for improvement. The committee created innovative programs to address sick leave and mandatory overtime. The home is on an enterprise budget and is earning money which has enabled the county to invest in some improvements in the facility (Blumner et al. 1998). Privatization is no longer on the agenda.

While the county privatized bus service, it brought bus maintenance back in house. The Meals on Wheels program was contracted out to the hospital food service, and the county kitchen was closed. The reverse privatization at the airport actually increased county support but resulted in increased airport traffic. The self-funded health plan involved cooperation with the community college and the nursing home and has resulted in improved service, claims processing, and cost avoidance of close to $3 million over the past six years.

These brief case descriptions of complex restructuring illustrate how local governments employ a range of restructuring options that either enhance or reduce the public sector role in service provision. Restructuring is not a one-way shift from government to market provision. These governments are sharp and entrepreneurial. Guided by vigilance over costs, service quality, and citizen satisfaction, government remains an important player in structuring the local market for service delivery.

CONCLUSION

Local officials recognize the need for innovation to maintain and enhance service quality. They recognize the value of alternative approaches to service delivery but realize that economies of scale can be achieved through inter-municipal cooperation as well as privatization. While intermunicipal cooperation is clearly the preferred form of restructuring in New York state, privatization occupies an important place in the mix of restructuring options.

In recognizing the importance of market forces in increasing efficiency and reducing costs, local government officials are also keenly aware of local market conditions. They have carved out an important market structuring role for local government—ensuring service quality and competition. For many public services, especially in rural or isolated areas, there may only be one alternative service provider. In such cases, privatization merely replaces a private monopoly with a public one. Governments recognize the need to maintain capacity to provide services so they can ensure competition, if only a competition of two—public and private. They also emphasize the need to maintain public sector involvement in order to maintain service quality.

While competitive contracting has become popular in some municipalities (most notably Indianapolis and Phoenix), the reverse privatization described in this survey is related more to efforts to enhance service quality and secure greater local control over service delivery. Once governments think about a market for service delivery, it should come as no surprise that they think of themselves as an important player in that market in terms of setting cost and quality parameters. To move from this position to competing directly with private sector players in a broader range of services (beyond those typically provided by government) is a natural extension. From providing traditionally privatized services in house (self-funded health insurance, locally built bridges) to directly competing with the private sector (selling energy, print shop services, and highway services), local governments are becoming significant players in the market. With increasing emphasis on market provision, direct governmental entrepreneurship through reverse privatization or governmental expansion should be part of the mix.

ACKNOWLEDGMENTS

Research for this chapter was supported by USDA Hatch research funds administered by the Cornell Agricultural Experiment Station. Student assistants Michele Fei, Samuel Hammer, Norma Rantisi, Naomi Calvo, and Michael Ballard are thanked for their assistance in coding the data. Mary Hanak and Sandy Carroll, formerly of the County Legislators and Supervisors Association, are thanked for co-sponsoring the research and supporting survey development and implementation. My colleagues, Robert Hebdon and Amir Hefeitz, helped with data analysis as part of our larger research collaboration on Local Government Restructuring.

NOTE

1. The response rate was 47 percent for counties and 21 percent for townships. The sample was representative by population and income.

REFERENCES

Applebaum, Eileen, and Rosemary Batt. 1994. *The new American workplace.* Ithaca, NY: ILR Press, Cornell.

Bennett, Robert. 1990. Decentralization, intergovernmental relations and markets: Towards a post-welfare agenda? In *Decentralization, local governments and markets: Towards a post-welfare agenda,* ed. Robert Bennett, 1–26. Oxford: Clarendon Press.

Blumner, Nicole, Lindy Burt, Jon Gans, Lisa Goldberg, Kristin Guild, Young Sung Kim, Chang Kil Lee, Darth Vaughn, and Mildred Warner. 1998. *Aspiring to excellence: Comparative case studies of public sector labor management cooperation in New York State.* A Report from the Department of City and Regional Planning, Cornell University. Available online: <www.cce.cornell.edu/community/govt/restructuring/labor/reports/1998/report.html>.

Donahue, John D. 1989. *The privatization decision: Public ends, private means.* New York: Basic Books.

Hebdon, Robert, and Douglas Hyatt. 1996. Workplace innovation in the public sector: The case of the Office of the Ontario Registrar General. *Journal of Collective Negotiations in the Public Sector* 25(1): 63–81.

International City/County Management Association (ICMA). 1983. *The entrepreneur in local government,* ed. Barbara Moore. Washington, DC: ICMA.

Lauder, Ronald S. 1992. *Privatization for New York: Competing for a better future.* Report of the New York State Advisory Commission on Privatization, ed. E. S. Savas. Albany, NY.

Office of the State Comptroller. 1994. *Local government cooperative service provision.* Albany, NY: Office of the State Comptroller.

Orfield, Myron, 1997. *Metropolitics.* Washington, DC: Brookings Institution.

Osborne, David E., and Ted Gaebler. 1992. *Reinventing government: How the entrepreneurial spirit is transforming the public sector.* Reading, MA: Addison-Wesley.

Osborne, David E., and Peter Plastrick. 1997. Banishing bureaucracy. Reading, MA: Addison-Wesley.

KPMG Peat Marwick. 1998, September 14. *Practical privatization: Lessons from cities and markets.* Presentation at New York State Association of Counties Fall Seminar, Buffalo, NY.

Reason Foundation. 1997. *Privatization report.* Los Angeles: Reason Foundation.

Rusk, David. 1993. *Cities without suburbs.* Washington, DC: Woodrow Wilson Center Press.

Savas, E. S. 2000. *Privatization and public-private partnerships.* New York: Chatham House.

Sclar, Elliott D. 1997. *The privatization of public service: Lessons from case studies.* Washington, DC: Economic Policy Institute.

Sclar, Elliott D., K. H. Schaeffer, and Robert Brandwein. 1989. *The emperor's new clothes: Transit privatization and public policy.* Washington, DC: Economic Policy Institute.

Starr, Paul. 1987. *The limits of privatization.* Washington, DC: Economic Policy Institute.

Warner, Mildred E., and Robert Hebdon. 1997. *Survey of local government restructuring in New York state.* Ithaca, NY: Cornell University. Available online: <www.cce.cornell.edu/community/govt/restructuring/survey98>.

West, Jonathan, Evan Berman, and Mike Milakovich. 1994. Total Quality Management in local government. In *ICMA Yearbook 1994,* 14–25. Washington, DC: International City/County Management Association.

Young, Peter. 1992. The privatization experience in Britain. In *Privatization for New York: Competing for a better future,* ed. E. S. Savas, 288–304. A Report of the New York State Senate Advisory Commission on Privatization, Ronald S. Lauder, Chairman. New York: New York State Senate Advisory Commission on Privatization.

6

Providing Public Services through Long-Term Service Agreements

Douglas Herbst and David Seader

If essential public services are, in fact, public services, shouldn't the public sector provide the services? This question, although seemingly simple, is actually complex and does not offer a simple answer.

Many times in our travels throughout this country, we see signs that say, "Welcome to Anytown, USA, established 1823." When a governmental unit is established, it instantly is in the business of providing public services. Exactly which public services and at what level of service can vary. There are vast differences in the public services that were needed in 1823 and those needed in 2000. Consider the differences between a few of the more essential public services, such as fire protection, prison management, and public education in 1823 (remember the one-room schoolhouse on *Little House on the Prairie*?) and those same services in 2000.

Also, many of today's public services, such as treated public water supplies, distribution systems, and wastewater treatment systems did not exist in 1823. Today, web sites are used to communicate with the public. It would be interesting to go back in time and explain a web site to a mayor in 1823. The public services of today are many; some are complex and some are not; some are easy and some are troublesome; and some are costly and others are very costly.

OUTSOURCING SERVICES

Traditionally, government has looked to outside sources to provide services when the services needed were not "steady state," meaning that those services were not required day in and day out—usually more specialized services, only needed from time to time. These types of services, such as engineering and other consulting services (architectural, financial, legal) and construction activities, have traditionally been provided by the private sector. Most governments have engineering, legal, and financial departments but not necessarily at the level of sophistication and specialization often required for public service delivery.

Other services, such as snow removal, landscaping, and pool maintenance are contracted with private companies to spare the government the expense of maintaining a full-time staff to accomplish seasonal functions. Over time, government has also come to realize that other functions such as streetlight maintenance, building maintenance, custodial services, garbage collection, data processing and other computer services, fleet maintenance, and street maintenance could be contracted out to private sector specialists.

Typically, most contracted services are specific and short-term. For example, an engineering firm might be hired to design a new school; a construction contractor might be hired to make significant capital improvements at a water treatment facility; or a financial firm may be retained to assist in the municipal financing of a new fire department or government office complex.

Often these services are part of a sequential scheme involving two steps: (1) hire an engineer to study the feasibility of a new wastewater treatment facility and plan the facility with the preliminary engineering through preparation of the bidding documents; and (2) hire a construction contractor to build the facility. In addition, outside legal and financial expertise might be needed to issue bonds for the construction. Then, upon completion, the new facility is turned over to the government to operate.

FULL-SERVICE DELIVERY

In the past, not much consideration was given to contracting private sector entities to operate public service assets and deliver the full service. It was not considered feasible to hire external agencies for fire protection, prison management, or public education; however, time has shown that there are benefits to private sector operation of such services as fire protection, prisons, and educational systems.

By the same token, the public sector did not consider hiring a private sector firm to operate and maintain water or wastewater treatment services. In reality, water and wastewater services have been privately operated for more than 100 years. This has occurred through the use of regulated utilities, often referred to as "public utility companies." These companies are investor-owned, private companies providing services to the public. They are regulated by a state Public Service Commission or similar regulating body.

Today, when the term privatization is mentioned, there is often a knee-jerk reaction against private delivery of public services, when in fact, the approach has been in use for a long time. The reaction that privatization is new and untried comes from the perception that these "private" companies operating water and wastewater treatment systems were actually "public" utility companies.

Over time, issues have arisen that have prompted officials to seek new solutions to meet public service demands. Population issues, economic and technological growth demands, aging infrastructure in need of replacement, reductions in governmental funding, more stringent regulations and laws (environmental and otherwise), an increase in competing uses for limited resources, and a call to reinvent government have all been factors.

These forces place additional strain on already over-burdened governments. Governments are obligated to ensure that essential public services are provided, but they do not necessarily have to be the party delivering the services. Past experience has shown that there are benefits to engaging private sector partners in the provision of certain public services. It is then reasonable to suggest that the private sector can provide full-service capability (design/construct/operate and even finance) of municipal systems.

THE CONTRACT OPERATIONS CONCEPT

The idea of a private company operating a publicly owned asset had long been foreign, and in virtually all instances, public employees operated those assets. In one industry, however, events took place which led the way to what is termed "contract operations" or what is sometimes referred to as privatization. Initially, this industry dealt with short-term, relatively simple agreements and, later, long-term, rather complex agreements containing design/build and even finance obligations. The wastewater treatment industry, is the leader in regard to securing long-term contracts for the delivery of public services.

The arrival of the federal construction grants program in 1972 brought about the need for an alternative approach to public sector operation and maintenance (O&M) of wastewater systems. Under the program, local governments received grants (upwards of 75%) to build water pollution control facilities. This grant program was a result of the environmental movement in the early 1970s that also led to the creation of the EPA. At that time, it was determined that a massive infusion of federal funds was needed to clean up the nation's polluted waters.

When the first wave of grant-funded facilities was completed in the mid-to-late 1970s, many small communities faced a dilemma. New state-of-the-art wastewater treatment facilities now stood where there had been old, obsolete facilities or, in some cases, no facilities at all. These new facilities brought bigger problems. The federal government had provided construction funds but left it to the local governments to operate them.

Some small communities had trouble operating the new facilities because of a lack of properly trained staff and an inability to attract and retain qualified personnel. These problems led to the idea of a private company operating and maintaining the facility for the government. This approach eventually spread to drinking water facility O&M, and the number of communities utilizing contract O&M grew to include medium-size communities. Since the late 1970s, contract operations have grown into a major business involving a large number of firms operating many water and wastewater facilities.

EXAMPLES: BIGGER CITIES, BIGGER CONTRACTS

The trend to hire a private sector firm for treatment system O&M has recently expanded into large cities. From a historic perspective, the first large city to forge a partnership with a private firm for wastewater treatment was Oklahoma City in 1984. Since then, Oklahoma City's contract with its private partner has been renewed several times. When the most recent extension runs its course, the partnership will be 18 years old.

In this partnership, a unique contract add-on occurred recently in which the private sector partner implemented an effluent reuse project and formed a three-way arrangement with the city and a major area developer. The private sector partner designed, built, and financed the facilities to transport treated effluent to the developer for irrigation purposes. The project benefits all parties: the developer receives water for irrigation below potable water prices; the city receives revenue for the sale of its effluent; and the private sector partner shares in the revenue generated from the sale of the effluent. This is a vivid example of how long-term, public-private partnerships for water services can have beneficial developmental impacts for communities in addition to providing quality services at an affordable price.

Over time, other large cities have established public-private partnerships for treatment facility O&M. In 1990, Houston contracted out the O&M of a water treatment facility; New Orleans opted for private operations of its two wastewater treatment facilities in 1992; and Indianapolis contracted out the O&M of its two wastewater treatment facilities in 1994. Indianapolis decided to procure the private O&M of its collection system two years into its partnership. This procurement was won by the incumbent treatment facilities operator and increased the overall savings to the city by

$1 million per year. In addition, 18 months into the new collection system partnership, the city extended and consolidated both partnerships into a single ten-year partnership.

In 1997, the city of Cranston, Rhode Island, entered into a long-term partnership for its entire wastewater treatment system and realized additional O&M savings and significant capital cost-savings for the design/ build of needed capital improvements (previously, the treatment facility had been privately operated under a short-term arrangement). Also, significant financial benefits were achieved through private financing. The city's existing sewer debt, which accounted for about one-third of the city's total debt, was eliminated through a bond defeasance.

In addition, an up-front contract payment from the private sector partner enabled the city to eliminate all sewer fund liabilities to the general fund and have a positive cash balance moving forward. After this partnership was implemented, an effluent reuse project was established with treated effluent being sold as cooling water for a nearby power facility, providing an economic benefit to all parties.

In 1998, long-term O&M partnerships were established for Milwaukee's two wastewater treatment facilities and Atlanta's entire water treatment system. Milwaukee's contract is the largest in the nation for wastewater services and has projected savings of approximately $145 million over the life of the agreement. Atlanta's is the largest in the municipal water industry, with savings of up to 44 percent on O&M. The same year, Gary, Indiana, entered into a five-year arrangement for the private operation of its wastewater treatment facility and collection system.

The following cities have also entered into long-term public-private partnerships:

- Franklin, Ohio, which has two separate partnerships—one for a new water treatment facility and the other for a wastewater asset sale
- Gardner, Massachusetts, which entered into a partnership for its water and wastewater systems with capital improvements, including a new water treatment plant
- The Massachusetts Development Finance Agency, which is in a partnership with the town of Devens wastewater treatment system, an arrangement including capital improvements
- Taunton, Massachusetts, and Wilmington, Delaware, which have long-term partnerships with the private sector for the delivery of public services

The initial successes of water and wastewater privatization led the U.S. Conference of Mayors in 1997 to endorse a resolution supporting the use of public-private partnerships. Mayors also called for the state and federal governments to remove any barriers to public-private partnerships. In the resolution, the Conference supported partnerships as an effective method for the following:

- Improving efficiency in operation and maintenance of public water and wastewater infrastructure;
- Bringing existing facilities into compliance with environmental regulations;
- Stabilizing rates;
- Attracting private capital investment for improving, expanding, and developing clean water and drinking water infrastructure; and,
- Assisting in meeting existing and future federal and state environmental mandates. (Reason Public Policy Institute 1998)

SHORT-TERM CONTRACTING

There was a burst in the water and wastewater privatization market (private ownership) in the early- to mid-1980s when several privately financed and owned systems and facilities started. At the time, private ownership had become attractive due to several tax benefits in the form of lower service fees, resulting in significant savings to the public partner. The principal tax benefit was rapid (5-year) depreciation and an investment tax credit equal to approximately 10 percent of the capital investment.

In addition, capital cost-savings could be realized in the private sector design/build approach versus the traditional public approach of design/bid/build. With the passage of the 1986 Tax Reform Act, however, these tax benefits were all but eliminated, thus halting the once increasing momentum in private ownership of public service systems.

The contract O&M business in the water and wastewater market, however, continued to expand. By the mid-1990s, it had grown into a $1 billion-per-year business, with more than 1,500 water and wastewater facilities under private operation. Over the years, many O&M contracts, initially short-term in nature, were renewed, and the industry enjoyed a renewal rate of well over 90 percent. For those not renewed but reprocured, another service provider unseated the incumbent in some cases.

The delivery of public services by the private sector continued, proving that the public sector was satisfied with the arrangement and opted to renew or reprocure. Indirectly, many of the renewed/reprocured arrangements could be viewed as being "long term"; however, with the uncertainty of short-term contracts, there was little incentive to include design/build or financing of new facilities or other major capital improvements in partnership agreements.

From 1986 through 1997, contract operations agreements for water and wastewater facilities and systems were limited to five-year terms, as were similar service agreements in other industry segments in which publicly owned facilities were built with tax-exempt financing and operated by the private sector. This was due to Internal Revenue Service (IRS) rules implementing the Tax Reform Act of 1986 that related to such agreements, referred to as management contracts. In addition, all of these contracts had been required to include a termination-for-convenience clause, without penalty to the government, exercisable at the end of the third year of the contract.

Because of the short-term nature of these agreements, little could be done to utilize the many ways capital improvements could increase efficiencies and reduce costs. There are few capital improvements with a payback period of three years or less. Coupled with this condition was the fact that a three-year amortization did not encourage the public sector to include capital improvements in a contract of short duration. Consequently, in the beginning, the private sector could only achieve O&M savings ranging from 10 to 30 percent.

THE ADVENT OF LONG-TERM CONTRACTS

In 1997, the IRS removed the obstacle to long-term partnerships by issuing Revenue Procedure 97-13, allowing management contracts to have terms of at least 15 years and terms of up to twenty years for public utility property as defined by the IRS, which includes water and wastewater treatment systems.

In lengthening the allowable term of management contracts, however, the IRS also put severely limiting constraints on those agreements. The objective was to prevent the abuse of tax-exempt financing while allowing for private operation of assets. Chief among the limitations was that the private contractor could have no interest in the net revenues of the system (otherwise known as profit). Contractors could share in cost-savings or revenue enhancements, but not both. While this provision effectively precludes true concessionary arrangements with the private sector, it does open the door to innovative gain sharing provisions, which have become a standard part of the current crop of long-term contracts.

In another provision of the new rules, the private contractor is allowed to have up to 20 percent of its total contract remuneration as variable payment from cost-savings or revenue sharing formulae. These incentive clauses have invigorated the private sector to continually search for efficiencies in their managed facilities and systems, while giving the public the benefit of lower cost service with no further investment. This is a major benefit of long-term contracting.

Because of the change in rules that allows for twenty-year contracts, there is another major benefit for the public sector. Design/build of new facilities or capital improvements could now be included in a long-term management contract (or O&M contract), as well as could some measure of private financing, including up-front payments to the municipality, also known as concession fees.

With this flexibility, the term "public-private partnerships" can now refer to the many types of arrangements that currently exist. Today, partnerships can be much more than contract O&M agreements, and privatization (here meaning private ownership) is not required for a long-term relationship with the private sector. A partnership now can take many forms, from a short-term to a long-term operations contract, or to a long-term operations contract with design/build obligations in which financing is included. New facilities or systems can be built through a design/build/operate or a design/build/finance/operate partnership in which various lease concepts exist. All of this can be accomplished without the public sector relinquishing ownership. A sale and lease-back of new facilities or systems can be realized with private ownership, which can also be viewed as a public-private partnership.

These changes have provided the public sector with perhaps the optimum method of public service delivery, especially when new facilities and/or capital improvements are needed. The private sector can now provide public services over the long-term and be charged with significant responsibility and performance. The private partner can act as a long-term participant and take a long-term view regarding investment, creativity, and innovation. The two major benefits to this approach are (1) the cost-savings that can be achieved; and (2) risk shifting through the single point of accountability and responsibility tied to the private partner's guarantees of cost, performance, and timing.

Since the announcement of the new IRS regulations, a flurry of long-term water and wastewater contracts have been agreed to throughout the nation. According to a recent survey, in the past two years, more than 80 municipalities have begun the competitive process for contracts with initial terms of more than ten years (Reinhardt 1999). During the same period, 45 governments have agreed to O&M contracts of more than ten years. Revenues for the agreements are projected at nearly $5 billion, and cities are estimated to achieve annual operating savings of between 20 to 45 percent. Some of the details of long-term contracts signed in 1997 are listed in Table 6.1.

Long-term contracts also came about as other trends were forcing municipal officials to consider alternative approaches. State and federal grant programs that provided financial assistance in the 1970s were reduced during the 1980s just as water quality regulations were being tightened by the EPA. This confluence of events led to more consideration of public-private partnerships—especially after officials realized their cost-savings potential.

Cost-Savings Opportunities

The O&M cost-savings through private operation, ranging from 10 to 50 percent, have already been established, both in short-term and long-term contracting (Peterson 1994; Reason Public Policy Institute 1998, 1999;

Table 6.1
Long-Term Water/Wastewater Contracts Signed in 1997

	State	Contract Length	Water (mgd)	Wastewater (mgd)	Additional Comments
Evansville '97	IN	10	60	—	—
Buffalo Water, '97	NY	10	160	—	—
Seattle, '97	WA	25	120	—	DBO w/ public finance
Franklin, '97	OH	20	5	—	$6.5 M capital
Chester Borough, '97	NJ	20	—	0.1	—
Alpena, '96	MI	6	—	5.5	—
Toronto, '92	OH	10	—	1.8	$300,000 capital
Edison, '97	NJ	20	9.5	—	$6.7 M fee; $9.5 M capital
New Haven, '97	CT	15	—	40	Capital repair & replacement fund; $750,000 fee
Bessemer, '97	AL	20	12	—	—
Boonville*	IN	10	—	1.4	—
Kenner*	LA	10	—	10.6	—
Rockland*	MA	10	—	1.6	—
Pine River*	MN	10	—	0.1	—
Cranston, '97	RI	25	—	12	$48 M fee; $24 M capital
Freeport, '96	TX	20	—	1.5	—
Indianapolis, '97	IN	10	—	—	—
Manalapan, '97	NJ	20	<1	—	Concession fee paid annually based on number of new customers added
Hoboken, '94	NJ	20	—	4	$10 M fee; $8 M capital
No. Brunswick, '96	NJ	20	10	—	$7 M fee
Danbury, '97	CT	20	—	15.5	$10 M fee
Wilmington, '97	DE	20	—	105	$1 M fee; $15 M capital

*Existing contracts renewed in 1997.

Source: Public Works Financing March 1998, 5.

Reinhardt 1999). Many short-term contracts are now being converted into long-term agreements to take advantage of the more generous upside available to the public.

Many large cities have already benefited from reductions in O&M costs through private sector partnerships, including Oklahoma City (35%), New

Orleans (16%), Indianapolis (40%), Milwaukee (30%), and Atlanta (44%). Small- to mid-size communities have also realized savings, including Franklin, Ohio (30%), for its water plant; Huber Heights, Ohio (18%); West Haven, Connecticut (29%); and Fall River, Massachusetts (25%). There are also many more small- to mid-size communities throughout the country documenting substantial cost-savings through partnering with private sector firms.

Cost-savings opportunities in the water industry are driven by fierce competition from a variety of companies. Global, national, regional, and even local firms are competing for business in a multibillion dollar industry that is expected to grow in the future. Companies are continually buying and selling each other to gain market share and competitive advantage. The competitive nature of the industry should allow city officials to continue to realize cost-savings and improved levels of service.

Tied to the savings through O&M costs is the ability to reduce capital costs in the 10 to 50 percent range, utilizing a design/build approach for new facilities or capital improvements versus the traditional design/bid/build municipal approach. In Seattle, the design/build/operate approach saved the city more than 40 percent of the capital costs for a new water treatment facility. For many communities throughout the country, the fiscal realities of this millennium will compel municipal decision makers to seriously consider public-private partnerships.

Risk Management Benefits

Another major benefit is the risk management aspect of these new service delivery systems. The public sector partner can now give to its private sector partner the responsibilities of design/build/operate and maintain. This sole source accountability feature, backed with time, cost, and performance guarantees (with financially strong parent guarantees and other forms of security), is perhaps the optimum risk management arrangement for public service delivery. Public sector partners are protected to a large extent against cost overruns prevalent in traditional public works projects. The performance is guaranteed and, whether the performance failure is related to design, construction, or faulty equipment, the private partner is responsible for the failure. From the public partner's vantage point, the only issue is achieving performance.

With long-term contracts, a strict procurement process is needed to protect the integrity of the process; keep politics out of the selection; and insulate the process from favoritism, discrimination, and conflict of interest. Ultimately, the selection should be made on value for the cost and not low cost alone. Over time, public sector partners will become increasingly well-informed, sophisticated, and value-conscious and not be guided by "low bid" privatization proposals.

The benefits to private design/build/finance/operate arrangements are very powerful and are not present in the traditional public method of service delivery. The public sector will come to realize the significant nature of these benefits as more and more communities establish such partnerships. This service delivery option will then grow and may become the preferred approach in the future.

Addressing Concerns

Despite the many benefits to the design/build/operate approach for the delivery of public services, there are many detractors to this arrangement that cite the following disadvantages:

- Under design/build, the public sector partner does not really know what it is getting.
- With the design/build approach, the public sector can wind up with a "Chevy" when it wanted a "Cadillac."
- Under the design/build approach, the private sector will build a substandard facility that is not meant to withstand the test of time as many of the traditionally built assets have shown.
- Under a long-term contract, the public sector is in essence "selling its soul" and is locked into a monopolistic arrangement in which the public partner is at the mercy of the private partner after signing the contract.
- Under a long-term arrangement, the public sector loses control and the ability to achieve additional benefits in the future.

The key to the utilization of the design/build approach is to define what type of system is needed with as much specificity as possible in order to enable the private sector to understand what is required, whether it be a Chevy or Cadillac. The specifications, however, should be performance-based so as not to constrain the private sector but allow it to be flexible, creative, and innovative in the approach. Going beyond performance-based specifications can inhibit the private sector and limit the benefits to the public sector. The goal is to achieve the right balance by being as specific as is necessary to ensure the public sector knows what it wants and will be getting, without constraining the private sector. In fact, where privatization has failed, the reason cited most often is a lack of specificity in contract language (Ward 1998).

Consideration should also be given to the concept of allowing the private sector to propose alternatives that will comply with the legal requirements of the service being delivered, as well as the specific performance desired by the public partner. In fact, the Chevy may meet the needs of the community and, if properly operated and maintained, may provide reliable services over the same term as the Cadillac. In this case, the public sector partner may have wanted a Cadillac but after finding that the Chevy would meet the needs of the community, was then able to use the resulting cost-savings for other pressing financial needs.

Under the design/build/operate approach, there is an inherent incentive that the private partner will build a facility to perform and last over the long term because that same entity is required to operate and maintain the facility under a long-term contract. Because the private partner guarantees performance during the O&M period, it wants to build a facility that can meet the needs of the community. This total responsibility feature ensures that a substandard facility is not built and that all the considerations between capital costs and long-term O&M costs have been considered. In addition, the entire design/build/operate proposal is being developed amid a procurement process in which the competitive marketplace drives the private sector firms to propose the very best they have to offer at the best price they can offer.

Obtaining Maximum Benefits

The long-term nature of the design/build/operate arrangement ensures that maximum benefits can be delivered. Proper terms and conditions can ensure that the monopolistic concern is managed away. First and foremost, it is the inherent desire of the private sector to not lose a "client." The private sector has a keen awareness that losing a client because of poor performance can damage its reputation and inhibit its business growth potential. The reputation of a firm in a marketplace is paramount and often misunderstood and overlooked by public sector decision makers. It is a powerful driver to ensuring that the services are delivered in a high-quality and reliable manner.

Secondly, if the contract gives incentives for the parties to work together to keep current concerning steps toward further efficiencies and cost-savings, both parties can benefit from moving forward. The key is to have the future benefits shared in a manner that makes sense. There can also be various sharing arrangements within the contract; a one-size-fits-all type of arrangement does not necessarily have to be used.

Finally, as a policy decision, the public sector partner can include a termination-for-convenience clause so that an escape hatch is included. The concept is that the public sector partner has an out, and the private sector partner will be driven to perform day after day, with great incentive to establish a relationship that is built on trust and understanding and that continuously delivers benefits. In this way, the private sector partner keeps the public sector partner far away from the escape hatch and gives it no reason to consider using it.

If the escape hatch is used, however, the public sector partner must recognize that it will have to provide the private sector partner reimbursement for any outstanding indebtedness associated with the partnership that was amortized over the life of the contract, and for demobilization and transition costs. The reimbursement of transition costs is required because the private sector partner will be involved in the transition to some extent and should be paid accordingly.

In addition, the concept of a payment to the private sector partner to make up for lost profits should be considered in a termination-for-convenience clause. The private sector partner cannot expect to fully recover the lost profits since full profits are earned by delivering the services and taking the risks associated with that service delivery. A certain percentage of lost profits, acceptable to both parties, should be considered, however. The entire cost to the private sector partner could be viewed as the cost to the public sector partner for the ability to terminate for convenience. In actuality, however, the cost for the convenience termination would only be the payment for lost profits because other costs are justified and reimbursable. This would only govern termination for convenience, since termination for cause by either party or termination permitted by the contract due to a Force Majeure event would be governed by other terms and conditions specific to the situation.

Increased Control

With long-term and short-term contracts, public sector control is actually increased because service delivery is now wrapped into a contract with requirements and responsibilities that can be monitored and enforced. This is the control that counts and the type of control that increases under private sector operation. The type of control that is given up is the day-to-day administrative burdens, regulatory compliance duties, and technical functions. Giving up this kind of control is a benefit to establishing a partnership with the private sector for the delivery of public services.

ADDITIONAL BENEFITS FOR THE COMMUNITY

With long-term contracts, the private sector partner has the opportunity to establish a strong relationship with the community—to become a good corporate citizen and good neighbor by being actively involved. While price is important in the selection of a private partner, it should only be one of several factors considered when reviewing proposals. A private company's involvement and commitment to the communities in which it works should also be a factor in the selection process.

A strong community involvement program is an important aspect of a private firm's reputation and market image. Strengthening ties with the community allows the company to become a participant in the community; establish emotional links with local decision makers; and focus on delivering more than reliable, high-quality services. The private sector partner should be committed to and have an investment in the community. Generally, the employees that will be transitioned to the private sector firm live in the area and become supporters of the private firm's community involvement efforts. Such involvement is through civic, community, and charitable activities and contributes to the improvement of the quality of life.

How Long-Term Contract Pricing Adds Benefits

The basic payment scheme in long-term operating contracts is to set a base rate for the totality of services in the first year and then escalate that cost over time by using a standard inflation factor such as the Consumer Price Index. This fixed payment usually does not include costs over which the private contractor has no control, such as energy costs, which become pass-through under the contract. The contract should also allow for changes in remuneration due to changes in contract conditions, such as the increase in the system's service area or service population, but basically, these are fixed-payment contracts.

Fixed-payment contracts mean that potential contractors compete for the contract based on first-year total costs. Given the competitive nature of the contract operations business, the public has received great benefit from competitive pricing. In some cases, a successful contractor may even price the first-year fixed payment at or below its own cost of service. But if it does, how does it then turn a profit on the contract? Because the agreement is long term, the contractor can make up for early annual losses or break even by keeping cost increases below the escalation factor in the contract. Some private providers estimate that it can take up to ten years to start making profits. Profitable operation can also be the result of finding additional cost-savings or revenue enhancement opportunities in the system and getting the incentive payments for such items.

This mechanism assures the public of the long-term dedication of the contractor, who must maintain good results and good relations over the long haul in order to reap the contract's benefits. It also means that the contractor must always have a proper incentive to look after the public's interest in the implementation of the contract.

A downside risk to the public is that the contractor will skimp on O&M to achieve the same result. Actual costs lower than the contract allow more profit. This risk can be mitigated substantially through proper contract drafting and monitoring. For example, most contracts provide for a maintenance budget to be agreed upon each year with spending only on maintenance, giving the contractor no incentive to refrain from proper maintenance. In addition, the contract may provide for the public sector partner to pick up the cost of anything but routine maintenance, again giving the contractor no reason to skimp.

The most important benefit to the municipality of the pricing of long-term contracts may be that the contractor can afford to offer additional services, concessions, or investments by having time to make up the costs of those additional offers over time. Thus, the contractor may make its own investments in automation or preventative maintenance that pay off over the long term, if it assures the contractor of lower costs in the out years through which it can get a return on such investments.

The most important additional benefit that contractors can offer cities through long-term arrangements is a painless, no-damage transition of public employees to the contractor's payroll. Most cities, for reasons of both fairness and political necessity, require that contractors selected for the long-term O&M contract guarantee that no current workers in the system are laid off for a given amount of time, somewhere between one and three years. The only allowable staff decreases would be through attrition or termination for cause after the private takeover. This means that the contractor cannot get down to an optimal staffing level except over time—an investment that the municipality requires the contractor to make.

Most vendors of O&M services routinely offer no layoff policies in their bids, sometimes for the life of the contract because the long-term nature of the relationship allows them to manage that investment and come out whole over time. The same mechanism can work for other city-imposed contract costs such as community investments, set-asides for local businesses, or other noncommercial aspects of the contract.

Private sector operating efficiencies that save money for cities can also influence water rates paid by customers. In New Brunswick, New Jersey, a financial study commissioned by the city estimated a savings of approximately $46 million over twenty years through an O&M contract. Officials were able to raise rates at a much slower pace than would have been possible under city management. In fact, officials determined that projected increases over the next twenty years will be less than increases during the past twenty years (Ward 1998).

Many local officials also cite the stability and peace of mind that a long-term agreement brings. A long-term contract allows a private firm to complete necessary capital improvements and upgrades without having the city issuing RFPs each time. Public and private officials are also better able to plan for the future with long-term contracts.

Concession Payments

Another aspect of long-term contracts is that they provide the ability to structure a concession payment, which is an up-front cash payment made to the public sector partner. This payment is usually a monetization of the savings to be realized over the term of the contract. Concession payments can be used to purchase assets, repair/replace assets, or for a variety of purposes provided such uses are allowable under local and state law. In many cases, water and sewerage finances are set up as an enterprise fund, separate from the general fund of a city, and any revenues created by those systems are required to remain in the enterprise fund for like purposes. In other instances, the transfer of revenues off-system are precluded or severely restricted by bond covenants of outstanding system debt. This is not to say that ways have not been found to transfer net revenues to the general fund through payments-in-lieu-of-taxes (PILOT) or via franchise fees. These types of mechanisms usually hold up under scrutiny if fairly applied to the water and wastewater systems.

Cranston, Rhode Island, used its $48 million concession to help fund mandated capital improvements. In a slightly different twist, Danbury, Connecticut, officials decided to take only a percentage of up-front savings ($10 million) in a concession fee. The terms of the fee agreement are left up to municipal officials.

An interesting view of concession payments is that they can be used in other infrastructure areas where capital is harder to come by (e.g., education) or where precious general obligation debt capacity cannot or will not be used. This is especially true because the use of general obligation debt usually requires a public authorizing referendum while long-term contracting and concession payments do not, giving public officials much more flexibility. Such was the case in 1998 when the mayor of Birmingham, Alabama, wanted to use the proceeds of the sale or lease of the city's water system to fund needed school improvements.

The public sector partner should recognize, however, that a concession payment is simply a loan and will be repaid during the term of the contract. If the contract is terminated, the outstanding principal amount must be repaid to the private sector partner. Also, if the payment is used to fund an ongoing program, the public sector partner should ensure that another revenue source is available when the concession runs out in order to continue the program.

By the same token, when the funds are used to "jump start" a program, a revenue source will be needed to continue the program because the money will not be well-spent if the program dies after the jump start. In the event a concession payment is included in a long-term contract, a clause that gives the public partner the flexibility to pay off the concession fee and/or replace it with municipal debt should also be included.

The use of up-front concession payments also may complicate a long-term transaction by raising the suspicion that it represents a lease of the system rather than an O&M contract. Without careful structuring, the federal government may consider such a payment a trigger for the repayment under Executive Order 12803 of outstanding grants previously made to the system by the federal government or a violation of the management contract rules of Rev. Proc. 97-13. Even with these possibilities, the monetization of savings available from a long-term contract represents a powerful potential tool for fiscal management on the part of municipalities, and its use may be further tested in numerous situations in the near future.

Private Sector Financing

Long-term contracts also provide the option for private sector financing of projects, though not within the IRS-sanctioned management contract framework. Although municipal financing is more cost-effective on face value, the entire life cycle cost of service with private financing (i.e., impact on user rates) should be analyzed and compared to the tax-exempt option and, if politically acceptable, private sector financing may be used. This holds true especially in instances in which constraints exist to municipal financing or the ability for municipal finance is better preserved for other worthy uses.

The transaction in Cranston, Rhode Island, is an excellent example of this alternative. In Cranston, the private contractor not only could operate the wastewater system more cost-effectively but could also provide the needed capital improvements at a fraction of the cost of the proposed traditional public design, even considering the financing cost differential. In addition, the private vendor guaranteed that the less expensive alternative would meet water quality regulatory standards. This set of conditions may exist with numerous other U.S. water and wastewater systems.

Private financing in a long-term project can also be used as bridge financing or construction financing in anticipation of government grants or loans. In addition, private financing can be used for small capital needs and repaid on a useful life amortization schedule. When a sufficient number of small capital improvements are made to justify municipal financing, private sector financing can be taken out and replaced with municipal financing. Private financing provides added flexibility for interim financing and can enable the public sector partner to accomplish capital improvements or make repairs or replacements in a timely manner.

CONCLUSION

The need for upgraded water and wastewater systems in the United States is enormous. Cities face hundreds of billions of dollars worth of needed capital repairs and improvements in the coming years. Mandated treatment plant upgrades will also be required across the nation. City officials will need alternative methods of financing improvements instead of relying on rate increases.

Relaxed IRS rules on long-term contracts have enabled the water industry to step in and meet the needs of cities. In every region of the country and in large and small cities, innovative partnerships are emerging that enable private sector firms to use their experience and expertise to help upgrade the infrastructures of cash-strapped municipalities. Long-term agreements create win-win outcomes for private industry and the public sector, with improved service, lower costs, and opportunities for capital investment to meet the needs of the future.

The future growth of long-term agreements for delivery of public services will depend on building a critical mass of successful partnerships between the public and private sectors. These positive experiences will lead the drive towards acceptance of the long-term, public-private partnership approach as a bona fide, established, and beneficial service delivery option. Once this is accomplished in one infrastructure segment, other segments can then use it as a further catalyst to promote growth or as a springboard to initiate growth. As the water industry is demonstrating, the delivery of public services under long-term partnerships is an idea whose time has come. It is a significant option that can deliver substantial benefits, and more and more public sector decision makers throughout the country are evaluating its potential use.

REFERENCES

Peterson, W. A. 1994. Privatization at a crossroads. *Water Environment & Technology* (November): 56–60.

Reason Public Policy Institute. 1998. *Privatization '98: 12th annual report on privatization.* Los Angeles: Reason Public Policy Institute.

Reason Public Policy Institute. 1999. *Privatization '99: 13th annual report on privatization.* Los Angeles: Reason Public Policy Institute.

Reinhardt, William. 1999. Water/wastewater privatization hits a growth spurt. *Public Works Financing* (March): 20–25.

Ward, Janet. 1998. The pros and cons of long-term privatization. *American City and County* (May): 54–62.

7

The Role of Information Management in Making Competition Work

Bridget M. Anderson

How great are the savings one can expect from competition? Historically, public sector entities have focused on service delivery and not necessarily on competitiveness; therefore, this has been a difficult question to answer. Before the savings question can be answered, two fundamental but extremely important questions must be asked: (1) What services does the government provide? and (2) How much does it cost to provide each service?

Cost analysis is an important consideration in determining competitiveness, as this is the baseline from which all "make or buy" decisions will be made. In fact, the cost tool, coupled with performance measurement and process improvement tools, provides management with the type of useful information necessary to select the appropriate service delivery method. These tools, both financial and managerial, enable employees to be held accountable and to operate like a business. In addition, these tools should be coupled with an information technology system infrastructure that allows for flexible and timely determination of the costs of each service provided by the government.

Governments have many diversified needs for effectively and efficiently providing services into the twenty-first century. Meeting these needs requires governments to undergo managerial cultural change. Government's plans for the future should include the following:

- Increased emphasis on Activity-Based Costing (ABC) and Activity-Based Management (ABM)
- Implementation of managed competition

- Implementation of performance measures
- Implementation of flexible performance budgeting
- Ability to perform performance audits

Many governments have already begun some of these initiatives but are now considering creating an information system infrastructure that will allow for flexible and timely determination of costs at the activity level as well as providing traditional fund accounting information. To begin the process, a government must evaluate and understand the underlying mission, the supporting business requirements and responsibilities, and the existing processes to ensure that an effective information technology and business improvement solution is implemented. Consequently, the approach used in developing an effective Activity-Based Costing/Management (ABC/M) solution for evaluating the competitiveness of the government must effectively link a business analysis with a technical analysis.

ABC/M is the key component in the overall approach and it will help the government attain its ultimate objective of being able to instantly and accurately assess the cost of various activities conducted within the government. The result will be to use this information to provide better and more cost-effective services to citizens and constituents.

A robust and functionally driven applications environment is important in maximizing an organization's ability to effectively conduct ABC. Although many applications may not be critical to the initial development of the ABC model, such a model can be significantly more difficult to implement and maintain without automated processes and effective decision making capability based upon real-time and enterprise-wide performance data availability. Generally, the current automated processes do not adequately support the long-term successful implementation of ABC. New automated processes include an enterprise-wide information system that captures institutional data with minimal, manual entry/reentry and reconciliation, enabling faster and better management decisions. Before concentrating on factors associated with new or upgraded enterprise systems, the government should first work to resolve the following five critical application issues (if applicable):

1. Functional and technical quality of existing financial-related applications causing questionable ability to support ABC on a long-term basis
2. Closing of application gaps in potential ABC functions
3. Detailed ABC (functional) requirements definition
4. Development of software evaluation and selection criteria to ensure ABC requirements are met
5. Portfolio management of functional applications to help enable internal charge-back for IT services rendered

First, in terms of the functional and technical quality of existing institutional applications and processes, several issues may serve as an impediment to successful ABC implementation on a long-term basis. In terms of functional quality, it is not unusual to find a lack of user friendliness and adaptability of the existing applications that worsen the current trend of satellite tool development and disparity in application architecture. Consequently, users may find that they cannot track activity data with the systems that they currently have. Users will therefore spend more time reconciling data between systems to come up with the total organizational figures required to effectively measure business-unit and government-wide performance.

In terms of technical quality, data accuracy and long-term maintainability may be of concern because some institutional systems may not be easily maintained, modified, and/or integrated with other applications. Multiple applications performing similar functions take more time, effort, and money to support, and they result in data redundancy and inaccuracy. Furthermore, current institutional systems may have inadequate (often a single point of contact) and unresponsive (remote vendor and restricted hours) user support available to assist the end user base, which can be a learning curve when ABC becomes a factor.

Second, if gaps exist in application coverage of critical business functions across the government, the successful implementation of an automated ABC environment could be inhibited. Gaps in important business functions such as budgeting, work order, time/labor, and fixed assets tracking will impede successful capture of accurate, enterprise-wide activity and performance data, which are critical in an ABC environment. Nonautomation of these critical functions—even in a current costing environment—may indicate that decision makers are not receiving the timely, accurate, and useful data necessary to manage government business.

Third, when applications are purchased or developed without a full understanding of the functional environment and business drivers they are intended to support, they often do not adequately meet user needs, business unit needs, or the needs of the entire organization. This is also partly due to the lack of a detailed, comprehensive user requirements definition and analyses being conducted prior to application acquisition. Because this user requirements definition process is not being performed consistently and comprehensively, users across various business units may duplicate applications and application functions, contributing to other issues as mentioned previously.

As a new costing model is implemented throughout a government, it will be imperative for those responsible for the overall IT application evaluation and purchase to understand the functional requirements of ABC before deciding upon any potential enterprise-wide technology solution. This will help ensure that a technically proficient system can successfully perform in the designated ABC environment and vice versa.

The issues related to IT must be addressed in order to successfully implement a costing/competition program on a long-term basis; however, the tools and methodologies required can be successfully implemented on a shorter-term basis while the IT infrastructure, no matter how simple or complex, is being designed.

The tools and methodologies used in the success stories discussed in this chapter were implemented using fairly straightforward technology infrastructures while a longer-term strategy was contemplated. Consequently, we have found that a successful implementation generally starts with a series of pilot projects. This approach allows a transfer of knowledge about ABC/M to take place between the implementation team and other individuals in the government, which assists in the transformation of the cultural behavior of the employees.

IMPLEMENTING A SUCCESSFUL ABC
AND COMPETITIVENESS METHODOLOGY

The initial step in the competitiveness process focuses on evaluating an organization's competitiveness by determining the services provided and the associated costs. This approach enables a government to obtain an understanding of the business and financial objectives and how its performance can be compared to others. In order for the government to succeed in being more efficient and responsive (i.e., being more competitive), additional tools must be explored. It must research tools that have been successfully implemented in other governmental entities. The tools most effectively used in the competitiveness process are ABC, process improvements/reengineering, performance measures, benchmarking, and pay-for-performance.

Before any of these tools can be implemented, an identification of the government's services and customers must be performed so that elected officials, management, and employees have a clear understanding of their operating environment. Only then can they make informed decisions on whether it is appropriate to continue to deliver these services. In addition, management needs to identify any services that they do not provide, but perhaps should, to best serve its customers.

The true cost of providing services in each area must be identified in order to find where efficiencies can be gained and to determine if any of the areas should be subjected to a managed competition effort. A natural progression for the government is to implement ABC to further assist management, not only in determining the cost of provided services but also in determining types and levels of services in order to improve operating efficiencies. Furthermore, the results of the ABC program can be incorporated into the government's budgetary process and can provide meaningful benchmarks both internally and externally.

Consider the following example of how the State of Iowa, Department of Transportation, has effectively used costing, performance measurement, and benchmarking tools to evaluate their competitiveness. In May 1996, the Iowa governor asked the Department of Transportation to conduct two pilot competition projects—(1) sign shop and (2) pavement markings—to guide future competitive efforts. The initial step was to determine current costs, make suggestions for improving operations, and submit a cost proposal to help the department compete with outside vendors in providing the service. The consultants worked closely with the sign shop and pavement markings teams in order to complete the following:

- Define activities
- Collect and analyze appropriate current cost and allocation methods using ABC
- Reengineer the service delivery approach
- Train union and management personnel
- Prepare bids
- Calculate cost-savings

The following is an excerpt of the Iowa Department of Transportation's Pavement Markings ABC Results (Table 7.1) with some discussion of its analysis of the results. As is clear, the cost of performing the various pavement marking activities varies considerably among the state regions; however, once the paint crews were armed with the total and unit cost information, they were able to compare the information by region and analyze the fluctuations by like activity. The result was an overall decrease in costs with an increase in quality of service provided. This was accomplished by identifying desirable staffing levels, mix of equipment, and a reconfiguration of the pavement marking routes.

Table 7.1
Iowa Department of Transportation, Pavement Markings ABC Results

Region	Centerline/No Passing	Edge Line	Curb and Other
Region 1	$131.89	$134.37	$24.56
Region 2	$178.81	$115.63	$35.30
Region 3	$180.23	$140.28	$21.00
Region 4	$232.17	$129.33	$26.69
Region 5	$234.72	$123.02	$27.33
Region 6	$238.52	$154.20	$16.32

Sources: Obtained from KPMG LLP materials: client reports, KPMG developed training materials, and marketing materials.

The employees had never had access to detailed cost information prior to the ABC analysis. Once given this information, management and employees took ownership of the results and moved ahead to change the way they provide services. They were ready to participate in the managed competition pilot program that was being implemented. The employees then took the ABC results, reengineered the way they provided services, and submitted a winning proposal.

In the pavement marking project, the state employees won the competition, saving the state approximately $350,000 (10 percent), from the previous year—the closest outside vendor proposal was about $500,000 higher. The sign shop retained the right to produce highway signs, while an outside vendor was selected to produce the graphic displays. The sign shop committed to increasing its output and filling excess capacity with no increase in budget. No employees were replaced or lost their jobs as a result of the project.

Consider another example of how the tools of competition have been successfully implemented. Nestled between the Great Basin Desert and the Sierra Nevada Mountains, with some of the best skiing in the country and a booming gaming industry, Reno, Nevada, is a city with something for everyone. Although Reno is home to a thriving tourist industry, its resident population of 300,000 makes Reno, by most standards, relatively "small," truly living up to its reputation as "the biggest little city in the world."

When the city of Reno decided to examine how much public services cost, like most governments in cities of this size, its goal was not to revamp the budget by putting all services out to competitive bid in the open market. Instead, city officials simply wanted to know what they actually spent and on what items in order to establish a baseline for costs and to see where money might be saved.

Reno decided to implement ABC to gauge the real costs of providing services—the first step in improving government and business processes. The city selected five service areas as ABC pilots: (1) street sweeping, (2) sewer line cleaning, (3) vehicle preventative maintenance, (4) emergency medical response, and (5) work card processing. Furthermore, because city employees were trained on how to use ABC on an ongoing basis, the city has been able to cost other service departments on its own in areas such as the public works, police, and finance departments, as well as the City Attorney's and City Clerk's offices.

The following are the steps that must be taken to become a successful government:

1. *Performance Measurement.* Governments and businesses alike cannot maximize efficiency and cut costs without measuring current effectiveness and establishing baselines. An ABC methodology enables cities to systematically evaluate the

effectiveness and efficiency of resources, quantify results, and establish clear accountability.

2. *Benchmarking.* While performance measurement shows an organization where it stands, benchmarking compares it to competitors or peers. Comparing operations to the best practices of others can enable organizations to expedite improvements in the way they work.

3. *Process Reengineering.* Reengineering is a high-level process improvement tool used to identify customer needs and then find a way to meet those needs by working faster, smarter, and cheaper than before. Reengineering is not about cutting positions but about improving the way in which work is performed.

ABC provides real performance indicators in which costs can be measured on a per-employee, per-task, or per-project basis. City officials can determine which divisions incur the greatest costs, begin to examine the reasons why, and choose whether business process reengineering or outsourcing may be appropriate.

ABC also lets public officials present tangible data to voters, city councils, or boards of supervisors. Reno's budget manager points out, "One of the good things about ABC is you can create a budget scenario . . . and take that to the voters. For example, if you know you can do one less plan review and, with the money saved, hire half a patrol person [you have the data to back that initiative]." And although Reno's thriving economy shows no signs of a downturn, in cities where the economy does turn or for those cities facing a budget crisis, ABC would provide the data to support a tax increase.

Reno achieved savings in the street sweeping activity under the Streets Division. The city defines street sweeping as two main activities: (1) regular routes and (2) special events. Local officials found that the special event sweeping cost the city more than the regular sweeping due to the overtime hours incurred. Because of the special nature of these activities, the city can charge specific organizations for this service since it was done for their special events. In addition, the city effectively reduced costs for equipment because it had several excess sweepers on hand in case of breakdowns and so on. The reduction in the sweeper fleet as well as other operational improvements has led to significant savings of over 20 percent.

Of course, cities that want to take ABC to the next level can consider business process reengineering and sending services out to competitive bid as the city of Indianapolis did on a large scale; others may opt to outsource certain services as Reno did. In the areas in which Reno put contracts up for bid, it located areas of inefficiency, identified which services were cost-effective for the city to continue performing, and determined a future date when services could be more effectively outsourced. Reno's savings have more than paid for the cost of the ABC implementation. As a management tool, ABC/M helped Reno focus on what it does rather than on what it spends. It is a methodology intended to drive and support strategic planning, process reengineering, quality management, value chain analysis, and performance measurement.

ABC is most effective when used to:

- baseline the cost of activities and outputs.
- determine what is driving these costs.
- identify targets for process improvements.
- identify cost reduction opportunities.

(See Figure 7.1 for a diagram of the implementation of ABC/M.)
The value of ABC/M lies in its ability to:

- determine costs and establish a baseline.
- provide a basis for future benchmarking and business process reengineering.
- enable cities to put services up to competitive bid.
- act as a leave-behind tool for long-term usage.
- provide real performance indicators such as per-employee or per-project cost.
- provide hard data for voters and city council members.

After the organization's competitiveness and baseline costs have been determined, it is time for implementing the competition cycle. Each step in the managed competition cycle can be linked to the competition tools previously discussed. (See Table 7.2 for a depiction of the link between the steps in the managed competition cycle and the competition tools.)

The city of Indianapolis is probably the best example of how a government has successfully integrated competition tools and the competition

Figure 7.1
ABC/M Implementation: Organization-Wide Approach

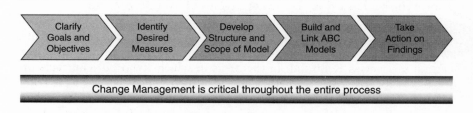

Sources: Obtained from KPMG LLP materials: client reports, KPMG developed training materials, and marketing materials.

process. Taken together, the savings that can be attributed to the mayor's competition and management policies exceed $550 million over 16 years. The city's competitive initiatives drive alone resulted in approximately $360 million of these savings, while additional efforts, such as reengineering, project cancellations, staff reductions primarily through attrition, and decisions to discontinue services, are estimated to exceed $45 million over seven years. (See Table 7.3 for a sample of Indianapolis's savings.) By establishing a baseline for costs and putting services up for bid, Indianapolis saved on big-ticket items, including wastewater treatment and sewer maintenance, as well as on smaller areas of need. The achievements for Indianapolis are as follows:

- Over 70 city services competitively bid, outsourced, or cosourced
- Over $550 million saved over 16 years
- Budget reduced by $119 million in 1997 versus a 15-year budgetary trend line

Table 7.2
The Competition Cycle and Competition Tools Matrix

	1	2	3	4	5	6	7
1. Identify Barriers	✔		✔	✔	✔	✔	
2. Select the Service	✔	✔	✔	✔	✔	✔	✔
3. Prepare RFP; Solicit Response; Select Vendor	✔	✔	✔	✔	✔	✔	✔
4. Prepare Contract and Monitor	✔	✔	✔	✔		✔	✔

1=Costing; 2=Performance Measures; 3=Performance Budgeting; 4=Benchmarking; 5=Organizational Assessment; 6=Business Process Improvement; 7=Gainsharing.

Sources: Obtained from KPMG LLP materials: client reports, KPMG developed training materials, and marketing materials.

Table 7.3
Sample of Savings by Indianapolis (in millions)

Service Area	Prior Cost	New Cost
Information Technology	$107	$81
AWT & Sewer O&M	$505	$316
Solid Waste Collection	$139	$104
Fleet Services	$20	$16
Print Copy Services	$7.4	$3.5
Microfilm Services	$3.7	$1.9

Sources: Obtained from KPMG LLP materials: client reports, KPMG developed training materials, and marketing materials.

- City's fund balances increased to more than $100 million in 1997 from $22 million in 1992
- Over $360 million saved by competitive initiatives drive
- Shifted to performance-based budgeting

Identify Barriers

A first step in the competition cycle is to identify potential barriers that could jeopardize the success of the managed competition effort. It is important to overcome these barriers in order for the government and employees to unleash their competitive spirit and creativity. This is absolutely essential in creating a level playing field for the employees and the private sector alike.

Generally, the majority of the barriers will be in three broad categories: (1) collective bargaining agreements, (2) personnel laws, and (3) procurement laws; however, a review and analysis of potential barriers will show that barriers are not limited to these areas. The competition team should review the respective collective bargaining agreements and personnel laws to determine the effect that competition will have on them.

Barriers may also be identified that will require changes in legislation, rules, or orders. The competition team should work quickly to draft legislation, rules, and orders to overcome these barriers. We have found that governments may have had a well-thought-out, sensible managed competition policy and may have identified and corrected barriers during the implementation of the policy, yet, in the end, the policy failed due to a lack of communication.

Consequently, the government should create a public information campaign for its primary and potential stakeholders. This campaign can be the vehicle used by the agency to announce its successes and maintain open communication regarding the entire process. The government may want to consider establishing a separate communication vehicle such as a newsletter, video, or poster for internal purposes, which contains information relating to the overall status of the project and testimonies from employees who have been part of the process.

It is important that the employees are kept informed during this process, as part of its success depends on the willingness of employees to be flexible and to discuss and resolve problems as they arise. The city of San Jose, California, used an employee newsletter as a communication vehicle. Articles discussing the program and results to date were included; however, the most valuable component was the employee submissions to the newsletter, which included their impressions of the program; their role in the team; lessons learned; and, most importantly, their messages to those employees yet to go through the program.

Select the Service

To identify the best opportunities for competition candidates, certain levels of research should be performed. The research can be as simple and straightforward as using the "yellow pages" test to determine if competition does in fact exist in the marketplace to soliciting input from private sector entrepreneurs, vendors, and, of course, public employees and research organizations. No matter what method or combination of methods is used, data must be accumulated in order to perform the appropriate analysis. The service being provided and the related costs must be understood. There are examples of failed competitive efforts in which the homework was not done up-front. Trash collection is a typical example. An assumption was made that the right service was selected, and to compound the problem, the related costing analysis was not performed.

When determining the best services to consider, focus on the following issues:

- Select activities that provide for simple quantitative analysis in terms of measuring results.
- Start with activities with relatively small operational budgets.
- Include activities with internal customers as opposed to only those activities with external customers.
- Determine private marketplace interest in each identified activity.

Prepare Request for Proposals, Solicit Response, and Select Vendor

Strategies and proposer analysis are integral facets of the managed competition process and must be logically and methodically organized from the start. The team should ensure that a project plan, which specifies responsibilities and dates, is prepared along with a base cost analysis. Quantitative and qualitative performance measures should also be developed. (See Figure 7.2 for a summary of an approach to the preparation and solicitation cycle.)

Once a service or activity is identified, the competition team should work with procurement and contracting to develop a solicitation document in the form of a RFP. The team should work with the affected department to develop a statement of work from information gathered from the department, purchasing, contracting, other stakeholders, and previous experiences with other governmental entities. The team should ensure that the statement of work is not just a listing of what has historically been performed by the government but a written document which focuses on what should be done and the desired outcomes and outputs. This approach allows a level of flexibility to the proposers in determining the most effective means of performing the activity or service.

Figure 7.2
Preparation and Solicitation Cycle

Prepare for Competition	Prepare and Issue RFP	Evaluate Proposals	Contract Award

- Development of Project Management Plan
- Base Cost Analysis
- Development of Quantitative and Qualitative Performance Measures

- Development of Statement of Work
- Development of Draft and Final RFP
- Development of Evaluation Criteria

- Development of Project Methodologies to Adjust for Bilateral Inequities between Public and Private Sector Bidders
- Quantitative and Qualitative Analysis
- Effort Proposals and Costs
- Due Diligence Review of Bidders

- Development of Cost Savings
- Analysis
- "What If" Analysis

Sources: Obtained from KPMG LLP materials: client reports, KPMG developed training
        materials, and marketing materials.

The RFP will include a description of how the managed competition will be conducted; proposal instructions, including the general terms and conditions; how the external proposals will be evaluated; how the cost comparison will be made; and how the eventual winner will be monitored during the contract period. The RFPs will be finalized once feedback has been obtained on performance standards, evaluation criteria, and any ideas for improving the solicitation. This feedback is necessary to ensure that quality requirements are clearly defined and the statement of work does not limit innovation and creativity in service delivery.

There are several different methods for evaluating vendor responses; the choice depends upon the form of solicitation used. The evaluation criteria should be developed simultaneously with the development of the program requirements; therefore, a determination must be made as to which aspects of the RFP are mandatory and which are considered desirable.

When developing the evaluation criteria, the following items must be considered: technical (service) requirements, business requirements, and costs. Further, a determination of their importance must be made and weighted accordingly. The following is an excerpt from a performance evaluation criteria matrix (Table 7.4): "A reasonable balance between the technical and cost evaluation is needed. Do not sacrifice quality for price."

In addition, a savings calculation must be prepared to take into consideration such items as bid amounts, contracting monitoring costs, unavoidable costs, and transition costs. This will be an important step in the eval-

Table 7.4
Proposal Evaluation Criteria

Criteria	Government	Company A	Company B
Quality			
Methodology			
Resources			
Project Staff			
Organization of Resources			
Customer Service			
Communication			
Location			
Proximity			
Technical Approach			
Work Plan			
Transition Plan			
Response to Complaints/			
Special Requests			
Training			
Capacity			
Adequacy			
Documented Experience			
References			
Recent Experience			
Financial Stability			
Execution of Contract			
Cost Proposal			
Realistic			
Adequate			
Experience Identifiable			
Within Budget			
Performance-Based			

Sources: Obtained from KPMG LLP materials: client reports, KPMG developed training
   materials, and marketing materials.

uation process since it will identify the true savings from the managed competition effort and may be used to determine whether the government wants to go forward and award the contract to a vendor. A methodology should be developed for use on all managed competition efforts throughout the government to ensure consistency among the competition projects. (A sample of how an evaluation of the costs may look in addition to how a savings calculation may be performed is shown in Table 7.5.)

Table 7.5
Sample: Savings Calculation

Bid/Cost Proposal	Government	Company A (dollars)	Company B
Total Bid	300,000	250,000	500,000
Unavoidable Costs	(70,000)	—	—
Avoidable Cost of Service to the Government	230,000	250,000	500,000
Total Cost of Service	300,000	—	—
Add Contract Monitoring and Other Transition Costs	40,000	—	—
Adjusted Cost of Service	340,000	—	—
Cost of Service Prior to Competition	450,000	—	—
Savings to Government	90,000	—	—

Sources: Obtained from KPMG LLP materials: client reports, KPMG developed training materials, and marketing materials.

In evaluating the cost proposals, assuming the quality and scope of services is the same for all proposers, the evaluation team may initially want to consider awarding the contract to Company #1 as they have the lowest overall bid or cost proposal. After taking into account the government's avoidable and unavoidable cost of services, however, it may turn out that the government can actually perform the services more efficiently than Company #1. Once the determination is made as to the successful proposers, the evaluation team must go one step further and determine if there is an overall savings to the government once the new costs of contracting, such as contract monitoring, are added on. In the preceding example, the government saved more than 26 percent as a result of the managed competition effort.

Finally, a "what if" analysis will be prepared in the evaluation phase to ensure that the winning proposal is in the best interest of the government. This will be especially beneficial when flexibility is granted to the proposers for varying service levels, allowing a comparison to be performed between proposers for like conditions.

Contract Preparation and Monitoring

The government agency will retain the performance responsibility no matter who provides the service. Consequently, from the day service delivery begins to the end of the contract term, the contractor (either internal or external) is part of the local government. Thus, the government must ensure that the contractor is effective and efficient since any problems with the contractor's performance will be directly associated with the overall government's performance. The citizens do not care if the contractor is in house versus outside; if there is a problem, they will ultimately hold the government responsible. As a result, it is critical for the government to implement appropriate monitoring procedures.

We have found that the most successful approach in contract monitoring is to develop a transition plan and a monitoring plan. A well-defined and developed transition plan ensures a seamless transition between the existing and future provision of services. If the service remains in house, the transition plan will include details on how the government will make changes in service levels or processes to become more competitive or remain competitive.

A transition plan should be created, regardless of whether the government or another service provider is selected. The transition plan should be developed during the determination of services to be requested in the RFP process, which could involve a change in service level. Once the service provider has been selected, the transition plan can be finalized and implemented.

In addition, a methodology to administer and monitor either in-house performance if the service remains with the government or contract performance if an outside vendor is selected must be developed. As shown, contract administration and monitoring are both critical to ensure that the government receives the performance levels for the cost agreed upon during the proposal process. The methodology developed should include establishing a mechanism for ensuring compliance with the following:

- *Performance Measures.* Are the performance levels as defined in the contract being met?
- *Outcome Measures.* Are the outcome measures as defined in the contract being met?
- *Cost Construction.* Are the performance and outcome requirements being achieved within the costs defined in the contract?

In addition, the government agency must ascertain the appropriate performance and outcome measures that will be assessed as well as appropriate performance reporting mechanisms. It should use past experience along with current industry standards in determining various measures that could be used to monitor performance. Before monitoring can begin, the government and the contractor must achieve concurrence on the measures.

Another area critical to the success of the managed competition effort is overall customer satisfaction—that is, what services are important to residents and how well they are being provided. The government agency should establish a mechanism for customers (both internal and external) to formally provide feedback on services received that will be tied to the performance and outcome measures. This will entail establishing the criteria included in the survey instrument along with frequency of collection, tabulations, and reporting of the results. It is important that an independent party be involved in this process in order to maintain objectivity and retain the credibility of the process.

In the event of a performance breach, it may be necessary for a government to terminate a contractor. A breach of contract can be the result of various unplanned events occurring or tasks not being performed. The corrective action must be consistent with the guidelines established in the contract or memorandum of understanding. These guidelines must include specific details regarding the basis for, and the notification methods of, noncompliance, length of time to correct any deficiencies, penalties, and other issues. (See Table 7.6 for a chart depicting the various documents and analyses that will be prepared by the team throughout the competition cycle.)

CONCLUSION

Citizens are used to reliable, high-quality service virtually on demand from the private sector and they are now asking public organizations to do the same. Most governments are experiencing increasing demands for more and better services, yet the public and other recipients do not want to pay more.

Governments are facing the following challenges:

- People want better services, sooner.
- People want a more efficient, effective government.
- People are impatient for changes to occur.
- People want actions and decisions, not studies and theories.

By itself, a government agency cannot solve the issues it faces. Traditional means of coping with fiscal pressures such as increasing taxes or cutting services are no longer an option for most governments. This means governments will need to find ways to cut their costs. One of the most proven ways of doing so is by introducing competition into public sector operations;

Table 7.6
Documents and Analysis Required throughout Competition Cycle

1. Identify and Overcome the Barriers to Managed Competition	• "What if" analysis on successful or unsuccessful bid in relation to the impact on the collective bargaining agreement • Analysis of the impact of government personnel laws and regulations • Identification of procurement impediments which restrict the government's competitiveness with recommendations on how to overcome impediments • Potential draft legislation, rules, and orders required to implement managed competition
2. Select the Service	• Competition criteria • List of competition candidates
3. Preparation and Solicitation	• Definition of key team members' roles and responsibilities • Project management plan • Request for Proposal, including statement of work, performance measures, and evaluation criteria • Base cost analysis • Methodology for evaluating proposals including adjustments to create level playing field (i.e., avoidable/unavoidable cost determination) • Analysis of proposals, including calculation of cost savings
4. Prepare Contract and Monitor	• Transition plan which ensures a seamless transition between the existing and future provision of services, including identification of key milestones and tasks • Monitoring plan, including recommended performance measures, remediation strategies, and customer satisfaction analysis • Results of performance monitoring activities

Sources: Obtained from KPMG LLP materials: client reports, KPMG developed training materials, and marketing materials.

however, four points must be kept in mind for competition to be successful and sustainable: (1) the process shakes up the workforce and transforms attitudes; (2) the competition process must be done right—low bid does not necessarily achieve the desired results; (3) governments considering competition need good accounting systems or methods in order to compare their costs to those of alternative providers; and (4) competition requires effective monitoring and oversight in order to assure that expected results are achieved. Competition is key to improved services at a lower cost.

8

Impacts of Social Mandates in Contracting

Margaret M. "Peg" Swanton

There are currently two conflicting trends in government contracting. One such trend in both the private and the public sector is simplification—speeding up and reducing the cost of the procurement process. The other, occurring especially among some local and state governments, is the attempt to remedy societal ills through mandates on the government's suppliers. In direct contrast to the trend toward simplification, this trend actually complicates government procurement and must necessarily, from an economic viewpoint, increase costs.

Governments, however, largely fail to measure either the costs or the results of these social mandates and may not know the costs and do not measure the efficacy of the procurement process itself. By failing to measure costs and results, governments effectively hide the costs of these mandates and lose the opportunity to evaluate them and improve results.

The private sector is making substantial efforts to simplify the procurement process. The goals of this effort are to shorten the procurement cycle, allowing the organization to acquire needed resources more quickly and to decrease costs. A recent Microsoft advertisement noted that by implementing the new Microsoft-based corporate purchasing system, MasterCard saved up to $85 per transaction and reduced time requirements from four days to a day and a half. The advertisement noted that another firm saved $1 million in the first year.

Many government agencies, including the U.S. Department of Housing and Urban Development (HUD) (n.d.) which emphasizes its lack of "red tape," are also attempting to simplify and streamline the procurement process. Federal agencies are evaluating their procurement procedures and publishing results. The Tennessee Valley Authority (TVA) (n.d.) is developing paperless business processes, allowing their computers to communicate directly with those of their suppliers. The TVA projects sizable savings based on a reduced procurement process cycle and a decreased error rate. Speeding up the procurement process is also the goal of the Immigration and Naturalization Service's (INS) (n.d.) new team approach for information technology procurements. Such efforts are not limited to the federal government. The state of Massachusetts initiated a multistate cooperative purchasing system that not only offers reduced prices but also allows buyers to shop more efficiently (Newcombe 1998).

In contrast to this emphasis on streamlined operations, the other trend in government contracting complicates rather than simplifies the procurement process by requiring vendors to operate according to socially prescribed mandates. This chapter will address two sets of questions:

1. What are the issues being addressed? How are they being addressed? What has been the effect on procurement procedures?
2. How do governments assess the success or failure of this technique for addressing social ills?

THE ISSUES

Unemployment

The issue of unemployment has several facets: job loss for the specific individuals previously employed by the government, lack of employment opportunities for certain groups of people, and unemployment rates for the locality.

Individual job loss is one of the major reasons for protest against outsourcing. One union's protest stated, "What's wrong with outsourcing? In short, quite a lot" (Community and Public Sector Union n.d.). In DuPage County, Illinois, a 17-member task force, which was assigned the responsibility to investigate privatization of the county's mental health services, rejected the move. The task force cited loss of jobs for county employees as a principal reason for its decision against going private (Hudson 1998). When public or private organizations consider outsourcing, negative public reaction in the form of unfavorable media attention or workers' strikes are often the results. Furthermore, there are untoward political ramifications for government agencies that outsource—the larger the number of employees involved, the larger the issues. In 1995, when the Chicago School Finance Authority considered a recommendation to outsource facilities management at the Chicago Public Schools, the Coalition of the Chicago

Board of Education Unions (1995) warned that the jobs of "9,455 dedicated, hard-working employees would be terminated" (4).

There are also concerns about the lack of employment opportunities for certain groups, especially minorities and women. Many believe that governments offer better employment opportunities for women and minorities than the private sector. As a result, it is assumed that minorities and women will suffer most when governments streamline operations. For example, in the Chicago Board of Education example previously described, the Coalition of the Chicago Board of Education Unions (1995) claimed that it would be devastating to minorities:

Minorities are especially vulnerable to arrangements that reduce government because they make up a relatively large proportion of government employees. In a study done in 1980, 27.1% of all employed African Americans and 15.9% of Hispanics worked for government with a 6% rise per year. Of all African American managers and professionals, 53.5% are employed by government. (10)

Additionally, many cities and inner-ring suburbs see an exodus of jobs from their municipalities, with the end result being the erosion of their job pool and tax base. For example, statistics indicate that the overall unemployment rate for the city of Chicago is significantly higher than that of the metropolitan area overall. The overall unemployment rate was four percent as opposed to ten percent for the city. Chicago is not alone in this phenomenon; cities such as Detroit and Cleveland confront the same issue. When measuring wages rather than jobs, the picture is just as bleak with almost half of all wage and salary dollars earned in Chicago going to suburbanites, while only 11 percent of wages earned in the suburbs go to city residents (Persky 1994). To stem this perceived migration of jobs, many cities have enacted residency requirements for city employees and seek to extend those requirements to vendors.

Governments attempt to remedy the problems of unemployment through a variety of means, including adding hiring requirements to their contracts. For example, when the city of Monmouth, Illinois, contracted its public works functions, the vendor hired all current employees, recognized the union, paid comparable wages and benefits, and agreed that the workforce would be reduced only through attrition (Gillen and Johnson 1999, 7). When the city of Atlanta outsourced its drinking water system, all of the finalists agreed in principle to keep all 535 employees for the duration of the contract, voluntarily exceeding the city's three-year requirement. Vendors were permitted to use early retirement incentives, screening for alcohol and other drugs, cross training, and transfers within business centers to reduce employment to optimal levels (Public Works Financing 1998, 4). On the other hand, when the Bergen County Utilities Authority of Bergen County, New Jersey, attempted to privatize its waste transfer station, it required winning vendors to hire all employees at their current salary levels. Bergen County received no bids until it revised its bid requirements pertaining to hiring. Under the revision, the winning bidder was required to hire the agency's employees but was allowed to set wages (Snell 1999, 4).

Job losses for minorities and women are generally addressed through requirements to hire existing employees. The city of Chicago's McLaughlin ordinance, however, requires a minimum level of employment for women and minorities in certain construction contracts.

In addition, governments from the city of Chicago to Marin County, California, have enacted ordinances allowing preferences for local business. Marin County's code notes that there are multiple benefits to the local business preference:

It promotes the public interest to encourage the development and maintenance of local businesses in Marin County to insure a viable and balanced economy, provide local jobs for residents of the county, reduce commuter traffic, promote the development of the county's tax base, stimulate sales tax receipts, and enhance the number of and type of service available in Marin County for the benefit of its residents. ("Preference in Contracts and Purchases" n.d., Chapter 3.10)

Most such ordinances define local businesses as employing people within the government's jurisdiction. Marin County's code continues:

"Local business" means any business which: a) has its principal place of business in Marin; or b) has a business license issued in Marin County for a period of six months prior to any claim of preference; or c) maintains an office or other facility in Marin in which not less than five persons are employed substantially full time. ("Preference in Contracts and Purchases" n.d., Chapter 3.10)

Under such requirements, contracts are awarded to the low bidder, except that a qualified "local business" will be awarded the contract if the local business' bid does not exceed that of the nonlocal low bidder by more than a certain percentage of the total bid. Marin County allows a five percent preference on the price submitted by a local business. Cook County, Illinois, allows a two percent preference for local businesses ("Local Business Preference" n.d., Chapter 10, Section 38).

These mandates affect procurement procedures. For each, the government must explain the pertinent requirement or preference allowed. Vendors must supply the documentation to show that they complied (or will comply) with the requirement or that it can be considered for preferential treatment. The government must verify the accuracy of the vendors' assertions and monitor compliance during the term of the contract.

Low Wages

Coupled with fears that the private sector does not offer adequate employment opportunities for women and minorities, there is also a concern that private employers pay low wages. In the unions' rebuttal to the Chicago Public Schools proposal to outsource facilities management, it was noted that "When jobs are privatized, those employees who did not suffer a job loss did, however, suffer a substantial loss in wages, medical benefits, and benefit days" (The Coalition of Chicago Board of Education Unions 1995, 10).

In addition, even without outsourcing issues, many local governments have concerns about jobs that pay less than the local or federal poverty level. Welfare reform has emphasized moving welfare recipients into the workforce. The Personal Responsibility and Work Opportunity Reconciliation Act of 1996 contained limits on welfare benefits and stressed working. This added emphasis on work prompted local governments to consider the effect on their communities of a growing population supporting themselves on poverty-level jobs but denied welfare benefits.

In addition, some governments are reporting growing increases in wage inequality, including steep declines in wages at the bottom end of the wage scale. According to a recent report commissioned by the city of San Jose,

- While salaries have been growing for many skilled employees in the city's high-tech industries, working families have seen their earnings drop by more than 13% between 1989 and 1996.

- The cost of living in the area has skyrocketed, as the cost of a single family home has risen more than 20% in the last year alone, to over $340,000, and the average rent has risen by nearly 30% between 1995 and 1997, to $1,200 per month. (Benner and Rosner 1998, 2)

The San Jose report continued, noting that of all Silicon Valley jobs,

- 19% do not allow "a single adult to live alone without some form of public assistance."

- 40% do not sustain a single parent and child above the regional poverty level.

- 55% do not support a family of four. (Benner and Rosner 1998, 2)

Responding to concerns about low wages, many governments have enacted Living Wage Ordinances. As of August 1998, 16 cities, including Baltimore, Los Angeles, Oakland, Portland, St. Paul, and Chicago, have implemented such requirements (Benner and Rosner 1998). Living Wage Ordinances generally prescribe a minimum wage in excess of federal minimum wage requirements and a minimum package of benefits that must be paid by vendors who win city contracts. Companies that receive contracts of more than $100,000 from the city of Boston must pay at least a minimum hourly rate of $7.49/hour, which is equivalent to the minimum wage for city workers ("Boston Enacts Living Wage Rule" 1997). Los Angeles County requires that companies receiving contracts in excess of $25,000 pay full-time employees at least $8.32/hour or $9.46/hour if no health care benefits are provided, while Ypsilanti, Michigan's Living Wage Ordinance requires $8.50 or $10 without insurance (Association of Community Organizations for Reform Now 1999).

These mandates require that the government explain the requirement or preference; vendors must report information to document compliance; and the reported information must be verified. Meaningful implementation of the Living Wage Ordinance requires verification of employee compensation by audit.

Nonpayment of Child Support

The nonpayment of child support has obvious adverse effects on both the individual families involved and society as a whole because of the massive amounts of money due. Unpaid child support in Illinois alone amounted to more than $1.3 billion in 1997 ("Deadbeat Parents . . ." 1997, 1). By 1998, that balance had grown to $1.6 billion (Hynes 1999, 9). In addition, there is increasing recognition of the effect on society as a whole and of the link between poverty and the failure of parents to provide support. Forty-six percent of all single-parent families headed by women live in poverty, and sociologists attribute this to the failure of fathers to pay support (12). The Personal Responsibility and Work Opportunity Reconciliation Act of 1996 contains comprehensive child support enforcement measures, limitations on eligibility, and work requirements. It also emphasizes increasing child support collections in an efficient and cost-effective manner.

In an attempt to increase the collection of child support, some local governments have enacted requirements in addition to the federal requirements. For example, the Cook County, Illinois, Child Support Enforcement Ordinance, effective July 1, 1998, required that every applicant for county privilege be in full compliance with any child support order before the applicant is entitled to receive or renew that privilege. This ordinance specifies the following:

"Applicant" means any person or business entity, including all Substantial Owners, seeking issuance of a County Privilege or renewal of an existing county privilege.

"County Privilege" means any business license, including but not limited to liquor dealers' licenses, packaging goods licenses, tavern licenses, restaurant licenses, and gun licenses, real property license or lease; permit, including but not limited to building permits, zoning permits or approvals, environmental certificates; County Home Loan, and contracts exceeding the value of $10,000.

"Substantial Owner" means any person or persons who own or hold a twenty-five percent or more percentage of interest in any business entity seeking a County Privilege, including those shareholders, general or limited partners, beneficiaries and principals; except where a business entity is an individual or sole proprietorship, Substantial Owner means that individual or sole proprietorship.

As a result of such ordinances, governments must provide information and the necessary forms for prospective vendors. Vendors submitting bids are required to identify all "Substantial Owners" and provide the name, social security number, date of birth, home address, and phone number for each. The monitoring process requires that the information be verified and checked against a child support database.

Environmental Concerns

Although the country has been concerned about the environment for some time, and environmental concerns have led to a variety of effects on procurements, those concerns have had a fairly superficial effect on the environment itself. For example, some governments allow a preference for recycled paper, allowing them to pay more for recycled paper than for other paper products. Other governments require that vendors print proposals on recycled paper or on both sides of the page. A 1998 city of Chicago Request for Proposal stated submittals shall be prepared on 8 1/2 by 11 size, recycled paper (with no less than 20% post-consumer content), printed double sided and bound on the long side. It is the city's policy to encourage the use of reusable, recycled, recyclable, and chlorine-free printed materials in the submittal of all bids, proposals, reports, and other documents prepared in connection with this solicitation.

The state of New York includes a prohibition on the purchase of tropical hardwoods in its standard clauses for all state contracts. Contractors must certify that all wood products to be used under the contract are in accordance with (but not limited to) the specifications and provisions of State Finance Law Section 165 (*Standard clause* for all New York state contracts Appendix A).

The effect on procurement procedures parallels that of the previously discussed mandates. Governments must explain each requirement, and vendors must document compliance which the government must verify. The government must confirm that proposals are printed on recycled paper, that the product being procured is recycled or recyclable, and that the wood used is not a prohibited tropical hardwood.

Lack of Opportunity for Women and Minorities

Many individuals believe that minorities and women should be awarded preferential treatment in government contracting and other business opportunities due to prior discrimination. As President Lyndon B. Johnson said to the graduating class of Howard University, "It is not enough to open the gates of opportunity. All our citizens must have the opportunity to walk through those gates" (Americans United for Affirmative Action 1965). As result of political pressure to remedy prior discrimination, many governments responded by making certain requirements of their vendors. In 1965, the U.S. Department of Labor's Office of Federal Contract Compliance Programs implemented regulations requiring that vendors receiving contracts in excess of $40,000 agree to certain nondiscrimination regulations, including the submission of affirmative action plans. These plans documented how the organization ensured that applicants were employed and treated without regard to race, color, religion, sex, or national origin. The requirements on the federal government's contractors grew in scope from mandating affirmative action plans to directing contracts to minority- or women-owned firms. Many local and state governments implemented similar regulations. For example, Section 10-43.5 (a) of the Cook County, Illinois, ordinance states that Cook County's goal is "not less than 35% of the annual aggregate value of all contracts awarded by the County." Specifically, Cook County's goal is to award not less than 25 percent (30% for construction contracts) of the total annual dollar amount for county contracts to Minority Business Enterprises (MBEs) and 10 percent to Women Business Enterprises (WBEs). The *State of Indiana 1998 Procurement Manual* states, "invite small and minority-owned businesses to present their products and services for consideration in State procurements." Washington State (n.d.) also "encourages participation from minority- and women-owned business for purchasing."

Implementing such preferences entails three challenges: (1) defining minority or women ownership, (2) determining how to handle "preferences," and (3) structuring the program to avoid legal challenges.

The definition of a minority- or women-owned firm has been relatively simple, universal, and uncontested until recently. The traditional definition of minority or women ownership is a company in which members of minority groups or women own 51 percent of the firm. Recently there have been proposals to change that definition, at least for private sector purposes. The National Minority Supplier Development Council has proposed a change in that definition to allow minority firms more access to capital and better opportunities for growth. Their resolution would allow minority companies to sell stock and, in some cases, retain the council's certification, even if the stock sale results in minorities owning as little as 30 percent of the company. Harriet Michel, president of the council, stated, "Minority firms must be allowed the same opportunity to grow in this global economy, to be competitive and not to be defeated because they don't have access to capital" (Holmes 1999, 6). According to the council, too much emphasis has been placed on minority start-ups and not enough on nurturing them into the big leagues (Thomas 1999, B2).

The U.S. Hispanic Chamber of Commerce, Asian business groups, and a number of African-American leaders, however, oppose the change in definition. Earl G. Graves, Sr., publisher of *Black Enterprise Magazine,* stated, "If you have 51 percent, you have control; less than 51 percent, it is not control, you have an ownership stake" (Holmes 1999, 6). Other minority leaders have urged a delay in the vote, which had been scheduled for late October 1999, until the ramifications of the change can be studied more fully.*

While this controversy relates to private rather than public sector procurements, the federal government has also recently enacted changes which affect the determination of preferential status. In September 1998, the Small Business Administration (SBA) announced a new certification process expected to "reduce costs, prevent fraud and abuse, and ensure that the program is administered fairly." The new regulations will no longer allow firms to self-certify or identify themselves as disadvantaged. Instead, the SBA's Office of Disadvantaged Business Certification and Eligibility as well as a nationwide network of private certifiers will process applications and certify firms as disadvantaged. Some have protested this move over two issues:

1. "[T]he nation's two largest and most experienced certifiers of minority and women owned business—the National Minority Supplier Development Council (NMSDC) and the Women's Business Enterprise National Council (WBENC), respectively—were eliminated from consideration since neither organization provides certification to all possible SDB applicants (the NMSDC only certifies businesses owned by minorities; WBENC only certifies those owned by women)."

2. Certain for-profit businesses that bid on government contracts were selected as certifiers. "Is there a conflict of interest here? Would you want a potential competitor in possession of all your financial records—one of the requirements of the certification process?" (Conrad 1999)

In addition, and parallel to the NMSDC debate over the 51 percent ownership issue, the SBA (n.d.) has been criticized for its financial requirements regarding disadvantaged status. Individuals must have a net worth of less than $750,000, excluding the value of the business and personal residence. According to Carol Dougal and Hedy Ratner, copresidents of the Women's Business Development Center, that level is too low and will exclude many would-be participants (Russis 1999). Another organization indicated that especially in construction, many of the most successful firms are likely to lose their disadvantaged status, potentially delaying some highway construction projects. The organization also raised an issue about fairness; eligibility may depend on how the owner has structured wealth rather than actual wealth. For example, because an Individual Retirement Account is a personal asset, it is counted against the $750,000 limit. On the other hand, a pension plan is a corporate asset and is not counted. As a result, one firm may be certified as disadvantaged while another is not, even though the owners have identical net worths.

Applying the preferences in contracting allows the federal government to make use of a number of techniques. Firms certified as disadvantaged are eligible for price evaluation adjustments of up to ten percent in certain federal contracts. The SBA program also provides evaluation credits and, in some cases, monetary incentives for prime contractors who achieve subcontracting targets. In addition, it offers "set-aside" procurements for eligible businesses. The new HUBZone Empowerment Contracting Program allows certain small firms located in many urban or rural areas to qualify for sole-source and other federal contract benefits. The city of Chicago also makes use of a number of different approaches. It has used targeted procurements that limit bidding to city of Chicago certified MBE/WBE firms (see Specification No. B3-91039-08 for Janitorial Services issued by the Department of Purchases, Contracts, and Supplies, City of Chicago [July 1993]); required MBE/WBE participation for individual contracts; and recently issued an RFP for Professional Service Agreements, seeking a number of vendors that could be prequalified to provide services as needed. The RFP stated the following:

The city of Chicago is now seeking Minority Business Enterprise and Women Business Enterprise commitment on individual proposals at this time. The intent is to insure that among all contracts awarded as a result of this RFP, 16.9% and 4.5%, respectively, of all contracts will also be awarded to city of Chicago certified Minority Business Enterprises and city of Chicago certified Women Business Enterprises. (City of Chicago 1998)

Under this RFP, vendors were not required to subcontract services to MBE/WBE firms and the city met its responsibility to direct business to certified MBE/WBE in total rather than contract by contract. Other governments have chosen to implement this ordinance on a contract by contract basis; they require that a percentage of each contract be subcontracted to minority- or women-owned businesses.

Programs must be structured to avoid legal challenges. While many individuals believe that minorities and women should be awarded preferential treatment in government contracting, this belief is not universal. Preferences have been challenged in court—sometimes successfully. In *Richmond v. J. A. Croson* (1989), a nonminority firm successfully challenged the city's economic set-aside programs on the grounds that they were adopted without direct evidence that the city had discriminated against minority subcontractors. The decision established that programs that set aside certain contracts for minority- and women-owned businesses must be supported by firm evidence of prior discrimination within the local market area. Later decisions, including *Cone Corporation v. Hillsborough County* (1990) and *Coral Construction v. King County* (1991) helped to establish the definition of "local market area." The ruling in *Adarand Constructors, Inc. v. Pena, et al.* (1995) extended the strict scrutiny standard to federal programs. The ruling had two outcomes: (1) that federal minority or women business programs can be implemented or maintained only if there is evidence of discrimination and (2) that programs must be narrowly tailored to remedy that discrimination. Governments must define "market area," conduct disparity studies documenting evidence of discrimination, and tailor their affirmative action programs to address those issues or risk legal action. Programs must be reassessed and possibly changed with each court case. The new SBA requirements were written to comply with the Adarand decision.

Implementation of these mandates requires substantial additional paperwork to explain the requirement and to provide the forms to be completed. Compliance requires statistics on total contracts awarded as well as those given to firms that are entitled to preferential treatment. The status of those firms must be verified. Without such data, governments must comply with requirements on a contract-by-contract basis. When compliance is determined on a contract-by-contract basis, each vendor is required to recruit subcontractors or find other ways to meet the participation requirement. The government must review the information submitted by the low bidder and determine whether the vendor has complied with the ordinance. If a vendor is deemed noncompliant, the next vendor is evaluated for compliance. In some localities, the next step is to determine whether or not the next vendor's price is "competitive." If that vendor's price is considered competitive, the contract is awarded. ("Competitive cost level" is defined as exceeding 10 percent of the lowest bid price for that contract. It does not refer to an independently established market price.) If the price is noncompetitive, the contract is rebid. As a result of the legal challenges, those requirements may be changing, thus creating confusion on the part of both the government and the vendor.

ASSESSING SUCCESS OR FAILURE

In attempting to assess the success of social mandates, it is important to distinguish between the principle (such as ensuring parental financial support for children) and the technique chosen to implement it. Separating the two allows an evaluation of the technique without a debate about the goal itself. It allows the following questions:

- How effective is the technique at reaching stated goals?
- How much does it cost?
- Would another technique achieve better results at the same cost?
- Would another technique achieve the same results at lower cost?

In order to answer these questions, it is necessary to have information about results and costs before and after the implementation of the mandate. This information is generally lacking.

Interestingly, the same governments that do not analyze the results of their social mandates on the procurement costs frequently carefully examine the results of outsourcing arrangements. The General Services Administration, IT Management Practices Division (1998), noted that "outsourcing benefits those organizations which have the foresight to take the time to 'benchmark' the services required." The General Services Administration recommends that governments invest in understanding the costs of the current system as well as accounting for the full costs of the outsourced model in order to maximize the benefits of outsourcing.

While understanding the costs and the savings related to outsourcing can be a challenge, various organizations publish guidelines, including the federal publication, *OMB Circular A-76* (Office of Management and Budget OMG 1983), and the NLC's publication, *Municipal Service Delivery: Thinking Through the Privatization Option* (Fryklund, Weil, and McCullough 1997). Both publications offer advice about how to capture the full in-house costs. Thus, many governments measure the results—both the costs and the savings— of privatization efforts. They analyze the results and share those results with other organizations through publications such as *Privatization Watch,* which is published by the Reason Public Policy Institute.

Yet many governments fail to measure the results of their social mandates. Why do governments measure the costs and benefits of outsourcing but fail to quantify the results of those mandates? There are two probable reasons that governments analyze the results of outsourcing efforts:

1. They are frequently motivated to outsource due to the potential savings. Many governments face either shrinking budgets or pressure to reduce costs— sometimes both. Because they are motivated to reduce costs, they measure costs.

2. They can be under significant pressure to document savings. Thus, many organizations fully account for current costs and measure both the costs of outsourcing efforts and the results, including the number of potholes repaired or the number of children placed for adoption. They may also measure service quality (e.g., by counting and analyzing complaints).

By comparison, governments do not generally implement social mandates in order to decrease cost. They are neither subject to political pressure to prove that mandates reduce costs nor pressure to justify results. Indeed, some people fail to acknowledge that mandates increase costs and view success simply as passing the ordinance. They do not believe it is necessary to evaluate results. Consequently, governments do not know either the costs or the results of their social mandates. The result of that lack of measurement is that governments do not have the information needed to manage their operations. The general principle is that organizations can be managed by their results to improve results, but these governments do not have the quantifiable information necessary to make use of the feedback loop (Figure 8.1).

The desired result, or mission, establishes the focus for the entire enterprise. The organization operates in some environment. It has inputs and produces some actual result. The discrepancy between actual and desired results constitutes information about the success of the organization. By

Figure 8.1
The Feedback Loop

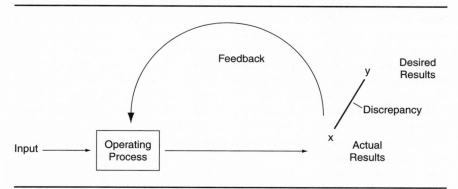

Source: Author.

recognizing and analyzing that discrepancy and using the results of that analysis as feedback to guide changes in the operating process (especially by answering the question, "Why did the discrepancy occur?"), management can redirect activities to bring actual results progressively closer to desired results.

Figure 8.1 illustrates the importance of using concrete information to evaluate and improve the results of operations. It can describe the organization as a whole or specific departments, each with its own goals, measured results, and operations controlled by feedback. A well-designed organization is structured as a nested set of feedback loops. The desired outcomes and operating processes are inextricably linked by this idea of a system anchored in its mission and controlled by feedback.

For example, *The Wall Street Journal* has complained for years about legislation requiring the use of particular technology for reducing emissions. When such legislation is passed without requiring later evaluations, the technology is locked in place. Without an assessment process, ten years later, manufacturing firms will still be required to install the required equipment even though new and better technology is available.

Looking specifically at the procurement function, Steven Kelman, Professor of Public Policy at the John F. Kennedy School of Government at Harvard University, recommends evaluating that function based on a simple criterion—how well it supports the mission of the organization. The evaluation process would require asking questions such as the following: "Did departments receive the goods or services when they were needed?" "Was the quality provided sufficient?" "Did the organization pay the best possible prices?"

To apply this concept specifically to social mandates in order to assess the effectiveness of, for example, the child support ordinances, it is necessary to measure and compare the difference between expected and actual collections and costs (including the effect on the procurement process and the organization as a whole.) By comparing actual to expected results, the government agency can use the feedback loop to fine-tune its operation. That is to say, it can introduce changes that would decrease prices paid, speed up the procurement process, increase child support collections, or achieve the same level of collections while decreasing costs. As Bill Gates (1999) explained in his book, *Business @ the Speed of Thought,* "How you gather, manage, and use information will determine whether you win or lose" (1).

Many governments fail to gather, manage, or use information about either the procurement process itself or social mandates implemented through the procurement processes. They fail to develop benchmarks against which current costs and current results can be measured. They fail to account for the costs associated with social mandates and fail to measure results. Without this information, the government is operating in the dark. It is unable to determine whether it is achieving its goals, whether it is doing so cost-effectively, or whether another technique would provide better results.

The remainder of this section will discuss the costs and measures of the effectiveness of social mandates. Because actual costs and results are largely unavailable, the discussion will be based on economic theory rather than data analysis.

Costs

There are two types of costs related to social mandates: (1) internal processing costs and (2) the costs of higher prices.

Governments incur two major internal costs: (1) administrative costs related to the procurement process and (2) the cost of delays in procuring needed resources. Administrative costs are the added financial burdens, including additional personnel, paper, and postage of the procurement effort. Vendors must be notified, information verified, and compliance monitored. These costs are largely hidden. Some of them are reflected in the budget of the department responsible for the procurement function; however, most agencies have no way to distinguish the costs of the social mandate from other procurement costs.

The private sector frequently makes use of techniques such as ABC to estimate the costs of specific business processes such as procurement. Firms know the costs of procuring different types of goods and services. Governments generally do not and may not know either the full costs of their procurement process or the costs of each social mandate added to that process. As has already been noted, without this information, it is impossible to assess the cost-effectiveness of the technique chosen to implement the mandate. The costs of child support initiatives, for example, include the costs of added paperwork and notifying potential vendors of the child support requirements, as well as monitoring costs. Meaningful implementation requires the agency to verify that (1) substantial owners have been properly identified and (2) they do not owe child support payments. The costs of local business preferences are similar. The government must notify potential vendors of the preference and monitor compliance by verifying reported local business status. It must also calculate preferences allowed. The Living Wage Ordinance requires extensive monitoring to meaningfully implement the ordinance.

The administrative costs of MBE/WBE requirements can be even higher. Some internal costs of MBE/WBE requirements are substantial and easily identified such as the cost of the department that certifies vendors as disadvantaged or minority- or women-owned. MBE/WBE firms are required to document both ownership and control by one or more minorities or women by providing information about or copies of the following:

- All current signed leases from all locations
- Current applicable licenses and permits
- Other certifications or denials
- Copies of stock certificates
- W-2s for all owners, officers, and managers, as well as a recent payroll register with copies of canceled payroll checks
- Bank resolutions and signature cards
- Contracts for the firm's three largest contracts in the last year
- Loan agreements
- Financial statements
- Tax returns
- Minutes of shareholders' and directors' meetings and more

The government must verify the information submitted to document that these firms are genuine, not front organizations, that women or minorities, in fact, own and operate the firms. The governmental review process generally includes site visits to the firm. According to the head of a large contract compliance department, this verification process and the determination of who is actually the decision maker in the firm can be very difficult as is illustrated in the following examples.

MBE/WBE Example 1. A woman owned a relatively small janitorial services firm. She was married to a man who was the president of a major firm in the same field. The woman's father owned the larger firm. She contended that she was completely independent and applied for WBE status. Her request was denied because her office was located within the office of the larger firm; she could not answer basic questions about her business, including the number of people on her board of directors and how jobs were priced. In addition, she was unable to describe contracts held by her firm, and the larger firm guaranteed work on a major contract for her firm.

MBE/WBE Example 2. A married couple, consisting of a Hispanic man and a white woman, owned a business together with the husband owning the majority of the stock. The firm was certified as minority owned. When he died, he left his stock to the woman's children from a prior marriage. Complaints were received when the firm maintained its MBE certification; however, investigation showed that the father of the children and the children themselves were Hispanic and that the children had indeed taken over the management of the firm.

MBE/WBE Example 3. A firm was founded, owned, and operated by a woman. She was successful, and the firm grew to a substantial size. As the firm grew, she spent less of her time managing the firm, hiring employees to handle operations while she devoted her time to sales. Although she was frequently out of the office and other personnel handled much of the day-to-day operations, her business was recertified because she maintained control of the firm, signed the checks, and was responsible for decisions.

Growth makes it especially difficult to determine who actually runs the business. "With a $100,000 firm, it is easy, but as the business grows, the owner gets farther and farther way from day-to-day operations. Many tasks are delegated to subordinates," stated an individual who works in the certification process. Another organization that certifies businesses as women-owned concurred that it can be difficult to determine who is actually controlling a family business. Their main reason for denying certification was that family involvement in the business made it unclear who the decision maker was. In spite of the obvious difficulties of determining who is running the business, the government can face major embarrassment when it makes a mistake.

MBE/WBE Example 4. A Chicago newspaper recently published an investigative report about a company certified as a women-owned firm, which secured city contracts based on that status. The complaint was not that the owner was actually a man but that:

- the woman-owner hid her relationship to her family by using her maiden name.
- day-to-day management of the firm was actually handled by male family members.
- sizable payments were made to those male family members.

The reporting of this story continued with a newspaper column:

I tried this experiment the other night at the Billy Goat Tavern.
Sam Sianis wasn't there, so Nick the bartender was the guinea pig.
I plopped down on a stool. Nick walked over with the bottled suds.
"Look at me, Nick," I said. "Look at me. What do you see?"

"I'm looking," said Nick. "You better eat something if you're going to drink."
How long did it take for Nick to realize that I am not one of the following:

a) a black woman
b) a Hispanic woman
c) a white woman

"Why you ask me crazy stuff?" Nick said. (Kass 1999, 3)

The column continues: "Like I said, the Duff story broke 68 days ago. That
was 1,632 hours ago. Or 97,920 minutes ago. Or 5,875,200 seconds ago, as
of noon on Thursday, if you prefer. It takes a team of City Hall payrollers that
long to determine if the Duffs are white guys, and they're still not sure." Of
course, the story would not have been so entertaining if it had explained that
the difficulty was verifying ownership and control of the business rather than
the sex of the individuals involved. As a result of the complications of determining MBE/WBE status and the risk of embarrassing news coverage for
errors, governments devote substantial resources to this effort.

There are additional costs of MBE/WBE requirements. When these
requirements are applied contract by contract, the government must verify
that each firm receiving a contract meet requirements or make "good faith
efforts" to meet requirements if they were indeed, not met. The costs of these
efforts combined with the certification process are not inconsequential;
Cook County has more than $800,000 for this effort in its current budget.

Of course, on the other hand, there is the argument that the full cost
of the process should not be allocated to the procurement function
because the MBE/WBE certification is used for purposes other than
securing government contracts. Regardless of what program the cost is
allocated to, it is a cost to the taxpayers. Other costs are largely hidden.
Like the social mandates already addressed, costs include added paperwork and notifying vendors of the requirements, plus the costs of monitoring compliance. MBE/WBE requirements entail significant added
paperwork to be prepared by vendors and reviewed and monitored by
the government.

The second major internal cost is the cost of delays. Delays in the procurement process add substantially to the costs of the process. The private
sector recognizes that an efficient and fast procurement process is cost-
effective. Many firms put significant effort into simplifying and speeding up
their procurement processes. As was stated earlier, MasterCard dramatically reduced its procurement cycle by changing software systems (from
four to one-and-a-half days). In comparison, the average procurement cycle
for county and state governments, as reported by the Center for Advanced
Purchasing Studies (n.d.), was 24 days.

With a lengthy procurement process, departments are forced to anticipate
their needs for goods and services well in advance. The need for advance

planning and employee efforts is increased. When procurements are delayed unexpectedly and departments cannot obtain resources when needed, pro-curement becomes a crisis. The mission of the department suffers. Employ-ees must find creative ways of making do with inadequate or inappropriate items, continue with paper procedures when they cannot obtain computers, or make barter arrangements with other departments. If handled in a rou-tine manner, tasks could be handled by subordinates who now absorb man-agement time and energies.

In economic terms, this type of cost is referred to as "opportunity cost." Employees could do something more productive than what they are actu-ally doing. The cost of delays is most visible when it continues long enough to justify another employee to handle the increased demands; however, this cost is not necessarily the cost of an additional clerical employee.

For example, a physician and department head at a big government-owned hospital reported that when her department's photocopier failed, the procurement process was extraordinarily slow. At the beginning, the clerical assistants "borrowed" use of other department's copiers. As the delay continued, the clerical employees in those departments became resentful and harassed her employees. The end result was that for an extended period of time, all photocopies needed by the department were made by doctors.

Opportunity costs, as in this example, are likely to be the most costly result of the current process that fails to measure the costs of social man-dates. The costs of delays are included in the costs of each department or organizational unit that relies on goods or resources procured from the out-side. The costs depend on how many delays the department faces, the dura-tion of those delays, and the skill of the department in facing them. Com-pared with the average cycle time reported by county and state governments, 24 days, a day or two delay is not significant; however, small increases accumulate. This is part of the reason for the significant difference between the 24-day procurement cycle reported by county and state gov-ernments and MasterCard's one-and-a-half days.

Some social mandates clearly add to procurement delays. If governments verify that substantial owners of vendors are properly reported and that they are not delinquent in child support payments before awarding the con-tract, the procurement is delayed.

MBE/WBE requirements also delay the procurement process, especially for those governments that have chosen to implement these ordinances on a contract-by-contract basis. Each vendor winning a contract is reviewed to assess compliance with MBE/WBE requirements. When a vendor is deemed noncompliant, the next vendor is evaluated for compliance. In addition, some governments, in an attempt to ensure that prices are not substantially increased due to these requirements, mandate rebidding if the lowest priced compliant bidder's bid price exceeded the competitive cost level. This requirement not only builds in delays by restarting the entire process but also doubles many processing costs. Some governments that require rebidding of noncompliant contracts count the procurement cycle to measure the time between the receipt of a requisition by the purchasing department and either the award or the cancellation of the contract. When a contract must be rebid, the contract is canceled and the procurement cycle is restarted. Thus, the average procurement cycle reported by the Center for Advanced Purchasing Studies may be understated.

Higher Prices.   According to economists, social mandates attached to the government procurement function necessarily increase prices paid for goods and services. Meeting requirements entails added transaction costs. In economic terms, these are the costs associated with a market transaction: the cost of finding and evaluating potential suppliers, matching buyers and sellers, negotiating contracts, and monitoring and enforcing contracts. These costs also include the costs of reviewing and meeting contract requirements.

Transaction costs do not include costs that the vendor would have incurred anyway. This is probably why there is little resistance to hiring requirements. Hiring the former employees makes sense from a business viewpoint. As one vendor stated, "We need to hire anyway to handle the project." Recruiting from among the former employees provides a ready source of new recruits, who are already trained to do the work. While additional training to learn the procedures of the new organization may be required, hiring the former employees is likely to be significantly less costly than recruiting from the general population. This of course assumes that appropriate work rules can be enforced and nonworking employees can be replaced.

Other transaction costs can be substantial. The Living Wage Ordinance may require vendors to pay more than their current wages or even more than prevailing wages in the community in order to be awarded a contract. If the total increased cost cannot be passed on to the customer (the government), the vendor is not likely to submit a bid. The net result is certainly forcing the government to pay higher prices and may limit the pool of vendors to those who do no private sector business.

The prices paid for goods and services procured under MBE/WBE requirements, especially when MBE/WBE requirements are implemented on a contract-by-contract basis, are also necessarily higher for several reasons. First, requirements force MBE/WBE participation in each government contract. The contract division requirement forces the prime contractor to incur added transaction costs. The vendor must locate, negotiate and contract with, and supervise subcontractors. Of course, any firm that wanted to use subcontractors for business reasons (e.g., to obtain specialized services or expertise) would do so. The vendor would have incurred these costs anyway. The price charged to the county must be high enough to cover all the internal costs that would not be incurred if the vendor were selling to a private sector buyer.

Second, MBE/WBEs also incur additional transaction costs. They must complete documentation proving that they are genuine and keep that documentation up-to-date. Again, the price charged to the county must be high enough to cover all the internal costs that would not be incurred if the vendor were selling to a private sector buyer. These costs are not immaterial. The number of companies certified as "small disadvantaged businesses" for federal contracts under new SBA requirements has fallen far short of the expected number—even after the deadline was extended twice. The "tepid response seems to indicate that small businesses think certification isn't worth the time and money" (Russis 1999, 33).

Third, while some purchases involve services (e.g., food service) that can be subdivided into economically meaningful units (food purchase, food transportation, dietician services, food preparation, cooking, and serving) that can be subcontracted, other purchases cannot be easily subcontracted. Many commodities purchased by governments, such as paper, squad cars, computers, and syringes, are unitary objects that cannot be meaningfully subdivided.

When the contract requires subcontracting, and the physical item cannot be subdivided, percentages can be met only by adding on services that can be performed by another firm. Often, this is an intermediate function of some sort—broker or distributor. Governments frequently require a "commercially useful function." Cook County's ordinance includes such a requirement, defining a commercially useful function as "the performance of real and actual services in the discharge of any contractual endeavor." Work must be done; the MBE/WBE requirement cannot be met simply by making a payment to an MBE/WBE that does no work.

The fact that work is done, however, does not necessarily mean that it would be done at all absent the ordinance. For example, MBE/WBE requirements frequently force governments to make purchases from distributors when the business world would customarily order directly from the manufacturer.

Fourth, firms doing business with the government on a regular basis would develop ongoing relationships with minority- and women-owned firms that would subcontract on such business. While these relationships would serve to lessen the added transaction costs, they could create artificial barriers to entry into the government market. Firms wishing to do business in the market must develop these relationships or, if it is perceived as too expensive to do so, opt not to bid. If the transaction costs are still higher than those for other business relationships, the MBE/WBE subcontractor is not likely to work with the prime contractor on nongovernment projects. The county will pay higher prices as the result of any restriction in the number of bidders.

In addition, some governments have implemented MBE/WBE require-ments in such a manner as to effectively hide the higher prices. As explained previously, MBE/WBE requirements can force governments to buy from distributors rather than from manufacturers. When manufacturing firms do not bid directly on government procurements, and prices are compared only among those vendors who submit bids, the government has no way to recognize the higher prices caused by the requirements.

Effectiveness of the Programs

While there is little effort to measure the effectiveness of social mandates attached to the procurement function, it is likely that many mandates are ineffective. This may be the case because governments sacrifice results by failing to systematically measure results. Experience has shown that people respond to the goals that are measured. Mark H. Moore, Professor of Crim-inal Justice Policy and Management at Harvard's Kennedy School of Gov-ernment, noted in a recent editorial in *The Wall Street Journal,* "What organizations measure, they get; what they fail to measure, they sacrifice to produce the effects they do measure" (Moore 1999, A22). Some ordinances contain no quantified goals, and others no requirements to measure actual results. For example, in spite of the significant emphasis on measuring the effectiveness of other child support collection efforts, there is little effort to measure how well the procurement function serves to collect such pay-ments. Some governments do not even identify collections attributed to enforcement via the purchasing process as opposed to those payments brought in through other sources.

There is also rarely any mechanism for assessing the overall effectiveness of policies to increase opportunities for minority- and women-owned firms. Governments sometimes assess results on a contract-by-contract basis with-out annual reports showing the percentage of contract dollars that go to such firms, without reports showing whether the pool of MBE/WBE firms receiving the government's business is expanding or remaining the same. There is no assessment of whether those vendors receiving government con-tracts under preferential terms become sustainable firms functioning in both the private and public sectors. In March 1995, the federal Glass Ceiling Commission (1995), headed by Elizabeth Dole, reviewed total federal efforts and concluded, "Progress has been disappointing." In addition, there appears to be no consensus, even among supporters of such programs, about the definition of success. Should the program be designed to help the firm enter the "big leagues" or should it provide assistance to small start-up firms, which when they meet a predetermined size are eliminated from preferences. Governments may state limitations, such as the SBA's eligibil-ity requirements for SDB status. Firms are excluded if the owner has amassed more than $750,000 in personal assets. Even when the government does not limit the size of firms or the wealth of its owners, the ability of a firm to expand may also be limited by the 51 percent rule. The size of the firm has become increasingly essential as both the private sector and the government try to minimize procurement transaction costs by contracting with smaller numbers of vendors to provide an increasing scope of goods and services. Some refer to this practice as "contract bundling." From an economic viewpoint, this practice helps to lower the costs of contracting out. On the other hand, the practice can obviously preclude competition from smaller firms. Because eligibility under SDB is limited, the ability of SDB firms to compete in the market is limited. As a result, the federal government issued rules limiting the flexibility of agencies to bundle contracts. It must be both necessary and justified to bundle contracts even though the practice is designed to minimize procurement costs.

The second reason mandates are likely to be ineffective overall is because they affect only a small number of individuals. Child support collection efforts tied to the procurement function affect a very small number of people. Only "Substantial Owners," persons who own more than 25 percent of the business, are required to report. Many firms such as large corporations or large professional partnerships are likely to have no Substantial Owners. Other firms have a single owner.

MBE/WBE requirements also benefit only a small pool of individuals, those who own businesses. The requirements ignore the much larger pool of individuals who are employees. Given this ordinance structure, governments favor the law firm controlled by minorities or women rather than the large firm with a stellar record of hiring and promotion to partnership. According to Dr. W. Avon Drake and Dr. Robert D. Holsworth, professors at Virginia Commonwealth University, set-aside policies had little to do with the aspirations of average black citizens. Discussing *Richmond v. J. A. Croson,* Dr. Holsworth stated, "If you want to examine [set-asides] as the critical strategy for moving [the Black community] forward, then you have to say it probably wasn't that relevant to the kind of issues that Richmond faces today" (Williams 1997).

Finally, there are other considerations that reduce the likelihood of effectiveness. It is unlikely that child support enforcement tied to procurement will be effective. Vendors are put on notice that they must pay child support in order to receive county contracts. It is more likely that any vendor deliberately not making child support payments will stop bidding on government procurements rather than pay them.

MBE/WBE requirements may also not meet the goal of developing viable independent businesses. If using a broker is the only way to meet the county's MBE/WBE requirement, then the county is encouraging minority- and women-owned firms to develop a market niche that does not exist in the private sector. This, in effect, keeps the firm dependent upon government business rather than helping it to compete in the market. As previously discussed, some argue that MBE/WBE status requirements may limit a firm's ability to grow and compete in the open market.

MBE/WBE requirements also have a built-in bias in favor of business ownership. Entrepreneurship is inherently risky, yet these ordinances hold this out as the only method qualifying a minority individual or a woman for preferential consideration.

CONCLUSION

When governments add social mandates to procurement processes and fail to evaluate the results or the costs of those mandates, they lose the opportunity to determine whether they are spending tax dollars effectively or whether alternative approaches to addressing social goals would be more effective. Failure to evaluate the procurement function based on how well it supports the mission of the organization compounds the problem. The government cannot answer the following questions:

- Does the Living Wage Ordinance make the biggest difference in the lives of the largest possible number of low-skilled workers, or would another option produce better results per dollar spent?
- Is the cost of child support collection efforts tied to procurement greater than the amounts collected? Could collections be increased at the same or decreased cost?
- Do MBE/WBE requirements offer improved business opportunities for a significant number of minorities and women? Or do the requirements benefit only a small number of individuals? What is the cost to the taxpayers? Do other options benefit a greater number of people at the same cost or benefit the same number of people at reduced cost?
- Do the social mandates interfere with the other functions of the government such as providing police and other services?

By analyzing results, accounting for costs, and using that information to fine tune the results of operations, governments can ensure that they are indeed making fiscally responsible decisions and getting the most benefit for the money spent. By failing to do so, they are ignoring the costs and opportunities for improved operations. As Michael Dell, president of Dell Computer Corporation, said to the City Club of Chicago recently, "If you don't know, you have to guess and guessing can be very expensive." It is time to stop guessing and start making informed decisions about social mandates tied to procurement.

*Editor's note: After this chapter was completed by the author, two developments occurred concerning the proposed change in definition of a minority- or woman-owned firm, referred to as the "Growth Initiative." The National Minority Supplier Development Council (NMSDC) Board of Directors decided at its meeting in October to postpone the vote on the Growth Initiative for three months in order to clarify understanding about its goals with other organizations, government agencies and the business community. According to a news release issued on February 1, 2000, by the NMSDC, the members of the Board of Directors indicated their approval of the Growth Initiative by a wide margin with 76 percent of the voters endorsing the plan. Harriet R. Michel, president of NMSDC, stated, "The Growth Initiative creates a new category—certified minority-controlled firms—that can retain minority status and control while accepting equity capital from institutional investors. This will allow minority companies to grow and be more competitive."

REFERENCES

Adarand Constructors, Inc. v. Pena, et al. 1995. 115 S.Ct. 2097 (U.S. Supreme Court 1995).

Americans United for Affirmative Action. 1965. Speech given by Lyndon B. Johnson to the graduating class of Howard University, June 4, 1965. Available online: <www.auaa.org/ timeline/1964.html>.

Association of Community Organizations for Reform Now. 1999. *Living wage successes: A compilation of living wage policies on the books.* Available online: <www.livingwage campaign.org/living-wage-wins.html>.

Benner, Chris, and Rachel Rosner. 1998. *A report on the benefits and impact of a Living Wage Ordinance on the City of San Jose.* San Jose, CA: Working Partnerships USA. Available online: <www.atwork.org/wp/lw/>.

Boston enacts living wage rule. 1997. *New York Times-Union* (August 14). Available online: <www.crisny.org/not-for/profit/unions/bos-815.htm>.

Center for Advanced Purchasing Studies. n.d. *Summary of state and county government benchmarks.* Available online: <www.capsresearch.org/research/ benches/State-County94.html>.

City of Chicago. 1998. *Request for proposal for professional services for the Department of Finance* (Specification No. B89180-404).

Coalition of the Chicago Board of Education Unions. 1995. *A reservoir of knowledge and experience: The employees of the Chicago Public Schools.* Submitted to the Chicago Board of Education, January 23, 1995.

Community and Public Sector Union. n.d. *Info Tech News.* Available online: <www.cpsu.org/it/ it2509.htm>.

Cone Corporation v. Hillsborough County. 1990. 908 F.2d 908 (11th Cir. 1990).

Conrad, Ginger. 1999. Publisher's page. *Minority Business Entrepreneur (MBE) Magazine* (January/February). Available online: <www.mbemag.com/htm/ jan-febpub.html>.

Coral Construction v. King County. 1991. 941 F.2d 910 (9th Cir. 1991).

Deadbeat parents slip past watchdogs. 1997. *Chicago Tribune* (March 2): 1.

Fryklund, Inge, Vivian Weil, and Harriet McCullough. 1997. *Municipal service delivery: Thinking through the privatization option.* Washington, DC: National League of Cities.

Gates, Bill. 1999. *Business @ the speed of thought: Using a digital nervous system.* New York: Warner Brothers, Inc.

General Services Administration, IT Management Practices Division. 1998. *White paper: Outsourcing information technology.* Available online: <www.itpolicy. gsa.gov/mkm/gsaepp/finalout.htm>.

Gillen, Shawn J., and Robin A. Johnson. 1999. Small town enters into cutting-edge public-private partnership. *Privatization Watch* (267) (March): 7.

Glass Ceiling Commission. 1995. *Good for business: Making use of the nation's human capital.* Available online: <www.auaa.org/timeline/1992.html>.

Holmes, Steven A. 1999. What is a minority-owned business? *The New York Times* (October 12): 6.

Hudson, Wade. 1998. Privatizing mental health services. *Privatization Watch* (264) (November).

Hynes, Daniel W. 1999. *Receivables report: Calendar year ended December 31, 1998.* Springfield, IL: Office of the Comptroller.

Immigration and Naturalization Service (INS). n.d. *Ideas that work.* Available online: <www.itpolicy.gsa.gov/mkm/gsaepp/ideas/ins1.htm>.

Kass, John. 1999. Unsure if they're men or women? Just ask Nick. *Chicago Tribune* (September 30): 3.

Local business preference. n.d. *Cook County (Illinois) ordinance* (Chapter 3, Section 38).

Moore, Mark H. 1999. Private-sector lessons for New York's finest. *The Wall Street Journal* (April 12): A22.

Newcombe, Tod (Features Editor). 1998. Multistate online procurement project underway. *Government Internet Guide.* Available online: <www.govtech.net/ publications/ govinternetguide/gig98/multistate.shtm>.

Office of Management and Budget (OMB). 1983. *OMB Circular No. A-76 revised, performance of commercial activities.* Washington, DC: Executive Office of the President, OMB.

Persky, Joseph. 1994. *Suburban workers and city jobs: Chicago construction employment in a divided economy.* Unpublished manuscript.

Preference in contracts and purchases. n.d. *Marin County (California) code* (Chapter 3.10).

Public Works Financing (pwfinance@aol.com). 1998. Atlanta gets 44 percent savings on water contract. *Privatization Watch* (264) (December).

Richmond v. J. A. Croson. 1989. 488 U.S. 469.

Russis, Martha. 1999. Certifiably unmoved. *Crain's Chicago Businesses* (October 11).

Small Business Administration (SBA). 1998. SBA details new certification process for small disadvantaged business. *SBA News Release* (Release #98-78, September 21). Available online: <www.sbaonline.sba.gov/news/current/ 98-78.html>.

SBA. n.d. *Small disadvantaged business: Eligibility requirements.* Available online: <www.sba. gov/sdb/section06c.html>.

Snell, Lisa. 1999. Solid waste privatization. *Privatization Watch* (267) (March).

Standard clause for all New York State contracts (Appendix A). Available online: <www.ogs. state.ny.us/procurecounc/A.

State of Indiana. 1998. Support of small and minority-owned businesses. Chapter 3: Ethics: Guidelines for ethical procurement practices. *State of Indiana 1998 procurement manual.* Available online: <www.state.in.us/idoa/proc/procnbk/ index.html>.

Tennessee Valley Authority. n.d. *Paperless ordering under blanket contracts.* Available online: <www.itpolicy.gsa.gov/mkm/gsaepp/ideas/tva2a.htm>.

Thomas, Paulette. 1999. Groups call for delay of vote on minority-owned business. *The Wall Street Journal* (October 26): B2.

U.S. Department of Housing and Urban Development (HUD). n.d. *Frequently asked questions about HUD contracting.* Available online: <www.hud.gov/cts/ctsfaq.html>.

Washington State. (n.d.). *A guide to general administration policies.* Available online: <www.wa.gov/dis/dbww/goods/gaguide.html>.

Williams, Michael Paul. 1997. Affirmative Action: Choices and priorities. *Richmond Times-Dispatch* (August 18). Available online: <www.gateway-va.com/pages/cols/mike/ 0818mike.html>.

PART III

Results and Future Prospects

Privatization and Managed Competition: Management Fad or Long-Term Systematic Change for Cities?

Robin A. Johnson and Norman Walzer

For many years, local governments across the United States have contracted with the private sector for public service delivery. Municipal governments provide the greatest variety of local services, including police and fire protection, street maintenance, solid waste collection, water treatment, and sewage services. Municipalities, therefore, have the greatest opportunities to contract and, historically, have contracted refuse collection, tree trimming, and fleet maintenance, among other services.

The latest wave of privatization and competitive practices began in the late 1970s and coincided with several trends that forced officials into efforts toward greater efficiency and cost-savings. Proposition 13 in California in 1978 and ballot initiatives in Massachusetts, Michigan, and other states limited revenue-raising capabilities. The Conservative Movement ushered in by the Reagan administration also brought greater pressures to reduce the size and cost of government at all levels. In response, public officials increasingly looked to contract for the provision of services (e.g., privatization, outsourcing, or contracting) or remove public sector responsibility for services (asset sales and load shedding).

Intergovernmental relations changed as federal grant funding for services decreased sharply in the 1980s, with responsibility for more services transferred to the local and state governments. Also, cities faced continuing unfunded intergovernmental mandates especially for environmental services such as water and wastewater treatment.

Concurrently, innovative public leaders in Indianapolis, Charlotte, and Philadelphia, for example, began efforts in the 1980s and 1990s to find greater efficiencies in municipal government and to improve the quality of services through innovative contracting agreements. Officials in Phoenix developed a managed competition plan, which allows city employees to compete for public solid waste collection contracts. Previous competition schemes usually allowed only private sector bidding for public contracts.

The search for efficiencies and accountability in public spending caused Osborne and Gaebler's (1992) *Reinventing Government: How the Entrepreneurial Spirit Is Transforming the Public Sector* to become a standard reference for government reform. The National Performance Review under Vice President Gore brought further impetus for change. Interest in privatization and competitive government moved beyond ideological and political boundaries to become two of the more popular and successful management practices, stimulating innovation in municipalities of all sizes.

In fact, the National League of Cities (NLC), in a recent nationwide study of cities, reported a "change to a more business-oriented approach to local government . . . with many citizens looking to the city to provide core services in a more efficient manner" (Woodwell 1998, 27). Wellington Webb, mayor of Denver and president of the U.S. Conference of Mayors (USCM) said recently that city officials must "run their cities like private businesses with a public mission" (U.S. Conference of Mayors 1999).

Finally, a recent report on challenges facing local governments in the new economy recommends using competition and community, rather than bureaucracy, to provide essential public services (Bonnett 1999). Clearly, the paradigm has shifted from purely public approaches to providing basic public services to one of competition, choice, and innovative public-private partnerships. The role of partnerships extends beyond providing traditional public services to building economic development capacity as well, both in the United States and in Europe (Walzer and Jacobs 1998).

While the successes and limitations of privatization and competitive strategies are documented elsewhere in this volume (chapters by Savas, Donahue, Moore, and Hudson), less is known about systematic changes in local government management practices that create a competitive environment. Also, trends in contracting and competition during the 1990s have not been well-documented. Is the pace of privatization slowing due to improved economic conditions, or do cities contract more often for services now than in the past? Are privatization and competition merely the latest management fads, or are they efforts by local officials to institutionalize change and alter the culture of public organizations long term? Are cities creating policies and programs that promote competitive practices to help ensure the long-term success of privatization initiatives?

This chapter examines competitive practices in municipalities and sheds light on these issues based on information from surveys conducted by the ICMA in 1988 and 1997. Overall, 447 cities responding to both surveys are included in this analysis, allowing a comparison of changes over time. Some questions are further examined for a subset of cities that contract services. Combined, the surveys represent a reasonably complete data set on contracting, managed competition, and related management practices in cities.

This chapter has four main sections: (1) the trends toward increased privatization among U.S. cities are documented; (2) management practices used systematically to evaluate the potential of public-private partnerships, managed competition, and contracting are described in an attempt to determine their importance in ensuring success; (3) challenges faced by public officials attempting to change operating practices, especially with greater involvement by the private sector, are documented with special attention paid to working with public employees and unions; and (4) approaches used by city officials to monitor the success of managed competition, contracting, and public-private partnerships are presented.

TRENDS IN PUBLIC SERVICE DELIVERY

Much has been written about specific services that are considered likely candidates for managed competition and/or privatization and the characteristics of cities that contract most often. Services that are tangible, clearly specified, easily measured and monitored, and have identified users are usually best suited for contracting (Donahue 1989). For this reason, refuse collection is among the early services provided through contracts in many cities with substantial documentation of cost-savings to taxpayers (Savas 1977).

Not all cities are likely candidates for providing services under a contractual arrangement. Urban and suburban areas with competitive and developed markets for local services offer more opportunities than sparsely populated rural areas with fewer potential providers of services or with markets too small to be attractive to providers (Schneider 1988). A study using ICMA data from medium-sized cities found privatization more likely in wealthy, fiscally sound, and suburban cities (Greene 1996). Thus, financial condition is but one of the factors that enters into privatization decisions.

Several factors affecting local public finance suggested a movement towards greater privatization of services in the 1990s. Certainly, unfunded intergovernmental mandates, tax limitations, devolution of services to local governments, and greater public acceptance of privatization set the stage for local public decision makers to find lower-cost ways to provide services. Passage of the Governmental Performance and Results Act (GPRA) in 1993 focused attention on greater accountability in government spending and encouraged the application of private sector management practices. More sophisticated budgeting and management systems have increased the ability of local public officials to evaluate private company bids to provide services and have helped public officials evaluate the full cost of services provided by city employees.

Since fiscal conditions are an important element in deciding to privatize services, improved economic and financial conditions in recent years may have removed some of this impetus to privatize. In a National League of Cities (NLC) survey (1999), 75 percent of responding cities said they were better able to meet their financial needs than they were in 1998.

ICMA surveys that periodically track service delivery are used to analyze contracting trends. The surveys are sent to all cities with a population of 10,000 or more; one in eight cities with a population of less than 10,000 is contacted as well. Previous research has examined trends in contracting using ICMA surveys from 1982, 1988, and 1992. While contracting did not increase substantially during the mid-1980s (Morley 1989), usage accelerated during the subsequent five years as cities increased privatization because of continued financial pressures (Miranda and Andersen 1994).

The ICMA surveys list services that are commonly provided by municipalities and ask respondents to report the delivery system(s) for each service. The 1988 survey listed 71 services, and the 1997 survey listed 64. Results show a shift from in-house delivery of services to alternate means such as contracting with private firms and other governments. For example, the percentage of cities reporting services provided entirely or in part by in-house employees declined in 60 of the 64 service categories during the ten-year period examined.

Contracts with private firms increased for many services, with more than half (36) of the services listed increasing in private delivery between 1988 and 1997 (Table 9.1). Among the services shifting most towards private provision during the time period are gas operation and management

Table 9.1
Municipal Services with Largest Increase in Privatization, 1988–1997

Service (Does not include new services contracted)	Percent Increase
Gas operation and management	254.1
Electricity operations and management	199.2
Insect/rodent control	94.0
Water distribution	83.9
Solid waste disposal	67.3
Building security	59.2
Maintenance/administration of cemeteries	48.4
Commercial solid waste collection	43.9
Disposal of sludge	30.9
Residential solid waste collection	20.2

Source: ICMA's *Profile of Alternative Delivery Approaches* Survey 1988; ICMA's *Profile of Local Government Service Delivery Choices* Survey 1997.

(254.1%), electricity operations and management (199.2%), insect/rodent control (94.0%), water distribution (83.9%), solid waste disposal (67.3%), and building security (59.2%). The increase in contracting for water services may have resulted from changes in IRS regulations that loosened restrictions on long-term contracts.

Cities now contract for services that previously were provided exclusively inhouse. In 18 service categories, there were no cases of privatization reported in 1988, and in at least one case, ten years later (Table 9.2). Services contracted were usually health and human services (six services) and public safety (five services), partly because of the difficulties in measuring the services provided. For example, none of the responding cities in the sample reported privatized ambulance services in 1988 compared with 73 cities reporting private provision of ambulance services in 1997. This finding signifies a shift in privatization from traditional public works services to other areas.

Table 9.2
New Services Contracted, 1988–1997

Public Works/Transportation
  None
Public Utilities
  Utility meter reading
Public Safety
  Police/fire communications
  Fire prevention/suppression
  Emergency medical service
  Ambulance service
  Traffic control/parking enforcement
Health and Human Services
  Sanitary inspection
  Animal control
  Operation of animal shelters
  Operation of day care facilities
  Operation/management of hospitals
  Operation of homeless shelters
Parks and Recreation
  Operation of libraries
  Operation of museums
Support Functions
  Payroll
  Tax assessing

Source: ICMA's *Profile of Alternative Delivery Approaches* Survey 1988; ICMA's *Profile of Local Government Service Delivery Choices* Survey 1997.

In cities that have privatized services, the percentage of services contracted increased during the past ten years. In 1988, on average, cities contracted 9.58 percent of the 71 services with private firms compared with 10.66 percent of 64 services in 1997. The fact that not all of the same services were included in both surveys makes a strict comparison difficult, but the comparisons clearly show a broadening in the range of services contracted.

Definite patterns are found in the types of services for which cities tend to contract with the private sector based on the 1997 survey (Table 9.3). These services are usually irregular (vehicle towing), specialized (legal services), require a large capital investment (electricity operation and management), or have adequate private sector competition (solid waste collection and disposal).

In addition to contracting with a private provider, cities have used other approaches to lowering the cost of providing services. One method found most often in solid waste and utility services is franchising. A franchise agreement with a private firm differs from a contract because of the method of payment. A franchise agreement involves payment by citizens directly to a private provider while a contract entails payment by a government to the provider.

In the 1997 ICMA results, 17.1 percent of cities report franchises for commercial solid waste collection and 12.8 percent for residential solid waste collection. Thus, 73.1 percent of cities have privatized commercial solid waste collection through either franchises or contracting agreements. More than half (51.8%) of the cities report residential collection through one of the two private delivery systems.

Table 9.3
Municipal Services Most Likely to be Contracted, 1997

Service	Percent
Vehicle towing and storage	78.3
Gas operation and management	55.6
Legal services	49.9
Commercial solid waste collection	49.8
Operation of day care facilities	40.6
Disposal of hazardous materials	38.7
Operation/management of hospitals	38.2
Electricity operations and management	37.1
Residential solid waste collection	36.9
Solid waste disposal	33.8

Source: Adapted from ICMA's *Profile of Local Government Service Delivery Choices* Survey 1997.

Contracting for solid waste collection services exists across the United States and has risen in recent years. Our results are similar to other recent research findings. A 1995 survey of 66 large U.S. cities reported half of the respondents had privatized solid waste collection services (Dilger, Moffett, and Struyk 1997). A survey by The Mercer Group showed a steady increase in contracting for refuse collection services during the past ten years (The Mercer Group 1997). In 1997, 54 percent of the respondents reported privatized solid waste collection, nearly double the 30 percent from 1987.

Another measure of the extent to which privatization exists, and how it has changed, is the percentage or number of contracted services in each city. Approximately the same percentage of cities report contracting for more than 10 percent of the services (213 in 1988 and 209 in 1997); however, the number of cities reporting 20 percent or more privatized services increased from 45 in 1988 to 69 in 1997, and the number with 30 percent or greater went from two to 25.

Somewhat unexpectedly, cities reporting the most privatized services in 1997 are located mainly in the eastern and upper Midwestern states, including Worcester, Massachusetts (33); Northbrook, Illinois (29); Manchester, Connecticut (27); and Cambridge, Massachusetts (26). Previous research (Greene 1996) reported that privatization was more prevalent in cities in the far western states. In the current study, Garden Grove, California, with 27 contracted services and Upland, California, with 26, are examples.

While privatization has increased in the responding cities in the past ten years, contracting is by no means growing dramatically, at least by the measures used here. The scope of services contracting has broadened, however, especially for public safety and health and human services. Apparently, cities are experimenting with various levels of privatization and increasing or reducing private contracts to meet local needs. Also true, however, is that differences in levels of contracting could account for variations in responses.

DECISION-MAKING PROCESS: TOWARD A SYSTEMATIC APPROACH?

Contracting for a service and/or creating a more competitive environment for service delivery must be approached cautiously to obtain the best results for the city. The U.S. General Accounting Office (USGAO), in a review of competitive practices of local and state governments, recommends establishing a formal structure to organize and analyze a competitive/privatization initiative (Brostek 1997). A case study of privatization in state governments identified several pitfalls that can occur without an established decision-making process (Wallin 1997). The federal government has an approach (Office of Management and Budget Circular A-76) that can be adapted for local use (Prager and Desai 1996). These and other designs can

assist in implementing a privatization effort and provide an overall framework to enhance effective decision making.

City officials responding to the ICMA survey are definitely interested in
contracting, and a large majority reported a feasibility study in the previous
five years (Table 9.4). Most cities (79.6%) indicated that they had considered private service delivery in the five years previous to 1997, suggesting a
growing acceptance of privatization as a viable option and highlighting the
need for a consistent methodology.

Indianapolis, Houston, Austin, and Philadelphia have formal evaluation
approaches. For example, Indianapolis and Philadelphia have developed
systematic approaches to evaluate both privatization and competition for
services. A commission in Indianapolis includes both public and private sec-

Table 9.4
Cities Studying the Feasibility of Adopting Privatization

	1997	
	Percent	Number
Has your local government studied the feasibility of adopting private service delivery within the past five years?		
No	20.4	71
Yes	79.6	277
If *yes,* which of the following factors spurred your local government's decision to study the feasibility of adopting private delivery alternatives within the last five years? *(Check all applicable.)*		
External fiscal pressures, including restrictions placed on raising taxes, e.g. Proposition 13	49.6	134
Internal attempts to decrease costs of service delivery	90.7	245
State or federal mandates tied to intergovernmental financing	8.9	24
Change in political climate emphasizing a decreased role for government	22.2	60
Active citizen group favoring privatization	8.1	22
Unsolicited proposals presented by potential service providers	17.0	46
Concerns about government liability	11.1	30
Other	9.3	25

n = 447 (doesn't include cities that did not contract in
1988 and/or 1997)

Source: Adapted from ICMA's *Profile of Local Government Service Delivery Choices*
         Survey 1997.

tor representatives and analyzes costs, competitiveness, and performance evaluation. The Indianapolis model of managed competition allows public employees to bid for contracts. Philadelphia includes a 19-point checklist in its Competitive Contracting Program that city employees use in evaluating contracting for services.

Cost factors remain important as cities consider privatization. Among cities reporting a study of the feasibility of privatization in the past five years, 90.7 percent said internal attempts to decrease costs of service delivery was the main factor causing them to consider privatization. The second most important factor, reported by 49.6 percent of respondents, is external fiscal pressures such as restrictions placed on the ability to raise taxes.

In spite of the economic recovery during the 1990s, cities face continuing financial challenges on a daily basis. Public officials must balance demands for more and better services with public opposition to tax increases. Cities must also become more competitive in the race for jobs and development opportunities in order to meet the shifting challenges of the global economy. The search for greater efficiency inevitably leads to a review of private sector alternatives. A strong local economy may only temporarily lessen the interest in these alternatives.

The third strongest factor causing an examination of privatization is the change in political climate, emphasizing smaller government as reported by 22.2 percent of respondents. Citizens are less concerned about public or private provision of services, as long as they are provided in a cost-effective manner. Many elected officials have moved beyond partisan political and ideological concerns and now focus on quality and cost of services rather than on public versus private provider. From the Clinton administration to state capitols to many city halls, there has been greater acceptance of market-based solutions and public-private partnerships to solve problems rather than a purely governmental approach (Osborne and Gaebler 1992).

Local officials have significant incentives to be more pragmatic and less ideological in evaluating service delivery options. Cities provide basic services to citizens and are held accountable on a daily basis. They are also more likely to deal directly with constituents, especially in the case of small cities. State and federal officials, on the other hand, receive face-to-face feedback less often. State and federal governments can also more easily transfer responsibility for services to local governments. City officials have few alternatives to providing services other than load-shedding or service sharing and cannot simply shift responsibility for a service onto another entity.

State and federal mandates are less likely to spur a privatization decision; they were reported by only 8.9 percent of officials in 1997. Along with the findings about mandates, only 11.1 percent of officials reported liability as a consideration. These results may reflect the fact that mandates and liability issues often involve environmental services that must comply with Environmental Protection Agency (EPA) regulations and require a high degree of risk management. The lack of concern expressed in the survey could reflect better contract specifications and performance standards set by city officials. As cities gain experience with privatization and create more sophisticated policies and procedures, they can lessen, if not eliminate, many of the liability concerns that are usually associated with contracting services.

In-House Sources

According to the ICMA survey data, cities have increased their reliance on in-house sources to assist in evaluating the feasibility of a privatization initiative (Table 9.5). Cities also use a wider variety of sources for assistance in the evaluation process. The number of responses increased between 1988 and 1997 for every in-house source listed on the survey. For example, the number of cities that involved city managers/chief administrative officers in the evaluation process increased from 75.9 percent to 90.4 percent. Department heads are the next most likely to be involved in the process (72.2% in 1988 to 83.4% in 1997).

Cities are also involving financial officers more often because of the crucial role that cost comparisons play in the competitive process. Accurate

Table 9.5
Trends in Involvement in Evaluation of Privatization

Who inside your local government was involved in evaluating the feasibility of private service delivery? *(Check all applicable.)*

	1988		1997		Pct. Change
	Percent	Number	Percent	Number	1988–1997
Manager/CAO	75.9	265	90.4	283	19.1
Assistant manager/CAO	34.4	120	40.3	126	17.1
Management and/or budget analysts	22.1	77	25.6	80	15.8
Department heads	72.2	252	83.4	261	15.5
Finance/accounting officer	41.0	143	53.4	167	30.2
Attorney	25.5	89	33.5	105	31.5
Procurement/purchasing officer	14.0	49	16.9	53	20.6
Line employees	8.3	29	17.9	56	115.3
Elected officials	37.2	130	47.0	147	26.1
Other	2.6	9	5.8	18	123.0

Source: ICMA's *Profile of Alternative Delivery Approaches* Survey 1988; ICMA's *Profile of Local Government Service Delivery Choices* Survey 1997.

and complete cost data for public services are necessary for an effective competitive process. For example, 53.4 percent of responding cities involved their finance/accounting officer in 1997, an increase from 41.0 percent in 1988. Approximately one-quarter (25.6%) of cities use a management and/or budget analyst, and 16.9 percent involve a procurement/purchasing officer, both increases from ten years ago.

The largest increase in participation in the evaluation process (115.3%) involves line employees, which will be discussed in the next section. In addition, 33.5 percent of cities report that municipal attorneys have a role in the process, reflecting the importance of legal issues when contracting services.

Outside Sources

City officials rely most often on potential service deliverers (67.1%) and professional consultants (43.3%) as outside sources of information; however, cities have reduced their reliance on external sources for evaluations in five of the six categories during the past ten years.

One of the categories that experienced an increase during this period is service recipients/consumers, climbing from 10.9 percent in 1988 to 15.4 percent in 1997. Increased use of these groups suggests that city officials focus more on customer satisfaction and public involvement for controversial issues. Citizen and customer involvement can help build a political case for privatization, shield against potential opposition, and ensure against a charge of favoritism or corruption in the privatization decision-making process.

The survey did not ask respondents to tie specific services being evaluated for contracting to sources of analysis. For instance, did cities involve line employees in an evaluation of all services to be contracted or only those who were directly affected? Seasonal services, such as tree trimming, may not impact employees directly, leaving city officials free to contract without much input. Other services, such as refuse collection and water treatment, which require large numbers of employees for a full year of service, might be better candidates for greater involvement in the decision-making process.

Cities seem better able to obtain sufficient information on privatization alternatives and to build on previous experiences than they were in the past. The number of officials reporting a lack of evidence on the effectiveness of privatization declined in the past ten years, from 27.5 percent in 1988 to 22.5 percent in 1997. In a survey of municipalities in Illinois, lack of information was the leading obstacle to privatization as reported by 42.8 percent of respondents in 1996, but respondents were more likely to include officials from small communities who were less likely to have adequate information about contracting trends (Johnson and Walzer 1996).

Overall, the findings suggest that U.S. cities are becoming more systematic in their approaches to contracting. More in-house resources are used in the evaluation process, giving employees as well as managers a stake in the success of the initiative. Well-developed privatization or competitive initiatives involve many technical, financial, and legal issues that require expertise from a variety of sources. They also demand citizen and employee input to help provide accurate information and encourage an open process. Cities increasingly involve many players in the process, including the public and line employees, in order to help make proper decisions.

MANAGED COMPETITION AND EMPLOYEE TRANSITION

As privatization and competitive contracting evolved, more city officials realized the importance of creating strategies to involve employees in the decision-making process and to ensure that they are treated fairly during the switch to a competitive environment. A common misconception about privatization is that employees are always negatively affected by contracting for services. Past research studies have documented how most employees are not displaced by contracting. In fact, many benefit because of greater opportunities with the private firms that provide services under contract (U.S. Department of Labor, National Commission on Employment Policy [NCEP] 1989; Stein 1990; USGAO 1985). Little research exists, however, on whether cities have formal policies to provide fair treatment of displaced employees. The NCEP study examined 28 local governments and found 76 percent of them had some type of labor policy. The ICMA survey data offer an opportunity to explore this issue and move beyond purely anecdotal information.

Evaluation

The ICMA survey included several questions regarding attempts by cities to cushion the impact of privatization on employees. Some cities (17.9%) report involving line employees in the evaluation process to determine the feasibility of a privatization initiative. This figure is more than double the number reporting a similar finding in 1988 (8.3%) and represents the largest percentage increase of any category during the past ten years. These figures are relatively low compared with other categories, but the fact remains that more cities report involving employees as they attempt to smooth the transition process and lessen, if not eliminate, a potential source of opposition to contracting.

As cities gain more experience with privatization and aid in the successful transition of public employees, they gain more confidence that they can demonstrate the benefits of privatization to employees affected by new initiatives. Much literature exists to suggest that involvement of employees in the decision-making process can minimize the potential conflict over workforce changes such as privatization (Frost, Wakely, and Ruth 1974; Whitaker and Jenne 1995; Yager 1994).

Recent trends in privatization demonstrate how public employees can benefit from a transition to the private sector. In recent long-term agreements involving the privatization of water services in Atlanta and Milwaukee, private firms agreed to equal or better pay and benefits and no layoffs without cause for the full ten-year term of the contracts (Reason Public Policy Institute 1999). Employees can also thrive in a competitive environment in small communities. In a similar long-term agreement in Monmouth, Illinois (population 9,500), the local union voted to endorse privatization of public works services with similar employee protections (Gillen and Johnson 1999).

Involvement of line employees in privatization decisions increases with size of city—30.4 percent of cities with populations of more than 100,000 were reporting this activity compared with 11.1 percent of cities with populations of less than 10,000. With more employees and, therefore, greater potential for dissatisfaction and opposition, it makes sense for larger cities to be more proactive in engaging employees in the evaluation process. Also, large cities are more likely to have unionized workforces, which is also a factor in the amount of employee involvement in decisions (Jackson 1997).

Simply involving employees in the evaluation process may not be sufficient. As established by previous research, the extent, nature, and degree of involvement as well as the current state of labor relations are crucial factors in determining the outcomes (Yager 1994). A great deal of skepticism, if not outright hostility, to privatization still exists among public employees.

Opposition

The ICMA survey data reveal that opposition from line employees is the leading obstacle to privatization according to 63.5 percent of responding officials. Opposition from line employees, in fact, was one of only two categories that had increased between 1988 and 1997, while eight other categories showed decreases. This finding suggests that officials encounter fewer obstacles to contracting initiatives overall but still face strong opposition from employees.

Cities have found ways to contract for services while avoiding potential opposition. For example, some cities (28.9 percent) undertook privatization on a trial basis, but, obviously, this approach does not work well for services such as solid waste collection that essentially require a longer-term commitment. Services better designed for temporary contracts include seasonal activities such as tree-trimming or snow-plowing where public employees can assume responsibility if the contracting experiment fails. Other cities privatize only new (26.0 percent) or growing (25.0 percent) services since no current employees are involved, and contracts for an expansion of services are usually easier to implement than those affecting current employees.

Employee Programs

Of the cities that contract services, 30.4 percent reported a program to minimize the effects of privatization on public employees, approximately three times the number responding to a similar question in the 1988 survey. These programs are more prevalent in larger cities, with 42.9 percent of respondents of cities with populations of more than 100,000 reporting these efforts but only 20.6 percent in cities with populations of 10,000–25,000. None of the cities with populations of less than 10,000 report employee transition programs. This issue is explored in greater detail in Chapter 10.

Managed Competition

A final personnel strategy addressed in the ICMA surveys involves allowing government departments to compete with the private sector in the bidding process. As started by Phoenix, Arizona, in the 1970s and prominently implemented by Indianapolis in the 1990s, these managed competition programs empower employees to structure bids, conduct cost comparisons, and change the service delivery paradigm. By dividing cities into service delivery districts, public officials instilled competition between public employees and private firms to better compare efficiencies. Also, they do not abandon the service altogether in case private delivery fails and the city must resume overall responsibility. This type of managed competition seems better suited to cities with populations larger than 100,000 (Savas 1977) and is sustainable over the long term (Ammons and Hill 1995).

Managed competition among cities that contract services has exhibited major growth during the past ten years. The number of cities that allowed departments to bid nearly tripled from 13.5 percent in 1988 to 34.8 percent in 1997. This may partly reflect widely cited successes in Phoenix and Indianapolis that have been replicated by local officials seeking ways to implement competitive practices successfully within the city.

Managed competition is more common in large cities with 35.7 percent of 1997 survey respondents in cities with populations of more than 100,000 reporting that they allow city departments to compete. By comparison, none of the cities with populations of less than 10,000 report that they use managed competition to deliver services. This finding is not surprising since large cities have more resources and expertise to develop and implement managed competition systems. Indianapolis invested funds to train employees on cost accounting and bid preparations before employees could participate in the bidding process. Smaller cities may find it easier to bid a service involving only the private sector and include a provision requiring the winning bidder to hire the current workforce to overcome potential opposition; however, more cities with populations smaller than 100,000 are adopting managed competition as shown by survey findings.

Pekin, Illinois (population 32,000), is an example of a small city that developed a system similar to managed competition programs elsewhere. Officials in Pekin regularly conduct analyses of private and public costs for various services. For example, the city divided the solid waste management system into three components—(1) garbage, (2) yard waste, and (3) recycling—and sought the lowest cost provider for each. Through rigorous cost comparisons and aggressive bidding, Pekin saved approximately $100,000 annually by contracting garbage disposal and keeping yard waste and recycling services in house. Officials also analyzed the potential for bringing ambulance services in house but decided to keep the current private provider after determining it was more cost-effective.

Whether cities decide to privatize services or adopt a model of managed competition, they are increasingly seeking ways to involve employees to soften the transition process and lessen a source of opposition. Growth in the use of employee strategies appears to be formalizing a role for employees at the policy level and making permanent changes in organizational structures and relationships and labor-management relations.

MONITORING AND PERFORMANCE EVALUATION

Following the lead of the private sector, many public agencies are measuring performance of services to ensure cost-effectiveness and quality. Firms such as Intel and Hewlett Packard market sophisticated software packages designed to monitor the performance of contractors. Whether services are performed in house or through alternative means, the drive to measure performance will continue to increase in the future due to citizen demand and financial imperatives.

Cities must institute effective strategies for monitoring contractor performance when privatizing services. Simply turning a service over to a private firm without oversight can result in lower-quality services and higher costs. It is not unusual to see privatization agreements fail because of confusion and misunderstandings over the roles and responsibilities of the parties. An effective monitoring agreement protects the public interest by ensuring that the private firm fulfills its contractual obligations and meets performance criteria. Ultimately, public officials who vote to privatize a service are still held accountable by voters.

For services involving environmental regulations, such as solid waste disposal and water and wastewater treatment, monitoring contractor performance has a greater importance. Officials must be assured that contractors will meet EPA standards which protect public health and safety. In addition, cities could remain subject to financial penalties because of noncompliance; therefore, cities must have the in-house technical capabilities to develop an effective monitoring contract and also have the capacity to properly oversee contractor performance.

Because of the key role that contract monitoring plays in the success of a privatization agreement, it is important to examine municipal trends regarding performance measurement and contract evaluation. The growth in privatization during the past two decades and the involvement of more technical services has increased the importance of systematic attempts by cities to oversee contractor performance. In fact, the ICMA survey included several questions about contract monitoring and evaluation.

Evaluation

The number of cities reporting techniques to systematically evaluate the performance of private service delivery has remained steady over the past ten years, declining slightly from 62.4 percent in 1988 to 60.2 percent in 1997. Responses vary by size, with 76.5 percent of cities with populations of 100,000 or more currently reporting oversight techniques compared with 25 percent of cities with populations of less than 10,000 residents. Smaller cities have fewer staff and resources to effectively monitor a contract, which may account for some of the difference.

Apparently, more cities are developing sufficient in-house expertise to oversee contract management responsibilities. The number of cities reporting lack of staff with sufficient contract management background declined from 12.3 percent in 1988 to 3.8 percent in 1997. Combined with the earlier finding that a larger number and variety of in-house staff is engaged in evaluating privatization opportunities, these facts suggest that cities are developing institutional structures to consider contracting on a more systematic basis.

Areas of Evaluation

The ICMA survey followed up with questions about which service delivery aspects are evaluated and which techniques are used by cities. Officials reporting that cities monitored contractor performance were given a list of service delivery aspects that could be evaluated. Most officials from cities that contract identified cost (87%) and compliance with delivery standards specified in the contract (84.1%) as the leading topics. Another 64.7 percent reported that citizen satisfaction is also evaluated.

Obviously, cost factors are important for city officials to monitor because cost pressures are usually a driving force in the promotion of privatization in the first place. Cities contract with private firms mainly to save money which means that privatization agreements are ultimately judged by their ability to reduce costs. Some private firms offer guaranteed prices for services and have contractual provisions to cover costs exceeding that amount. For services provided in a competitive market, public officials can drive a hard bargain for cost and service quality guarantees.

While cost is a major consideration in evaluating the success of privatization, quality of services is another important measurement tool. Cities can assure that contractors meet quality and performance standards by enumerating specific tasks or performance measures in the contract. They may even include provisions for fines of contractors if they do not meet performance criteria. Performance guarantees and penalties are especially important for services involving intergovernmental mandates such as EPA regulations. In Evansville, Indiana, for example, the city's private partner that provides wastewater treatment pays a $500 fine for customer claims that the city determines were not handled properly and $5,000 for emergency complaints (Danks 1997). An effective monitoring contract can help overcome concern among opponents over loss of control that can occur in a privatization agreement.

Citizen satisfaction with contracted services is vital to the long-range success of privatization. Some officials and residents may initially fear the private takeover of public services and anticipate a diminished quality of performance. Contractors must ensure a smooth transition and continued emphasis on customer service to overcome those fears.

Survey findings show that city officials take their oversight responsibilities seriously and seek further protections to consistently serve the public interest through contracting agreements. It can also be inferred that as cities contract additional services, they learn new techniques with which to evaluate contracts and, therefore, are able to drive a harder bargain during the proposal and negotiation stages.

In Atlanta, officials developed a two-tier bid system that asked contractors for a best and final offer. The system, while controversial among contractors, provided extra assurance to city officials and citizens that the public interest was protected and the quality of service improved. Further experience will without doubt lead to more innovative approaches and newer advances to ensure that privatization saves tax dollars while maintaining or improving the quality of service.

Most cities that evaluate private sector service delivery use more than one of the oversight tools listed. For example, 20.6 percent of survey respondents report examining two aspects of private service delivery, and 30.1 percent say that they evaluate all three areas. A multifaceted approach ensures that cost is not the only way to measure success, with quality and citizen satisfaction also being key considerations.

Techniques

A variety of techniques exist for municipal officials to systematically evaluate private sector vendors. The ICMA survey asked city officials who have monitoring systems in place to identify specific techniques used to oversee contractors. The highest rated response according to the 1997 data is monitoring citizen complaints, which was reported by 74.1 percent of responding officials. Cities can develop systems for tracking complaints for specific contracted services to gauge customer satisfaction and service quality.

Elected officials are more sensitive to citizen complaints since failure to address them could lead to voter dissatisfaction at the polls. Also, angry citizens may be more apt to call their alderman than a private contractor, which may be perceived by the public as a quicker way to get a response. In fact, 24 percent of cities reported that they kept service complaint mechanisms in house as a way to ensure success of privatization. This finding occurred more often in smaller cities where loss of control is a more salient issue.

The second most popular form of oversight as reported by city officials is analyzing data and records, with 73 percent reporting this technique. Such data and records could involve demographic and/or financial information that helps officials evaluate service delivery; however, officials must be sure that the data received is reliable. Sometimes, cities must rely on records and performance data supplied by contractors. Cities should have employees and systems in place to provide independent collection and analysis of data to ensure quality and performance.

Conducting field inspections was reported by 69.8 percent of city officials as a technique used to monitor contractors. This could involve overseeing street maintenance work at a construction site or inspecting tree trimming after completion to ensure it has been done according to specifications. Sometimes it is better to observe contractor performance directly than to rely on other methods of evaluation, especially when it involves technical specifications written into the contract.

The final category listed on the survey was conducting citizen surveys, reported by 36.5 percent of respondents. The number increased from 20.9 percent in 1988, the largest increase for monitoring techniques in the survey. It is also consistent with 17.6 percent of cities who reported that they surveyed citizens as a strategy to guarantee the success of a privatization initiative. As part of a renewed emphasis on customer satisfaction, some cities have requested that citizens complete surveys to measure performance. Often, the surveys are given to citizens after they receive a service. For example, street crews may distribute surveys to citizens living on a street that has just undergone routine maintenance or repair. This allows instant feedback and potentially elicits suggestions for service improvements.

Generally, it is wise for cities to use a variety of monitoring techniques. A single approach may not provide a proper overall picture of performance. Using several alternative oversight strategies can help city officials make sure a private firm meets performance standards and fulfills contractual obligations. In the ICMA survey, 46.2 percent of city officials reported multiple monitoring techniques, with 18.1 percent using two, 19.2 percent using three, and 8.9 percent adopting four.

These findings suggest that cities are increasing and varying their use of monitoring techniques in an effort to assure service quality. The concern is with the roughly 40 percent of cities that do not systematically evaluate private vendors. This group could include cities which only contract a few services or cities which only contract those services that are seasonal, such as tree trimming or snow plowing, which may not require extensive oversight techniques. While the overall percentage of cities with monitoring systems has remained about the same over the past ten years, some cities would be advised to develop systems in the future even if they do not contract for many services.

CONCLUSION

Municipal officials seem to be taking a pragmatic, systematic approach in considering privatization of public services. As the use of privatization and competitive government practices have increased during the past two decades, city officials have adapted other cities' successful practices in order to meet local needs. They also have instituted formal policies that help ensure successful evaluation, implementation, and monitoring of contracting agreements.

The ICMA survey data show that cities contracted more in 1997 than they did ten years earlier although the growth is slower than one might have expected. Improved economic and financial conditions of cities may be one explanation for why more privatization has not occurred; however, the scope of services contracted has expanded dramatically with cities increasingly contracting with private firms for public safety and health and human services.

While privatization and managed competition have increased in recent years, city officials are gaining sophistication in the successful implementation of contracts. More officials and administrators in city government, including finance officers and line employees, are involved in the decision process. In fact, all categories of city officials listed on the survey showed increases in involvement in the decisions—a sign that officials are reaching out to many groups for input.

Cities are also increasingly involving the public in the evaluation process by consulting with customers and recipients of city services. By involving a wide range of people and groups in the evaluation process, city officials are gathering pertinent information, building public support, and making sure that the public interest is protected.

Another key finding from the ICMA survey data is that cities are increasingly involving employees in the evaluation process in order to reduce any negative impacts. While opposition from line employees remains the leading obstacle to privatization, officials are taking measures designed to soften the impact of contracting agreements, providing more information to affected employees, and attempting to overcome some of the hostility. More cities are involving line employees in studying the feasibility of privatization and developing programs to minimize the effect on displaced workers.

Substantially more cities are adopting managed competition programs that allow public employees and managers to compete with private firms in the bidding process. The growth of managed competition is a sign that city officials are more interested in efficient provision of services than just a private sector solution. Overall, increases in managed competition and policies designed to minimize the impact on employees show that city officials are devising innovative strategies that ensure fairness to employees.

More cities are also taking a systematic approach to evaluating and monitoring contractor performance. Cities are moving beyond an emphasis on cost to closely examine performance standards specified in contracts and measuring citizen satisfaction. To properly evaluate more aspects of contractor performance, cities are increasingly using a greater variety of monitoring techniques. A systematic approach to monitoring contractor performance is vital to enhance the quality of service, customer satisfaction, and cost oversight. Without such systems, cities could be at the mercy of contractors to evaluate their own performance.

While states are often referred to as laboratories of democracy, cities also have widely experimented with new and innovative approaches to governance. As privatization and managed competition have become more popular since the 1970s, city officials have moved beyond ideology and political party to adapt these management techniques to meet specific local needs. The increasing adoption of systems, policies, and methodologies to bring about the successful implementation of privatization and managed competition is further evidence of the commitment to better services, lower costs, and a greater emphasis on customer service. As the use of alternate service delivery techniques continues to grow in the future, cities will remain laboratories where innovation, creativity, and pragmatic solutions can prosper.

REFERENCES

Ammons, David, and Debra Hill. 1995. The viability of public-private competition as a long-term service delivery strategy. *Public Productivity and Management Review* 19(1): 12–24.

Bonnett, Tom. 1999. *Governance in the digital age: The impact of the global economy, information technology, and economic deregulation on state and local government*. Washington, DC: National League of Cities.

Brostek, Michael. 1997. *Privatization: Lessons learned by state and local governments*. Washington, DC: U.S. General Accounting Office.

Danks, Jack J. 1997. The Evansville, Indiana story: Breaking new ground in public-private partnerships with contract management. *Council Insights* (The National Council for Public-Private Partnerships) (August).

Dilger, Robert J., Randolph R. Moffett, and Linda Struyk. 1997. Privatization of municipal services in America's largest cities. *Public Administration Review* 57(1): 21–26.

Donahue, John D. 1989. *The privatization decision: Public ends, private means.* New York: Basic Books.

Frost, C., J. H. Wakely, and R. A. Ruth. 1974. *Organizational development.* Englewood Cliffs, NJ: Prentice-Hall.

Gillen, Shawn J., and Robin A. Johnson. 1999. Small town enters into cutting-edge public-private partnership. *Privatization Watch* (267) (March): 7.

Greene, Jeffrey D. 1996. Cities and privatization: Examining the effect of fiscal stress, location, and wealth in medium-sized cities. *Policy Studies Journal* 24(1): 135–144.

Jackson, Cynthia. 1997. Strategies for managing tensions between public employment and private service delivery. *Public Productivity and Management Review* 21(2): 119–136.

Johnson, Robin A., and Norman Walzer. 1996. *Competition for city services: Has the time arrived?* Springfield, IL: Office of the Comptroller.

The Mercer Group. 1997. *1997 privatization survey.* Atlanta, GA: The Mercer Group.

Miranda, Rowan, and Karlyn Andersen. 1994. Private service delivery in local government, 1982–1992. In *International City/County Management Association municipal yearbook 1994,* 26–35. Washington, DC: ICMA.

Morley, Elaine. 1989. Patterns in the use of alternate service delivery approaches. In *International City/County Management Association municipal yearbook 1989,* 33–44. Washington, DC: ICMA.

National League of Cities (NLC). 1999. *New NLC report finds cities investing in infrastructure, public safety, human needs; Annual fiscal survey shows continuing improvement and optimism for most cities; New analysis of municipal funding sources exposes revenue structure policy issues.* Available online: <www.nlc.org/pres-fs.htm>.

Osborne, David, and Ted Gaebler. 1992. *Reinventing government: How the entrepreneurial spirit is transforming the public sector.* New York: Addison-Wesley.

Prager, Jonas, and Swati Desai. 1996. Privatizing local government operations: Lessons from federal contracting out methodology. *Public Productivity & Management Review* 20(2): 185–203.

Reason Public Policy Institute. 1999. *Privatization '99: 13th annual report on privatization.* Los Angeles: Reason Public Policy Institute.

Savas, E. S. 1977. *The organization and efficiency of solid waste collection.* Lexington, MA: Lexington Books.

Schneider, Mark. 1988. *The competitive city.* Pittsburgh: University of Pittsburgh Press.

Stein, Robert M. 1990. *Urban alternatives: Public and private markets in the provision of local services.* Pittsburgh: University of Pittsburgh Press.

U.S. Conference of Mayors. 1999. *Webb calls for new partnership with America's communities.* Available online: <www.usmayors.org/uscm/US_Mayor_newspaper/documents/ 6_28_99/coverstory.htm>.

U.S. Department of Labor, National Commission on Employment Policy (NCEP). 1989. *The long-term implications of privatization.* Washington, DC: U.S. Department of Labor.

U.S. General Accounting Office (USGAO). 1985. *DoD functions contracted out under OMB Circular A-76: Costs and status of certain displaced workers.* Washington, DC: USGAO.

Wallin, Bruce. 1997. The need for a privatization process: Lessons from development and implementation. *Public Administration Review* 57(1): 11–20.

Walzer, Norman, and Brian D. Jacobs, eds. 1998. *Public-private partnerships for local economic development.* New York: Praeger Publishers.

Whitaker, G. P., and K. Jenne. 1995. Improving city manager's leadership. *State and Local Government Review* 27: 84–94.

Woodwell, Jamie. 1998. *Major factors affecting America's cities.* Washington, DC: National League of Cities.

Yager, E. M. 1994. An organizational perspective on municipal contracting decisions. *National Civic Review* (winter/spring): 73–77.

10

Impact of Privatization and Managed Competition on Public Employees

Christi Clark, Robin A. Johnson, and James L. Mercer

It is clear that just about everything affecting the provision of public services is in the midst of profound change. During the past two decades, public officials have increasingly embraced the tenets of "reinventing government" by trying to squeeze more efficiency from public operations and adopting management practices and techniques from the private sector. Everything from public enterprises like airports, public transit, and wastewater treatment to public programs such as youth detention, road maintenance, and park management have come under intense scrutiny. The pressure to continuously improve—usually without additional funding—has shaped the public sector landscape in ways that have changed its nature and affected its employees.

Contracting out the management of public assets and provision of services is not without pitfalls. While many look at privatization as simply a way to save money, it also has legal, managerial, and political implications. Yet, impressive success stories from around the country provide credible evidence that these strategies often produce substantial savings and performance results. Still, an issue that continues to plague privatization initiatives is how these strategies affect public employees.

Indeed, the employee issue lies at the center of the political questions concerning privatization and managed competition. Labor costs comprise approximately three-fourths of most municipal budgets (Rehfuss 1989). Thus, discussions of improved performance of government and cost-savings inevitably turn to the subject of personnel costs. Local officials struggle to balance the competing and sometimes contradictory goals of improving service quality, reducing costs, and lessening the impact on employees.

Without question, the opposition from public employee unions and the understandable anxiety of the employees themselves can pose a formidable obstacle to privatization. Employees fear loss of jobs, reduced benefits, or lower earnings, and they are uncertain about future working conditions, new policies, and job requirements. Public officials are often ill-prepared to reassure public workers, since they themselves do not know what the outcome will be when they first undertake a privatization study. While employees are seeking information and answers, public officials may respond with silence and secrecy in an effort to contain their plans until they become more certain.

For officials and employees alike, there are several well-circulated studies that show how privatization has affected employees in areas such as employment and benefits. These reports have done little to overcome the negative perceptions of employees and their unions, however. Communities are finding that other issues, such as communication, employee involvement, and training, are also crucial in managing a privatization initiative.

In fact, some public officials believe that the problems with government efficiency and performance do not lie with employees but, rather, with government structure and systems. In the city of Indianapolis (1999), officials empowered employees and produced remarkable results: "It is not the city workers who make for inefficiencies in government. Rather, the restrictions within government itself are usually to blame for the high cost and low quality that many have come to expect from government services. Too often the government traps good people in bad systems. If the systems are changed and the workers are liberated from bureaucratic constraints, they can compete against private sector providers, and often win."

This chapter examines recent innovations that have changed the way governments and private providers have approached employee issues through alternative service delivery. First, several areas in which employees can be affected by privatization are explored based upon previous research and recent innovative examples. Special focus is placed on how managed competition changes the dynamic of the public workplace. Also, the impact of privatization and managed competition on public managers and administrators is explored as an important area that has received little notice. Finally, the authors examine trends they see continuing into the future.

IMPACTS ON EMPLOYEES

For public employees, there are five primary areas of potential impact and ways they will need assistance that should interest public officials: (1) loss of jobs, (2) wages and benefits, (3) building trust, (4) coping with change, and (5) enabling the leadership. What does the research tell us about each of these areas, and how are communities working to help employees through privatization?

Loss of Jobs

In 1989, the National Commission on Employment Policy (NCEP), a research division of the U.S. Department of Labor, produced a comprehensive report on the effects of privatization on employees from city and county jurisdictions (U.S. Department of Labor, National Commission on Employment Policy [NCEP] 1989). The study encompassed 34 privatization initiatives and tracked the employment status of more than 2,000 workers. The results were impressive. The study found that private contractors who were taking over services formerly provided by the government hired more than half of the public sector workers; another 24 percent of the workers transferred to other government positions; 7 percent of the workers retired; and only 7 percent were laid off.

Similar results are reflected in a 1985 U.S. General Accounting Office (USGAO) study of job layoffs which followed a Department of Defense downsizing and privatization initiative. The report found that 94 percent of the 9,650 employees affected by the program were transitioned into other public sector positions or retired voluntarily. Half of the remaining 6 percent were employed with the private contractor and only 3 percent were laid off.

A recent study of privatization in Illinois municipalities found that only three percent of the 516 responding cities reported layoffs due to contracting (Johnson and Walzer 1996). Nearly two-thirds (64.9 percent) of the municipalities reported no displacement of affected employees while 10.8 percent transferred employees to other government jobs; 5.4 percent reported that employees were hired by the private contractor; 5.1 percent said the affected employees retired; and 9.8 percent reported a combination of these strategies.

These results demonstrate a legitimate and effective effort to protect public workers from privatization-related job displacement. In a recent RFP process in Atlanta, for example, four finalists seeking to run Atlanta's drinking water system all agreed in principle to a no-layoff policy for the 535 public employees of the city water department. Other strategies such as giving displaced workers preferential consideration for government job openings or creating new job classifications and career opportunities for workers are also viable options.

The city of Philadelphia provides an excellent example of the kinds of measures that can be taken to minimize job displacement effects. As part of the mayor's Competitive Contracting Program (CCP) introduced in 1992, the city implemented several programs designed to assist public workers in the transitions required by privatization and public-private competitions. In addition to establishing a Redeployment Office to match the skills of displaced employees to position openings in other departments, the city created new job classifications. It also gave displaced employees preferential consideration for other city jobs and required private contractors to give right of first refusal to affected city workers. In one case, the city invited displaced prison food service workers to participate in special training for a newly created "correctional officer trainee" position.

Offering displaced workers early retirement packages or severance buy outs are also viable options for those workers who prefer them; however, since no one approach will meet the needs of every worker or every community, a combination of programs can help make sure that public employees are treated fairly and given every opportunity to continue employment.

Developing policies to avoid layoffs does not mean that the total workforce will not be impacted by privatization. In many recent cases, contractors taking over public operations are allowed to reduce the workforce only through attrition. This strategy enables firms to reach an optimal staffing level that increases efficiency and generates additional savings. It also allows firms to invest in efficiency-enhancing capital and equipment early in the contract period and recover the investment through reduced numbers of employees in later years.

Recent changes in IRS regulations that allow long-term water and wastewater contracts are also having an impact on labor relations. Contracts over a longer duration relieve pressure on private firms to reduce costs early as with a short-term contract. Most short-term contracts and all long-term contracts agreed to provide for reducing workforces through attrition rather than layoffs (Ward 1998).

Public officials who are committed to minimizing job displacement during a privatization or managed competition process have excellent options available and many examples or case studies of how they worked. Armed with information and creativity, they can design a program that will even support a "no-layoff" policy, determined to best meet the needs of the community.

Wages and Benefits

In the area of wages and benefits, several reports show that private sector compensation packages are comparable with those provided to public sector workers. The 1989 NCEP study includes a comparison of wages and benefits for public and private sector employees. There were more instances in which wages increased than decreased after privatization, and there was no indication that private firms paid lower wages.

Another study by the U.S. Department of Housing and Urban Development (HUD) in 1984 compared wage levels for eight services in 20 California cities (Stevens 1984). Half the cities performed the services in house; the other half contracted with the private sector to do the work. When wages for these jobs were evaluated, the findings revealed little difference in the wage levels between the public and private sectors, although where differences were noted, the private sector paid slightly less. Comparable benefit levels were also found.

Other sources, such as the 1991 U.S. Department of Labor report, *Employment Cost Indexes and Levels 1975–91,* show that some public sector employees, such as those working for public sanitation departments, fare better than their private sector counterparts. The 1989 NCEP study also noted differences in benefits, with government benefits packages often being more generous than those provided by the private sector; however, private sector offerings like 401K programs, stock options, profit sharing, and better opportunities for training and advancement can help offset benefit program differences where they exist.

Several strategies have been used successfully to alleviate potential wage and benefit differentials for workers affected by privatization. In some cases, private contractors may voluntarily agree to meet wage and benefit levels offered by the government agency or department. Recently, the city of Monmouth, Illinois, incorporated comparable wages and benefits for public workers as a contract requirement when negotiating to privatize all city public works services. Environmental Management Corporation (EMC), a private contractor already managing the town's wastewater treatment, was invited to provide a proposal to take over additional services such as street maintenance, billing, and garbage collection for the city. To win the contract, EMC agreed to the terms required by Monmouth officials, hiring all affected public workers at wages and benefit levels matching the city's compensation package. The firm also agreed to recognize and bargain in good faith with the employee union.

Government officials should, however, be aware that requiring contractors to hire public workers at the same wage and benefit levels may reduce the availability of some compensation programs typically offered by the private sector such as incentive pay plans and bonuses tied to performance. To give contractors flexibility in designing wage and benefit plans that align with operating strategies, officials may allow contractors to provide "comparable" compensation plans with reasonable guarantees for meeting or exceeding former compensation levels. This flexibility can also benefit workers who exceed performance expectations and can earn higher compensation than received in their former public positions.

For employees who remain employed by the city following a privatization, there are several ways to assure that workers are protected from any adverse wage or benefit consequences associated with privatization. Many can be placed in jobs with similar wage and benefit levels or be trained to perform new jobs. In addition, other kinds of job enrichment programs, such as free wellness programs, child care vouchers, and education benefits, can help maintain or improve the overall value of the compensation package for retained workers.

Building Trust

If the statistics tell us that privatization produces a minimal number of layoffs and that wages and benefits are frequently comparable or can be made so, why is it that public employees continue to be hostile about privatization and related strategies? And why do public unions continue to contest and block these plans, especially when there are many cases in which public firms agree to hire most or all of the public employees and recognize and bargain with their union?

It may come down to a matter of trust. Stephen Haines, president and founder of the Centre for Strategic Management, puts it simply when he says, "people support what they help create." Some government jurisdictions, including the state of Massachusetts, have found that privatization strategies are unnecessarily complicated and even thwarted when employee involvement is not a key component of the process. According to a 1997 USGAO report on lessons learned by six local and state governments, the initial failure of state officials to involve Massachusetts employee unions created tensions that eventually led to legislation making privatization in the state more difficult.

Public workers and their unions tend to become defensive when officials do not provide them with clear information or invite them to participate in discussions early on. In the absence of this inclusive approach, workers and unions can become entrenched in an adversarial position and subsequent efforts to bring employees to the table are viewed as "too little too late." Emotions and tempers, along with misinformation and rumors, can fuel distrust and division between city officials and their employees, sometimes requiring litigation to resolve.

To build trust and gain buy-in from public workers, officials must foster a spirit of teamwork and demonstrate sensitivity to the issues concerning them. In return, workers can provide valuable insights about the services they perform and offer suggestions for improving the quality of final decisions. Several models can be used to engage public employees in the process effectively, including the use of task forces, employee feedback processes, and cross functional teams.

When the city of Ann Arbor, Michigan, wanted to investigate the possibility of contracting out the city's solid waste collection services, the City Council decided to appoint a task force of department heads/managers; American Federation of State, County, and Municipal Employees (AFSCME) representatives; and sanitation workers. The initial purpose of the task force was to gather information and explore issues associated with privatization. Because of their work, the task force created a comprehensive report for the City Council outlining program costs, service issues, and the possible impact on sanitation workers.

By embracing a participative approach, Ann Arbor officials were able to consider information that might otherwise have been unavailable to them, which helped to solidify labor and management relations. Instead of creating an adversarial environment, this approach fostered teamwork and collaboration, since all key stakeholder groups were represented on the work team. The approach provided a forum to discuss diverse views and opinions, but all recommendations had to be supported by evidence and facts in order to gain credibility.

The findings of the task force convinced the city to engage in a public-private competition, allowing city workers an opportunity to compete with the private sector for the sanitation contract. The same cross functional task force appointed by the City Council for information gathering stayed together to develop their bid submittal. The city employees were subsequently awarded the work and began delivering improved services at costs tested against the market for efficiency and competitiveness.

Another strategy is for private firms to slowly build a relationship with municipalities by taking over certain functions that often lead to more responsibilities in future years. An example is the recent practice of management contracts, in which a city retains responsibility for pay and benefits, and a private firm assumes control over the day-to-day operations and management. The private firm increases efficiency in operations and saves tax dollars while employees remain employed by the city. While cost-savings may be less than in a more comprehensive arrangement, management contracts help to ease the public employees' fears over job security and working for the private sector. Once employees see the benefits of private management, they may be less inclined to automatically oppose a full privatization agreement.

Buffalo, New York, became the largest city in the United States to operate under a management contract for water services in 1997. The division's 160-member workforce remains as city employees and were guaranteed jobs for five years. Labor contracts were negotiated with four unions representing water department employees. The city continues to pay workers, and the private contractor will reimburse the city.

Coping with Change

There are some policies that governments can offer to ease the transition process for public employees going to work for private firms and for public departments that are allowed to bid on contracts in a new competitive environment. Change in any environment can be difficult, but it is especially challenging in the public sector where employee expectations of employment stability are higher than in the private sector. Public officials who take steps to ease the transition process usually see improved morale and less intense opposition.

In order for public managers and employees to bid against private firms, they must develop skills in several areas, including cost accounting and bid proposal structuring. Training assistance for public employees provides them with the tools they need in order to be able to increase efficiency and productivity in the new competitive environment.

Under "Cleveland Competes," the city's competition initiative, city officials must meet with unions before changes in service delivery take place. Employees are allowed an opportunity to suggest changes for improving efficiency, which could eliminate the need to privatize the service. The city returns a portion of the savings realized for employee skills enhancement and equipment upgrades.

Coral Gables, Florida, assists employees in cost accounting, bid proposal structuring, and business plan development to prepare them to bid for a contract on vehicle maintenance. Los Angeles County, California, funds training for employees who have been displaced by privatization by earmarking five percent of the savings achieved through privatization for training in developing new skills and enhancing existing ones. Phoenix, Indianapolis, and Charlotte municipal governments have also developed programs to train employees in cost accounting and bid specifications.

In some cities, government officials can smooth the transition process through enhanced long-term planning. For example, human resource departments are taking a more active role in the planning process to determine future employee needs. If there are plans to privatize a department in the near future, human resource managers begin preparations for employee transition as soon as possible. In Phoenix, strategies are put in place as soon as a contract is signed to smooth the transition process.

A third way of easing the transition to a more competitive environment in government is to address the concern over retirement benefits. Several studies have shown that retirement benefits are the key difference in compensation packages between the public and private sectors. Public pension systems are traditionally more generous than those in the private sector, and innovative public and private officials have developed ways to soften the transition. One method is to make pension benefits portable to the private contractor's plan or to roll the account over into an Individual Retirement Account (IRA). Ohio adopted pension portability legislation which allows public employees working for a private firm to continue making contributions to municipal pension plans.

A recent ruling by the IRS, however, will have major implications for pension issues in future privatization efforts, especially for water services. According to a recent agency ruling, newly privatized employees can continue to participate in a public pension system even though they are no longer public employees (Mahtesian 1999). Thus, private employers can make contributions into a public employee pension system, allowing contributions to compound instead of setting up new accounts from scratch. This ruling is significant both because it removes a potential barrier to privatization and because it allows employees a choice between private and public pension plans.

The 1997 USGAO report outlined several strategies needed to manage workforce transition. According to the report, effective transitioning strategies require employee involvement in the privatization decision-making process, training to provide skills for either competing against the private sector or monitoring contractor performance, and the creation of a safety net for displaced employees. The strategies will vary depending on local political factors and the relationship between political leaders and employees. Most officials said that the strategies were designed to bolster support for privatization as well as to mitigate employee concerns.

When faced with the possibility of dramatic change in their departments, public employees go through several phases that must be managed. Their first reaction is a sense of confusion, denial that the changes will really take place, and even shock as they start to imagine how the proposed changes might impact their lives. As the possibilities sink in, a "fight or flight" reaction may occur, in which employees either start organizing resistance to the change or try to find other ways of regaining some sense of control, including departure.

If these efforts are not effective in stopping the change process, employees may begin to believe they have lost all their options. At this phase, they can feel victimized and depressed or adopt an "I don't care" attitude. They can be uncommunicative and moody, and even the most conscientious employees may revert to doing only the minimum work required or engage in subversive or destructive behaviors.

Involving public employees early in any process that contemplates privatization creates a valuable two-way flow of information and can alert watchful officials to potential employee problems. By listening carefully to worker concerns, answering questions honestly, and keeping employees informed throughout the process, public officials can help reduce workforce fears. Helping employees through the first two phases expedites the change process. They will more quickly start to believe that they can get through the change, adjust to the new paradigm, and do well on the other side.

One way to help employees cope with the inevitable changes associated with privatization or public-private competition is to expose them to the knowledge and skills they need for success. When the city of Charlotte, North Carolina, decided to start competing with the private sector to provide public services, it created a training course known as "Competition 101" for mid-level supervisors and other employees. As part of the course, employees were divided into smaller groups to form business models of companies that might compete against the city for service contracts. According to remarks made by Charlotte city official David Cooke to the Reason Foundation's 21st Century Government Conference in 1996, employees who participated learned to think about what they would do differently and how they would implement changes to make the city more competitive. They were also asked to think about what they could do differently as individuals, driving home the need for personal responsibility. As Cooke remarked, "The employees know what it takes to be competitive. They know how to succeed" (16).

That kind of confidence can help employees perform better, meet the challenges of public-private competitions, and cope with the dynamics of change in their workplace. Many of these employees have never worked outside the public domain and may feel threatened and inadequate in the private sector world of performance objectives and productivity requirements. In all fairness to them, the terms of public employment have often included promises of job stability without clear expectations for either job performance or continuous improvement. Workers must be made to feel that they are up to the challenge and can accomplish the goals set for them in this new competitive environment.

Enabling the Leadership

While much is written about the impact of privatization and managed competition on public employees and the political questions facing elected officials, there has been little mention of the impact of the newly competitive environment on public managers and organizations. They are the forgotten yet vital cog in a successful transition process. The interests of managers and/or administrators must also be considered to ensure a successful venture.

Sometimes, public administrators, managers, and department heads resist changes in procedures, especially privatization, since it at least implies that a private firm can provide services more efficiently than in-house employees. Managed competition schemes may be more to their liking since they can demonstrate their ability to compete. In either case, the traditional methods of operations will change leading to anxiety, fear, and resentment.

There are a variety of advanced skills needed by public managers and, in some cases, employees in order for them to successfully operate in a competitive environment. Increased emphasis on contracting, performance, cost-savings, and accountability require public employees to develop skills that they have not traditionally used. The new skills and abilities involved with contracting services include the following:

- Developing bid specifications
- Contract monitoring
- Performance measurement
- Contract negotiation
- Accurately costing services

These advanced skills will require management systems that are more sophisticated and systematic than what now exists in most government agencies.

The changing nature of government work also challenges public managers. With contracting on the increase at all levels of government, more public officials are becoming contract managers than direct providers of services. This "hollowing out" of government is already apparent at the federal level where, for example, the Department of Energy has more contract than full-time employees (Ingraham 1995).

Overseeing contracts requires different skills and abilities than what some managers may possess. While many managers may have monitored contracts for seasonal or specialized services, such as tree trimming or labor negotiations, they have less experience dealing with long-term contracts with specific performance measures. This situation may have consequences for environmental services, such as water treatment, where a failure to perform could result in fines and restrictions on growth.

Some organizations are developing contract management skills in house to meet these challenges. While many private firms outsourced services and functions during the 1980s, surprisingly few have developed effective internal monitoring procedures. Hewlett Packard has a short training course for employees and the Department of Defense trains employees internally through an in-house "university" (Kettl, Ingraham, Sanders, and Horner 1996). Seminars are also held by universities and think tanks to develop contract management skills. Yet, the supply still falls far short of the demand.

Advanced expertise is required for negotiating a contract with a private firm especially for long-term contracts with specific performance measures. Contractors will usually have an experienced in-house attorney negotiating contracts, while municipal attorneys, whether in house or contractual, may have limited abilities in this area. Negotiating an inadequate contract may result in worse service and higher costs, and it could even threaten the public interest. In fact, there are few sources of expertise in the rapidly expanding field of long-term privatizations, especially in smaller communities.

In addition, some governments include performance measures in contracts they negotiate with contractors. Such performance-based contracting is another skill that is rare in public agencies but crucial for creating a level playing field for public-private competition.

Creating a more competitive environment in public operations requires a variety of enhanced skills and training for public managers and employees. In addition to contract monitoring and oversight, public managers must be able to adequately measure performance of public functions. Performance measurement has taken on added importance in recent years at all levels of government as elected officials seek to demonstrate greater performance and accountability to residents.

Measuring performance becomes vital when considering whether to privatize a service or keep its provision in house. Public officials may discover that in-house sources are providing services as efficiently and effectively as potential private contractors. Private firms will undoubtedly be able to provide some measure of effectiveness in their operations for comparison. Information systems to gather, document, and analyze this information will become more important for public agencies in the future, and few examples currently exist. Efforts are underway, however, in cities such as Indianapolis to develop systematic approaches to performance measurement and benchmarking. These approaches are more prevalent in larger cities because they have staff and resources to develop them, but they are needed in smaller communities as well.

Public managers and employees will need training to help accurately determine the costs of providing services. Calculating the full cost of providing services is important for comparisons between in-house and private service provision. Simply looking at line-item amounts from a traditional budget does not provide an accurate reading of total costs and excludes overhead and indirect costs altogether. Advanced costing approaches, such as Activity-Based Costing, are adapted from the private sector and are used frequently in larger governments such as in Indianapolis and San Diego County. Officials in Virginia created a computer program called COMPETE that operates on a PC and determines the fully allocated cost of any activity or function (Kittower 1998). Some governments hire consultants to accurately cost services while others train in-house managers and employees in accounting practices. Either way, determining the full cost of services is vital to a program of competitive contracting and is important for internal cost analysis as well.

For example, Indianapolis Mayor Goldsmith became a strong advocate of public-private competition and supported attempts to introduce competition for more than 150 services by late 1993. In an effort to help city employees cope with these sweeping changes, the city of Indianapolis and union officials identified seven key areas they felt would help public workers affected by these initiatives. The 1997 USGAO report lists them as follows: (1) knowledge of the existing government program, (2) ability to analyze work flows and processes, (3) ability to develop methods to eliminate inefficiencies, (4) knowledge of cost-estimation techniques, (5) ability to apply methods of financial analysis, (6) ability to determine and write concise and specific contract requirements to delineate exactly what the contractor is responsible for, and (7) knowledge of methods for monitoring the performance of contractors.

While this list can certainly benefit city workers at all levels, it has special relevance for public employees serving in leadership positions. Department heads and supervisors are frequently charged with responsibility for creating and managing the fact-finding process, communicating with anxious employees, evaluating complex issues, and rapidly developing new skills. These leaders know their people, their assets, and the job that gets done every day. Yet, they may know little about the professional management and analytical tools available to assist them.

The body of knowledge required for either a privatization or managed competition process is significant, and much of it will be new to public leaders. In competitive environments, different approaches to doing things are easily observed by all providers of the service and quickly adapted by their respective operations. In the public arena, however, these observations are not as easy to make since the field of view is mostly local. Consequently, public leaders may be ill-equipped to effectively respond to the sudden political demand for decisive action and innovative solutions.

Officials can create better results by assuring that their public leaders are enabled with the information and support they need to meet the challenge. Many communities do this by hiring outside consultants who specialize in areas like activity-based cost accounting or workflow analysis. These consultants should be instructed to assist and educate department heads as part of their assignment so that they can learn and grow in the process.

Officials can also encourage their public leaders to contact other communities that have successfully privatized or competed for the services under evaluation. They can fund field trips to those communities with best practices that can be learned from or duplicated. This will broaden the scope of knowledge and information available to a city and increase the confidence and capabilities of the public leaders affected.

Finally, any change in management processes requires excellent communication, strategic and tactical planning, organizational design, human relations skills, and a host of other sophisticated capabilities. To the extent that officials provide training and support for their department heads and supervisors, these workers will perform well and deliver value to the privatization or managed competition process. On the other hand, without this investment in people, the decisions of officials will only be as good as the scope of experience their workers have to offer. Good options might be overlooked and cost-savings reduced because public workers were not provided with the necessary tools needed to fully contribute their expertise to the process.

Any practice by officials that strengthens the skills, confidence, and growth of their public workers will greatly enhance the probability of success, whatever the government's chosen course of action. This is especially true when a community decides to allow city workers to compete in a managed competition process.

THE SPECIAL CHALLENGES OF MANAGED COMPETITION

Competition is the driving force that has led to cost-savings and improved quality in the provision of public services. One form of competition has been termed "managed competition." Managed competition may be defined as the process in which a public sector organization competes with a private company or companies to provide a public service. In many instances, internal functions and services are streamlined so that the local workforce can be competitive and continue operations. The taxpayer wins either way because of reduced cost and greater efficiencies. There have been some charges by the private sector that in-house competitors have an advantage and that the "playing field" is not always level in such competitions. Managed competition must occur in a controlled or managed process that clearly defines the steps to be followed and the roles of the participants.

In the latest nationwide survey of privatization practices of cities, counties, and special districts, The Mercer Group (1997) found that the most significant trend was for more local governments to use managed competition. This finding is supported by recent survey data from the ICMA which also shows increased use of managed competition by cities (Chapter 9).

There are a variety of pros and cons concerning managed competition that directly affect employee performance. Managed competition positively affects the workforce by awakening current employees and empowering them to develop more efficient work practices. The process further engenders internal innovation as employees strive to deliver services at less cost to keep their positions. Finally, managed competition has a beneficial impact by increasing training of public employees. If a no-layoff policy is in effect, employees will have the incentive to reduce labor costs without hurting coworkers.

Another managed competition tool used to increase performance of employees is gain sharing. Indianapolis and Charlotte have developed gain sharing programs that reward employees with part of any savings generated through managed competition. Usually, gain sharing agreements are structured in such a way that any monetary rewards are shared when savings are achieved beyond an agreed amount. Cities can also implement pay-for-performance schemes that provide financial incentives for increased productivity.

Managed competition includes some disadvantages that can negatively affect public employees as well. If a city workforce features high current labor costs, competitive schemes will require a reduction of labor costs either through wage reductions or downsizing. In addition, it may be more difficult for employees to obtain equipment or technology needed to reduce labor intensiveness of services. Not only will they face opposition from affected employees, elected officials must also be convinced to justify spending funds on equipment purchases.

The city of Phoenix pioneered this process during the past two decades under the leadership of former Public Works Director Ronald W. Jensen. The result of one area of managed competition in Phoenix over a ten-year period was a reduction in solid waste collection costs of 4.5 percent per year. This was accomplished by allowing the city's Public Works Department to bid against the private sector to provide solid waste services. The affect of this approach on city employees in the Public Works Department was that they received the resources and training necessary to compete in a highly competitive environment and to win bids against the private sector to provide public services.

The result was significant cost-savings to the city of Phoenix (more than $6 million in savings on one bid alone), a much more confident and competitive environment in the Public Works Department, and significantly increased morale among departmental employees. This approach to managed competition has caught hold and has been implemented in several other local governments across the country since its early introduction in Phoenix.

According to Jensen, the key to the success of the managed competition effort in Phoenix has been a spirit of competition and cooperation within the city organization. Both labor and management joined together in an all-out effort to be the winner over the private sector. The improvement in morale and working relationships was evident to all, with public support of the city's efforts at an all-time high. A sense of pride developed that stimulated all levels of the organization to work together towards achieving excellence in operations.

UNIONS AND GOVERNMENT ENTREPRENEURSHIP

No discussion of the changes occurring in public employment as a result of privatization and managed competition would be complete without examining two other issues: (1) unions and (2) government entrepreneurship. Because they are nascent trends, there is little available information; they are still worth exploring, however, because of their potential long-range impact.

Unions

Privatization of government services is affecting traditional relationships between unions and employers. Most local government employees belong to a handful of unions whose experience has involved bargaining with public officials. As public employees are transitioned to private firms through privatization and their union is recognized, they will bargain with private firms. For example, AFSCME, which represents a large number of local government employees has been bargaining more with private water companies during the recent wave of privatizations in the water industry. The consequences for the governments and private firms involved are mixed and will not be known without further experience. Milwaukee's wastewater privatization, which will be discussed in the following section, illustrates some of the issues involved.

Also, with more members working for private sector firms, unions such as AFSCME may seek further opportunities in nontraditional areas outside of the public realm. In Indiana, a local AFSCME chapter has already developed plans to organize more private sector workers (O'Malley 1999). This could create competition with other unions, impact traditional patterns of union representation, and create a counter-trend in which private sector unions mobilize to gain more public sector members.

Government Entrepreneurship

Employees empowered to bid for public contracts may begin to seek more work outside the contracted service area. With new skills to structure bids, analyze costs, and increase efficiency, employees can market their services to private firms, other governments, and nonprofit organizations to increase their job security and to raise their wages through gain sharing. Such an approach would change the organization and structure of local government and increase public employment.

Private sector firms that compete with public employee groups would naturally feel threatened with increased government entrepreneurship. They will want to ensure a level playing field and may raise philosophical objections about the proper role of government. For example, New York City's Sanitation Department developed a Contracting-In Program for repair services in which it bid for other departmental contracts after increasing efficiency in internal operations (Osborne and Gaebler 1992). In Indianapolis, employees in the fleet services department bid for outside work after a successful managed competition, winning contracts with townships, social service providers, and hospitals (Goldsmith 1998).

Both increased government entrepreneurship through managed competition and the changing role of unions as a result of privatization are issues that will become further developed in the future. Developing a definitive analysis for trends is difficult because both changes are new. Other recent changes and trends in privatization and managed competition allow for more speculation about future impacts on public employees.

A LOOK TO THE FUTURE

From major urban areas, such as Atlanta and Milwaukee, to smaller communities such as Farmersburg, Indiana, and Monmouth, Illinois, current public employees are being retained when public works services are contracted with private firms. Indeed, fair treatment of employees is becoming the rule rather than the exception.

Recent examples show that employees can clearly gain from privatization. In 1998, the Milwaukee Metropolitan Sewerage District (MMSD) agreed to a ten-year operations and maintenance contract in the largest wastewater contract ever. One of the main priorities of public officials was to prevent cost-savings from negatively impacting employees because earlier cost-cutting measures had led to staff reductions.

The private firm, United Water Services (UWS), reached agreement with MMSD and the employee union on several key issues related to employment. UWS agreed to equal or better pay and benefits and no layoffs without cause for the full ten-year length of the contract. The total number of employees will be reduced only through attrition to the optimum level. In exchange for the labor concessions, the union agreed not to oppose the privatization agreement.

The private firm will undergo an increased level of risk because of labor concessions. For example, workers were not allowed the right to strike as public employees but can do so as private sector employees. Since a strike as public employees would lead to cancellation of the contract, privatization has given employees considerable leverage through the right to strike.

Another innovative aspect of the Milwaukee contract deals with employee pension plans. All parties to the contract agreed to seek regulatory relief from certain restrictions on retirement plans. The formal request to labor and tax officials was approved which allowed all employees transferring to the private firm to remain under the public pension system. This could be another innovation that gains in popularity in the future, especially after a recent IRS ruling that loosens federal restrictions.

Atlanta's water privatization, the largest in the nation, is dealt with in Chapter 12. It is also noteworthy for innovative contract terms concerning treatment of employees.

Recent case studies of managed competition also demonstrate how public employees can benefit from changes in service delivery. Indianapolis provides the most dramatic example in its fleet services division (Goldsmith 1998). The department administrator, employees, and the local union collaborated to develop a winning proposal for fleet maintenance. What made the bid extraordinary was the union employees' willingness to forgo previously agreed-upon pay increases. Instead, the bid was structured to pay employees for performance from additional savings generated beyond the amount in the proposal. Employees ended up earning more through the incentive plan than they would have through negotiated pay raises.

Several trends are occurring simultaneously that encourage the movement towards labor-friendly policies during privatization. The trends will probably continue in the foreseeable future and could accelerate as successful case studies become more well-known:

- *Privatization of Infrastructure.* Environmental mandates, financial pressures, fewer sources of grant funding, and citizen opposition to tax increases are forcing local officials to examine privatization and public-private partnerships as a

208   Local Government Innovation

viable way to upgrade decaying infrastructures. This trend is occurring in all sizes of cities, especially in water and wastewater services. Public works and infrastructure services usually require a large number of employees, making consideration of workers and employee-friendly policies more likely.

- *Long-Term Contracts.* This issue can work both ways. Changes in IRS regulations concerning long-term contracts are having an indirect impact on employee issues and are encouraging long-term contracts. Conversely, the trend of retraining all current employees necessitates long-term deals. It can take ten years or more of increased operating efficiencies to pay for system upgrades needed in most cases, especially if the private firm contributes some of the capital. In addition, as previously noted, private firms usually need fewer employees than employed by the public agency. With no-layoff policies, it will take several years before the number of employees reaches an optimum level. In fact, some contracts will involve operating losses for the first years of a contract and will make money only as the number of employees is reduced. Thus, private firms need a longer-term contract to recoup losses when they retain all employees.

- *Managed Competition.* Recent studies by The Mercer Group and ICMA both point to increased use of managed competition by cities. Some smaller communities across the nation are experimenting with various forms of managed competition, all designed to ensure the best "bang for the buck" for taxpayers. Whether the answer is privatization or managed competition, employees can come out winners if they are ensured a place at the bargaining table.

- *Enhanced Skills.* In order to compete effectively, governments must train employees on advanced skills in accounting, performance measurement, contract monitoring, and bid specification development. Some cities, such as Indianapolis and Charlotte, have formalized processes for training employees and managers in the managed competition process, but further training efforts are needed. Partnerships between universities and government may be the best source for training local officials in advanced skills development.

- *Politics.* The political nature of the privatization debate is also changing and has turned the terms of the debate upside down. It was a Republican mayor who worked with employees and empowered unions in Indianapolis in a successful example of managed competition; it was a Democratic mayor who stared down unions in Philadelphia and won important concessions through privatization, and developed a successful program of managed competition; and it was a Democratic mayor in Atlanta who produced the largest water privatization in history while ensuring that employees were treated fairly. These examples show that ideology and partisan affiliation have been ignored in many cities as innovative officials seek to provide the best services possible for citizens.

CONCLUSION

Enormous changes have occurred in the public service delivery paradigm in the past twenty years, especially with regard to how public employees are treated. Further mutations and changes are expected to occur in the next twenty years as contracting continues to grow in all levels of government.

In the future, public employees can expect to experience continued pressure from better informed citizens for cost-effective local government service provision. There will be continued emphasis on privatization of public services, increased reliance on managed competition, greater automation of the workplace, and increased emphasis on measures of work performance. These should not be seen as threats to the public workforce but as challenges that will make for a more effective and productive workforce in the future.

Privatization and managed competition will continue to evolve as they have done during their growth periods of the past two decades. The fact that employee interests are considered early in the process instead as of an afterthought is an indication of how privatization has changed. Impacts on employees are clearly an issue that must be addressed and can be as important as potential cost-savings and performance enhancement.

Managed competition is an outgrowth of privatization and is another major change in the traditional public sector approach to service delivery. While more promising for larger local governments than smaller ones, managed competition holds the promise of an empowered workforce with enhanced skills providing quality services to the public.

REFERENCES

City of Indianapolis. 1999. *Competition initiative home page.* Available online: <www.IndyGov.org/mayor/comp/pt1/chp1/cfp.html>.
Cooke, David. 1996. Competition 101: Getting public units ready to compete. *Privatization '96.* Los Angeles: Reason Foundation.
Goldsmith, Stephen. 1998. Can-do unions: Competition brings out the best in government workers. *Policy Review* (March/April): 24–27.
Ingraham, Patricia Wallace. 1995. *The foundation of merit.* Baltimore: The Johns Hopkins University Press.
Johnson, Robin A., and Norman Walzer. 1996. *Competition for city services: Has the time arrived?* Springfield, IL: Office of the Comptroller.
Kettl, Donald F., Patricia W. Ingraham, Ronald P. Sanders, and Constance Horner. 1996. *Civil service reform: Building a government that works.* Washington, DC: Brookings Institution Press.
Kittower, Diane. 1998. Counting on competition. *Governing* (May): 63–74.
Mahtesian, Charles. 1999. Public pensions and privatization. *Governing* (September): 56.
The Mercer Group. 1997. *Privatization survey.* Atlanta: The Mercer Group.
O'Malley, Chris. 1999. AFSCME wins the chance to recruit employees from the private sector. *The Indianapolis Star* (May 15): C2.
Osborne, David, and Ted Gaebler. 1992. *Reinventing government: How the entrepreneurial spirit is transforming the public sector.* New York: Penguin Books.
Rehfuss, John A. 1989. *Contracting out in government.* San Francisco: Jossey-Bass.
Stevens, Barbara. 1984. *Delivering municipal services efficiently: A comparison of municipal and private service delivery.* Washington, DC: U.S. Department of Housing and Urban Development.

U.S. Department of Labor. 1991. *Employment cost indexes and levels 1975–91.* Washington, DC: U.S. Department of Labor.

U.S. Department of Labor, National Commission on Employment Policy (NCEP). 1989. *The long-term implications of privatization.* Washington, DC: U.S. Department of Labor.

U.S. General Accounting Office (USGAO). 1985. *Department of Defense functions contracted out under OMB circular A-76: Costs and status of certain displaced workers.* Washington, DC: USGAO.

USGAO. 1997. *Privatization: Lessons learned by state and local government.* Washington, DC: USGAO.

Ward, Janet. 1998. The pros and cons of long-term privatization. *American City and County* (May): 54–78.

11

Impact on Public Organizational Structure and Behavior: Managed Competition and Privatization

Ed Sizer

Cities across the nation observed during the past two decades that businesses had to restructure in order to survive; they came to the obvious conclusion that local governments would have to do the same. Cities had to find new ways to manage with limited resources. Charlotte, North Carolina, was not, nor had it been, in financial trouble, nor did it want to be. Nevertheless, it did not wait but began a strategy to stay ahead of the curve and started cutting back in late 1990.

This chapter will detail Charlotte's innovative approach to restructuring city government through managed competition and privatization. It will examine the process of how the city determines services for restructuring, and will look at the benefits and drawbacks of Charlotte's innovations. Several case studies which involve managed competition where both the city and private contractors won competitions will also be included. Readers will be able to comprehend how the movement to managed competition and privatization has impacted Charlotte's organizational structure and relationships. First, it is helpful to provide a brief background on conditions that led to the restructuring of Charlotte's city government.

In the past, Charlotte had successfully used functional consolidations of city and county services to reduce costs, improve services, and save tax dollars. During the 1980s, more than 14 major service departments were consolidated, including Building Standards, Planning, Purchasing, Utility, Animal Control, Emergency Management, Crime Lab, Action Line, First Responder, E-911, Landfills, Veterans Service, Elections Office, Tax Listings, and Tax Collections. In the 1990s, Parks and Recreation and Police Services were added to the list of successful consolidations. Consolidations would not be enough, however.

RIGHTSIZING

Faced with the financial realities of the 1990s and the need to embark on a long-term organizational change process, the Charlotte city manager presented the concept of "rightsizing" to the city council in January of 1992. The premise for the rightsizing discussions was to ask the council the following question: "If we were to design city services anew today, what would they look like?"

Rightsizing was set up in two tracks: one for policy and one for management. Both radically and deliberately altered the organizational structure. The policy track was established in order for City Council to decide what services to provide and how they should be financed. The management track was established to evaluate alternatives on how to organize resources for effective service delivery and alternatives which could improve methods and/or reduce costs in the delivery of services.

The initial focus of the rightsizing program was to save money, flatten the organization, and rethink how the city conducts its business to better position itself in the future. Beyond saving needed money, rightsizing was very much a workforce initiative and not just a budget initiative. Rightsizing empowered employees to make decisions at the lowest appropriate level, and it promoted quality and excellence, accountability, productivity, teamwork, and openness in the workforce. Rightsizing provided the avenue to reshape all city departments and services by addressing four fundamental questions.

1. What services should city government provide?
2. How should services be financed?
3. How should resources be organized to deliver services effectively?
4. What is the most efficient method of providing city services?

The values and priorities of the community, not the organization, were now determining city services. Rightsizing reestablished the citizen and customer service as top priorities. The main goal now is to achieve 100 percent of the established customer service objectives. Highest priority is given to the services that serve customers directly. In order to make rightsizing successful and lasting, the city focused on training, communication and information, customer service, and technology and innovation. To further emphasize the importance of the rightsizing initiative and to promote employee training and high customer service, the training and customer service functions of the city were placed in the City Manager's Office.

In March, 1993, the following accomplishments were presented:

• Reduction of 272 positions, with no layoffs, representing $5.1 million in savings
• Employee innovations resulting in $2.8 million of additional savings
• Reductions in department layers of management to no more than five
• Employee teams to accommodate a smaller workforce and improve service delivery
• Establishment of a Customer Service Center
• Reorganization from departments to a focus on nine "Key Businesses" (KBs)
• Prioritization of city services resulting from a Services Assessment Process
• Investment in training for employees to manage change and acquire new skills
• Investment in technology to facilitate reduction in management, clerical, and administrative staff

MAYORAL TASK FORCES

Concurrent with the initiatives of rightsizing and the reorganization into KBs, Charlotte Mayor Richard Vinroot (1991–1995) established three citizen task forces to (1) review the city organizational structure, (2) review employee compensation plans, and (3) review and design a plan to test privatization of services and assets. The work of the mayor's Organization Task Force contributed to the reorganization into KBs. The Mayor's Compensation Task Force led to the implementation of Pay for Performance, a new Pay and Classification System called Broadbanding and Managed Health Care for employees. The determination of the Mayor's Privatization Task Force brought the concept of managed competition to City Hall.

The Privatization Task Force focused on the privatization interest that was sweeping across municipalities throughout the United States. The Privatization Task Force was asked to evaluate services and/or facilities provided and managed by the city of Charlotte and to determine whether they could be delivered more effectively and efficiently by the private sector. Mayor Vinroot and the Charlotte City Council can be credited with initiating what has evolved into the city's successful managed competition process.

After a year of studying the existing operations and evaluating competition/ privatization practices in other jurisdictions, the Privatization Task Force recommended that the City Council foster competition between the public and private sectors in providing municipal services. The mayor's Privatization Task Force stated in their final report, "Competition is the primary force that keeps private businesses efficient and focused on customer needs. The city should have to compete and perform in the same manner as demanded for private business to continue performing services." Shortly after receiving the mayor's Privatization Task Force Final Report in June

Figure 11.1
Organizational Chart Prior to September 1993

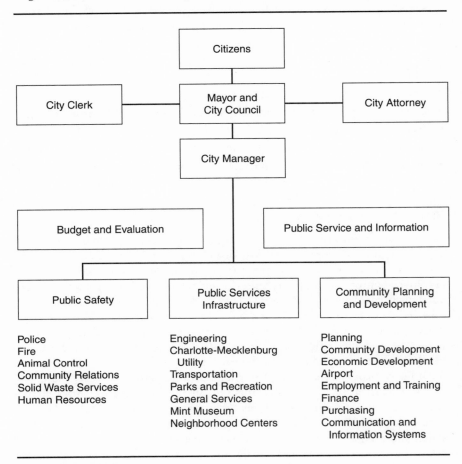

Source: City of Charlotte.

1993, Charlotte reorganized from 26 departments to nine KBs and four support businesses (Figures 11.1 and 11.2). With the change in the organizational structure, questions arose as to how the former departments— which were very focused on providing specific services—could be consolidated into larger and more encompassing service and support business units. In some cases, former departments became divisions of the new KBs. For example, the Equipment Management and Information Technology Departments became divisions in the key support business called Business Support Services.

Figure 11.2
Organizational Chart Today

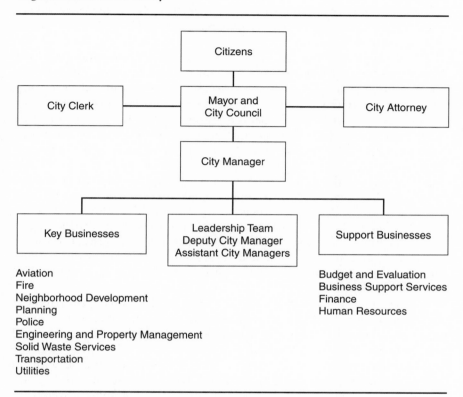

Source: City of Charlotte.

In order to refocus the organization around the nine KBs and the four support businesses, the city manager had the newly selected Key Business Executives (KBEs) develop business plans. The business plans were to include a vision and mission statement for each KB and outline what the KB Units would accomplish in the upcoming fiscal year, along with performance goals by which they could be measured. The business plan concept served the purpose of providing goals and direction for the KB Units, and it reinforced the city manager's initiative to bring private sector practices to government.

The business plans have evolved and become much wider in scope since they were first developed with the formation of the KB Units. Today, the business plans are the main tool by which the city manager conducts performance evaluations of the KBEs. The business plans are also the main reporting tool by which performance measurements for the Balanced Scorecard and City Council priorities are identified, tracked, and reported.

In October 1993, the City Council approved a policy statement and goals for services contracting that can be summed up as follows: "The city will seek the best service at the lowest cost either through city forces or the private sector. A competitive procurement process will determine who the service provider will be."

In November of 1993, the citizens' Privatization/Competition Advisory Committee (PCAC) was created to monitor the progress of implementing contracts for services, to recommend services to be considered for competition and privatization, and to advise on ways to improve current contracted services with service delivery problems. In July 1994, the City Council created services contracting guidelines, which were developed by staff and the PCAC, and which spelled out the steps in the competitive process.

Discussions of the potential impact that managed competition and the demands of a competitive marketplace might have on skilled, motivated employees led to the establishment of the Council's Employee Placement Policy in August 1994. The policy states that it is the city of Charlotte's goal to retain employees with good job performance and that in situations when employee positions are eliminated, every effort will be made to place employees who meet performance expectations and wish to continue with city employment.

In December 1994, after months of intense work involving employees at all organizational levels, the city's KBs released the first Five-Year Competition Plans. These plans, updated annually, established the competitive and outsourcing strategies for the next five years.

From May 1995 through June 1999, 52 different services, with an annual value of more than $18.5 million, were outsourced and 45 additional services, with an annual value of more than $24 million, were subjected to competition. The city employees' successes, not only in winning bids but actually performing the work for less than their bids, led to the City Council's approval of a Competition-Based Gainsharing Plan in June 1997.

The plan provides an employee incentive for exceeding performance and budget targets. All performance goals and budget expenditures must be achieved for employees to participate in the program. Expenditures are audited quarterly to determine operational savings below the bid amount. One-half of the savings are shared equally with employees. One-half of the savings remain with the bidding unit in a reserve account available for the purchase of new technology, employee training, and other items as needed. The distribution of incentives to employees is made quarterly with one-half of the total amount earned reserved for year-end distribution. The most recent plans developed by KBs for FY2000 through FY2004 identify 125 services, with an annual value of more than $64 million, targeted for competitive bidding or outsourcing.

MANAGED COMPETITION PROGRAM

Over the past several years, the city of Charlotte has implemented a managed competition program that has evolved and profoundly changed the way the city does business. It increased the efficiency and effectiveness of city services and resulted in significant cost-savings. Managed competition in Charlotte is an umbrella term for the host of activities contained in the city's competitive bid program. It entails a planned approach for service delivery, whether the service is outsourced (no public sector competition) or whether private sector firms are invited to compete against the public sector for the right to provide a specific service.

Managed competition is part of a larger strategy designed to address the problem of balancing scarce resources, little or no new revenues, and no property tax rate increases against escalating costs of and demands for city services. The city has not had a property tax rate increase since 1987, yet demands for and costs of services have continued to escalate, especially in four of the five highly visible and costly City Council focus areas.

Since 1995, the City Council has given priority to the following five focus areas: (1) Community Safety, (2) Transportation, (3) City-within-a-City, (4) Economic Development, and (5) Restructuring Government. The City Council further outlined some broad objectives for each area. These objectives helped provide staff with direction:

1. Community Safety—Provide public safety services to ensure that citizens feel safe; support programs which work to solve the root cause of crime and drug problems such as housing, jobs, and so on; and elicit the support of other organizations to reduce crime and the influence of drugs.
2. Transportation—Address the city's road and intersection improvement needs, accelerate sidewalk construction program; develop transit ways; and promote alternative methods of transportation.
3. City-within-a-City—Provide leadership and resources to make individuals and families self-reliant; and strengthen and revitalize deteriorated neighborhoods.
4. Economic Development—Support formation, retention, and expansion of business and initiatives that provide quality jobs.
5. Restructuring Government—Preserve the quality of life in the community through the fair and reasonable collection and balanced use of public funds; reduce dependence on the property tax as the major source of revenue; and improve business processes that strengthen the city's competitive position.

Managed competition also addresses the problems inherent in a monopoly. Whether it is private or public, a single service provider can foster an environment that stifles creativity, innovation, and a customer service orientation, while allowing inefficiency and higher costs. Until the program was put in place, the city had a monopoly on the provision of public services, many of which were services that the private sector firms also provided, including garbage collection, landscaping, operating water and wastewater treatment facilities, and building maintenance. Charlotte's managed competition program guidelines stipulate the following: "[T]he city shall use a competitive process in which private service providers are encouraged to compete with city business units for the opportunity to provide such services, and in which the option of delivering services through public employees and business units must be justified through the competitive bidding process." These guidelines effectively recognize and appropriately value the role of competition in the provision of public services.

Managed competition has fundamentally changed the way that the city does business. It developed a more entrepreneurial style of management and operation, incorporated strategic business plans into its overall operations, and adopted private sector costing and bidding methods.

Program Results and Policy Impact

The single most important achievement of managed competition has been to create a culture in which government is run like a business. This single achievement has enabled several other advances that can be attributed to this initiative. For example, managed competition required thinking about and approaching the public's business in new ways. City staff recognized early that if the city was to compete successfully, changes at all levels of the city organization were necessary.

Running the city government more like the private sector required several changes to existing practices. Traditional line-item budgeting was insufficient to capture costs, effect cost reductions, and enable service-delivery/reengineering improvements. The city implemented ABC and management to address this issue. ABC provides the framework in which KBs can identify the full costs for a specific activity or service level.

A citywide reorganization focusing on increasing overall accountability for service quality and cost efficiencies supported the change from traditional government to a more business-oriented approach. KBs were required to develop business plans. Decisions about human resources, budget, finance, and purchasing, formerly made by central administrative staff, were delegated to the KBEs. The change was significant and, in hindsight, critical to competing successfully with the private sector. KBs gained essential experience in business planning and operating more autonomously, making decisions about buying technology, redesigning jobs and service delivery systems, and reclassifying employees.

Some of the four support businesses established new working relationships with the nine KBs. Several support business units, such as the Business Support Service's fleet maintenance division, are entering into formal service agreements with the KBs they serve. All recognize their individual and collective contributions to the overhead costs of a specific service, and other city KBs have raised expectations for customer service.

New human resource policies mirroring the best private sector practices were developed to support the competitive culture. Employee gainsharing programs and incentives based on performance goals have been established. KBs were granted increased latitude in establishing new work schedules and modifying performance-based compensation guidelines. The city also committed substantial support to employee training programs that help employees develop new skills, stay current with technology, and participate in costing and process reengineering aspects of the managed competition program. This emphasis on skills development has enhanced service to citizens. It has also prepared employees for other employment opportunities within or outside the city organization.

MEASURES OF PROGRAM SUCCESS

The measures of success used in the managed competition activities are cost-savings, ability to fund high-priority service areas, new growth without new taxes, and the establishment of five-year competition plans. As Charlotte continues to grow both in population and size, the number of nonpublic safety employees per 1,000 population continues to decrease.

Recurring annual savings from managed competition, including those created by applying best practices learned by competing and controlling operating expenses through a process called optimization, were estimated at more than $11 million for FY99. Cost-savings from these and other city initiatives have enabled the city to reallocate resources to fund high-priority service areas by maintaining flat operating expenses since 1991 and without raising the property tax rate. A one-half cent property tax rate reduction was recommended for the FY2000 budget.

The impacts of the overall program are clearly revealed by comparing the changes that have occurred in staffing levels and payrolls in the Solid Waste and Police KBs (Figures 11.3 and 11.4) and in the reduction in the number of citywide support employees (Figure 11.5). Each KB—even Police and Fire—has a five-year competition plan which includes the following:

• A list of the services provided by the KB that are also available in the private sector
• A schedule for subjecting the services to competitive bidding or outsourcing
• Strategies for making the KB more competitive

Since 1994, the city has put 45 services out for competitive bid. Thirty-five contracts were awarded to city employees, and ten were outsourced to private firms. The following are some examples of new unit costs that have been reduced as a direct result of competition:

Figure 11.3
Impact of Competition on Number of Employees

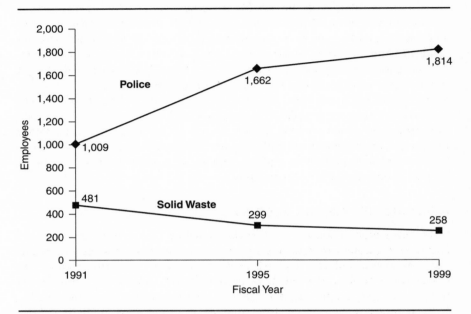

Source: City of Charlotte.

Service	Cost-Saving
Public Safety Vehicle Radio Installation	$162.00 per vehicle
Water Distribution Locate	$3.34 per locate
Specialized Transportation Services	$11.86 per customer trip
Street Tree Trimming (over 12" diameter)	$82.00 per tree
Residential Garbage Collection (4 basic services/week)	$6.48 per month
Residential Meter Reading	$0.40 per read
Multifamily Solid Waste Collection Services	$4.64 per dumpster/ $15.55 per compactor

During the next five years, 125 services with a total dollar value of $64 million are anticipated to be put out for competitive bid or outsourcing.

These plans have been instrumental in establishing the process of managed competition as a routine business approach. They enable the city to more effectively manage the process and coordinate the timing of competitive bids that impact one another (residential garbage collection and main-

Figure 11.4
Impact of Competition on Budget

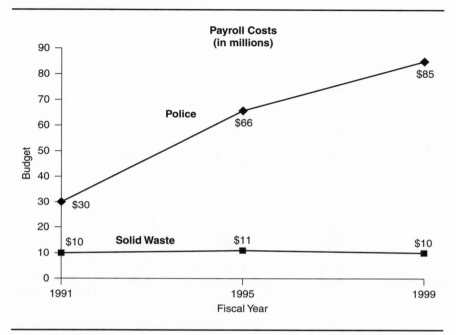

Source: City of Charlotte.

tenance of the city vehicle fleet). By anticipating competitive bid opportunities, the city can utilize a variety of strategies designed to maximize staffing flexibility and manage vacancies.

The city views every vacancy as an opportunity for change. If a position is determined to be essential, a KB may choose to contract for the position instead of hiring a full-time permanent employee. Taken together, these strategies increase the city's ability to plan for potential placements of high-performing employees in other vacant positions within the city if it chooses to outsource a service rather than compete, or if it loses a competitive bid. To date, 16 employees have been laid off, and the city has eliminated 837 nonpublic safety positions through managed competition. The remaining permanent positions that were eliminated included budgeted positions that were being held vacant, filled positions that were transferred to similar vacant positions in other service areas, and filled positions in which the employee was provided training to develop new skill sets and then placed in a vacant position within the city.

Figure 11.5
Impact of Support/Service Employees

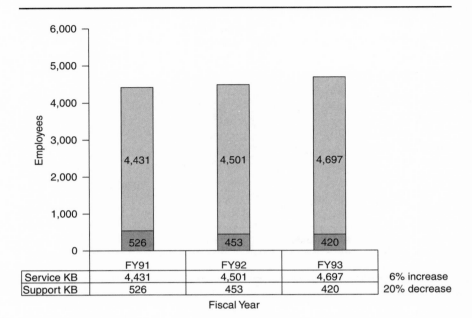

Source: City of Charlotte.

PROGRAM BENEFITS

The managed competition initiative is unique, and its effects are sweeping. It benefits all 522,000 residents of the city of Charlotte. By focusing on providing the best service at the lowest cost, managed competition enables the city not only to maintain a stable tax rate but also to reallocate the savings to fund high-priority service areas such as Community Safety and Transportation. Charlotte residents receive more and better services today than in 1987, the last time the property tax rate in Charlotte was increased. Public Safety and Transportation are two areas in which service enhancements are especially noteworthy.

As a by-product of the managed competition initiative, private sector organizations benefit from increased opportunities for services contracting. That is, private firms are invited to submit bids for services traditionally provided entirely by public entities (garbage collection, water and wastewater treatment plant operations, claims adjustments, vehicle maintenance, and special transportation service for people with disabilities). While these opportunities increase the total number of available contracting opportunities for private firms, the availability of such firms vary according to the specific service. In highly specialized areas such as electronic monitoring of red light intersections, only a handful of firms have the necessary expertise. In more routine service areas such as landscaping and grounds maintenance, there are a substantial number of potential private sector bidders.

MOST SIGNIFICANT REMAINING SHORTCOMINGS

Universal acceptance—in political, community, and city employee circles— of managed competition as the "right way" to provide public services has yet to solidify. There are those who believe privatization has no place in public service; private companies, they reason, have profit, not the public interest, at heart and would therefore gouge the unsuspecting taxpayer, leading to inflated costs for services and, perhaps, diminished quality.

There are those who maintain that the limits on the extent to which government can truly operate like a private business have led to the creation of policies and practices that look good on paper but do not bear up under the rigors of public sector scrutiny and everyday service delivery realities. Political decisions, and decisions based on the essential nature and role of government (i.e., for the common good), continue to supersede decisions made from a business perspective. On the other hand, some employees maintain that managed competition is a political tool simply designed to turn their jobs over to the private sector under the belief that the private sector is inherently better prepared to offer the services than the public sector. Taken together, these viewpoints, although diminishing with time, experience, and demonstrated results, remain a shortcoming of the program, preventing full acceptance of and participation in the process.

EVOLUTION OF THE PROGRAM IN CHARLOTTE

What began as a program favoring privatization has evolved to embrace public-private competition. Moreover, as the program has matured, the city government has grown in sophistication. Every competitive bid provides opportunities for organizational learning about all aspects of the bidding process, from developing RFPs and determining unit costs for service to reengineering service delivery methods and monitoring contractor (public or private) compliance with the established service expectations.

Earning the necessary trust and support of the CAC, and thus the City Council, has also been key to the evolution of the city's managed competition program. This committee has allowed city staff to demonstrate its ability to develop sound operational practices that can withstand the intense scrutiny of a very public and thorough review of any city bid. The committee remains committed to ensuring a fair and open process that has as its real beneficiary the citizens of the community.

Obstacles and Critics

Because the managed competition initiative requires substantial cultural and operating changes, most organizations will encounter obstacles to implementation. Charlotte's obstacles included overcoming employee resistance to change and fears of layoffs; acquiring the technical expertise to establish fully allocated costs for services; establishing credible evaluation, auditing, and monitoring processes; and dedicating the time to compete successfully.

The city dealt with these obstacles in several ways. An extensive employee education, information, and involvement plan was created to help employees adjust to and participate in implementing the necessary changes. The city hired outside experts to train staff in ABC methodology, to evaluate operating guidelines and competition methodology, to assist in developing RFPs, and to evaluate bids. Establishing the City Council-appointed PCAC was also key in providing credible evaluation, auditing, and monitoring. Five-Year Competition Plans provided the framework for establishing realistic timeframes for competitive processes.

The remaining obstacles include developing consistent application of and organizational proficiency with the costing methodology and the assignment of overheads to the city bid, producing timely cost information immediately after the end of a contract quarter, establishing clear service standards and plans for providing a service when a private contractor defaults on a contract, and developing written service delivery/quality standards for services for which no written standards existed because the city had always provided the service.

The most significant critics of the city's public-private competition program have been certain private sector contractors. Unsuccessful private bidders have claimed that the city had not accurately captured all costs of a service (a claim that independent evaluations dispute). These private firms have also argued that the competitive playing field favors the city because it pays no taxes and does not have to make a profit.

Others, including some employees and elected officials, are critical of the program because it disproportionately impacts minorities. A significant percentage of the services subjected to competition are in areas in which a majority of employees are African American (street maintenance, garbage collection, grounds maintenance, and water and sewer line installation and repair).

The program receives additional criticism from some elected officials, members of the PCAC, and citizen government watchdog groups who argue that the city should be competing major services more quickly and in larger amounts.

The city organization is continuing its education efforts to address the costing methodology and is establishing clear performance criteria and recovery plans when a contractor defaults. Similarly, as KBs prepare to competitively bid a service, staff members are developing written descriptions detailing all of the various components that make up a specific service.

Challenges

The city of Charlotte's success in winning bids per se brings about a list of new challenges. How, for instance, does one continue to keep the private sector interested in bidding for a certain service in "round 2 or 3" if the city has won previous competitions by a large margin? City officials have found that by involving the potential vendors before, during, and after the competitive process and by seeking their advice and suggestions throughout, the city is able to keep the private sector's interest. This results in a better overall process and product for the end customer, the taxpayer. For example, vendors are invited and encouraged to provide comments on draft Request for Qualifications (RFQs) and RFPs prior to issuance. Comments received are subsequently reviewed by staff and the PCAC for possible inclusion in the final documents.

In addition, after bids are received, an attempt is made to interview both the vendors that bid and those that chose not to bid to learn what caused the spread in bid amounts and why firms chose not to submit a bid. To the extent possible, lessons learned are incorporated in the next round of competitions for that and other services.

A similar challenge is to keep employees motivated in "round 2" when they feel their opportunity to win is lower, if not impossible, now that their total costing for the previous contract is public information and available to all for the asking. In all cases, employees have never bid their work exactly as they have previously performed it, and in most cases, they have performed the work for less than their bid. The same opportunities still exist in "round 2"—although some feel they are greatly diminished—and they continue to have the advantages of not having to include a profit or the payment of taxes in their proposals.

A third challenge, the solution for which is not known, is to find the right mix of bundling smaller services together for larger contracts to attract major companies and drive overall costs down, while at the same time trying to satisfy the conflicting goal of having smaller contracts to increase minority contractor participation. Large contracts also tend to include more of the city overhead costs in city bids and thereby make the private bids more competitive.

Help and Support along the Way

Early in the process, the Reason Foundation became both a major source of information about how the practice worked in other cities and a champion of Charlotte's emerging competition program. The cities of Phoenix and Indianapolis provided invaluable best practices and lessons-learned information that laid the groundwork for Charlotte's competition policy development. The mayor's Privatization Task Force of citizens was key in establishing the business case for a competitive process, and the PCAC has been integral in the development of the services contracting guidelines. This committee has become a strong supporter of city efforts in the area of managed competition. The City Council provides ongoing policy guidance and support for bid award recommendations.

ADAPTATION OF OTHER PROGRAMS

While the city of Charlotte has certainly borrowed from among the best practices exhibited in municipalities across the country, services contracting is not new to Charlotte. Like most other local governments, Charlotte has contracted with the private sector to provide many services for some time. As early as 1978, the city began outsourcing such services as street resurfacing, business garbage collection, multifamily garbage collection (1980), custodial services (1984), golf course management (1985), and ground maintenance (1986). Many of these services have just recently appeared on the privatization "radar screens" of other municipalities. In FY95, Charlotte awarded a total of $204 million in service and construction contracts to the private sector, up from $151 million the previous year. Charlotte improved on the practice of outsourcing by injecting public-private competition into the equation. The result has been a more streamlined, cost-efficient, and customer service-oriented government.

CITY COST EVALUATION AND REPLICATION

The city of Charlotte routinely subjects each competitively bid service to independent evaluation and audit. These evaluations are provided by the city's Internal Audit Division, the PCAC, and, in some cases, additional outside consultants. For example, the Raftelis Environmental Consulting Group provided an independent formal evaluation of the competition for operations and maintenance of water treatment and wastewater treatment plants (April 1996) and of the competition for the second quarter of the residential garbage collection contract (March 1997). Each review of every bid provides evaluative commentary on the process as a whole—the general approach, the guidelines, costing, and customer service.

In addition, Coopers & Lybrand was retained in early 1995 to evaluate the city's cost allocation/costing methodology. The firm reviewed the Guidelines for Services Contracting and the Cost Allocation Plan (how budgeted overhead costs are allocated to KBs), conducted employee interviews, and compared the methodology to commonly accepted industry practices. The Coopers & Lybrand review of April 18, 1995, found the following to be true: "The city's methodology is sound and is accomplishing the goal of rewarding those with good [insurance] loss experience and penalizing those with poor experience. . . . [T]he methodology is very responsive to claims experience and does not limit individual large losses."

The review recommended minor revisions to the Cost Allocation Projections ($29,218) that would then provide fully allocated overhead costs. It recommended changes to the standards for funding insurance losses and establishing limits for individual losses. The review also supported the city's expansion of ABC, stating, "[the expansion] is expected to improve overhead allocations further, provide more traceability of overhead costs and provide more definitive cost information to KB unit managers to help support their bid analyses."

Replicable within Other Jurisdictions

The managed competition program in Charlotte is quite replicable. City staff have fielded requests from municipalities from the United States, Canada, and abroad to assist in developing similar programs.

The process, including adopting operating guidelines, preparing the organization for competition, developing competition plans and timetables for competitive bidding, benchmarking services, drafting and responding to RFPs, evaluating bids, and monitoring contracts, is both logical and extensively documented. The guidelines for services contracting are clear. The costing methodology, while complex, is readily adaptable.

A key component to success in replicating this program is in establishing sound internal support systems (human resources, financial, general ledger) and credible, independent oversight with an outside committee like the PCAC.

The managed competition program has an annual operating budget of $50,000 (100% General Fund) to support the PCAC and $14,000 (100% General Fund) for staff support for the committee (Figure 11.6).

The lessons learned are too numerous to list, but here are just a few:

- There is no "cookie cutter" approach to the managed competition process.
- All services and their delivery methods are somewhat different. Some are equipment intensive, and some are labor intensive; consequently, the same approach to costing, RFP development, performance criteria, and gainsharing will not work for all.
- Experimenting is okay. Trying new work methods, equipment, and technology is encouraged prior to developing the RFP and bidding the work.
- Citizens must be involved as problem solvers. Citizens coming from a private sector environment bring an entirely new perspective to the table when discussing everything from the assignment of overhead to making a business decision such as to whom to award a contract.

Figure 11.6
Competition Process Overview

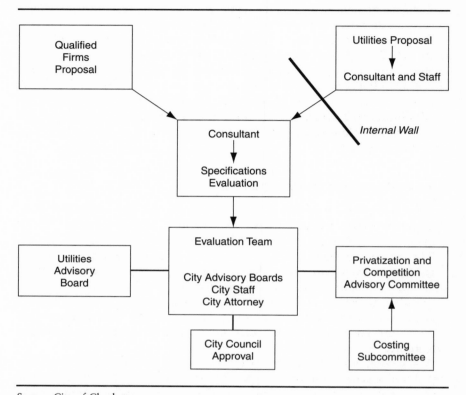

Source: City of Charlotte.

- Know your competition. Benchmarking with the private sector and contracting out a portion of the service to observe how they perform are just two approaches we have used to learn more about the private sector.

- Know your customers' expectations. Staying in tune with your customer is critical. Ensure that they have first-hand knowledge of what you are considering and are aware of all potential impacts contracting out may have on service delivery. Encourage their input in RFP development.

- Involve employees early. The grapevine is not the place for employees to learn that their jobs are in jeopardy. It is our experience that the best suggestions on how to reduce costs and become more competitive have come from employees.

- Involve Human Resources early. You should give HR as much lead time as possible to assist in the process of workforce reduction and employee placement in other departments when bidding a smaller workforce or if the city should lose the bid.

- You can do more with less. Time after time, internal bids have been significantly less than the historic/budgeted cost, and on several occasions, the private sector bid has been even lower.

- RFPs can be tricky. If the work has always been performed by city employees, writing the RFP can be very difficult. Check around and find a copy of a successful document from another city or other source. Don't be bashful, and don't forget that if the city wins, it must meet all of the requirements placed on the private sector bidders.

- Know the costs. To succeed, practitioners must be able to determine and be willing to disclose the total costs for the work even though only the "go away" costs actually end up in the bid. Once employees know the costs involved in performing the work, they will become strong advocates for cost reduction and be very vocal in pointing out areas for possible reductions.

- Costing is always an issue. Costing city services is and will always be an issue in the preparation and evaluation of bids. Overhead costs are currently the center of discussion.

MYTHS

Some of the common myths of the managed competition process include the following:

- "Experts" have all the answers. Experts do have some of the answers, but, in fact, most of the answers to the hard questions are readily available, using city staff and employees as resources.

- Thicker RFPs are better. Thinner RFPs with fewer detailed directions for service delivery allow for more creative and entrepreneurial ideas to be introduced by employee bid teams and private sector bidders.

- Large scale changes can occur without affecting employee morale. Employee morale will quickly become an issue anytime that change is introduced. The city must develop a plan of action to deal with it.

- Once all employees understand the vision and plan, they will play. The competition effort is intense, and keeping employees involved on a daily basis to keep them in the game is just one part of it.

- Teams always work. Teams must be given the opportunity to fail and fail again before they succeed. Some will never succeed in this environment.

- Once you have achieved the necessary results, further change is not required. Getting the results you predicted is just the first step. Not only must they be duplicated time after time, but process improvement and additional cost reductions are generally necessary to retain the work in the future. Competition is not just one leg of a 440 race; it's a marathon.

- Having all the answers to any and all employee questions is necessary. First of all, if the process must wait until all of the answers are known, it will never start, and soon the employees will be out of business. Answers will come as city officials and employees work through the process, and the answers will be right for that service at that time.

- Departures from the plan will fail. How many times has a detour on a well-planned trip resulted in a better experience for travelers? The same is true with managed competition. Don't be afraid to try new things or to go in new directions in an effort to create a better product. The results may be astounding.

- Communication is essential. One of the most important keys to this process is to Communicate, Communicate, Communicate, and then Communicate again.

CASE STUDY—WATER TREATMENT PLANT

The Charlotte-Mecklenburg Utility KB (Utilities) is the largest public utility providing water and sewer services in the state of North Carolina. It serves a population of more than 555,000 in the city of Charlotte and Mecklenburg County. It has more than 170,000 service connections and 5,650 miles of pipeline and operates three water plants and five wastewater treatment plants with an annual operating budget of $100 million and 729 employees.

The Vest Water Treatment Plant, a 24.8 million-gallons-per-day facility, was selected for managed competition for two reasons: (1) the scope of work for the operation and maintenance of this facility could be readily identified and (2) no major construction was planned for the facility within the proposed contract period.

The primary goals of the competition included determining the most cost-effective service provider, promoting competition from the private sector, utilizing objective evaluation criteria, and establishing a level playing field. An internal wall (Figure 11.7) was established within Utilities to separate those assigned to work with the procurement documents and proposal evaluation (procurement team) from those preparing the staff proposal (bid team). Separate outside consultants were retained for each group to assist throughout the process.

A two-step process was used. Ten firms responded to the RFQs. An RFP, while still in draft form, was issued to give the proposers an opportunity to provide comments concerning content and format. The final RFP was issued to the nine qualified firms, and six of these submitted proposals. Proposals were reviewed and evaluated by a six-person evaluation team, which included two citizen members from the PCAC and the Utilities Advisory, two nonutilities city staff members, and two members of the utility's management staff. Technical support for proposal evaluation was provided by an outside consultant.

CMCon-Op (the city bidding unit) submitted the lowest bid for the Vest plant operations contract. The net present values of annual fees submitted for the five-year contract ranged from a low of $2.5 million to a high of $5.5 million with a second lowest bid of $3.2 million. The CMCon-Op bid,

Figure 11.7
Solid Waste Positions, FY94–FY99

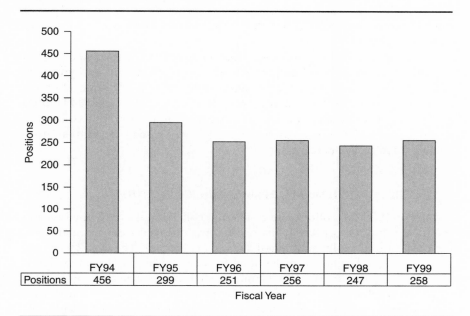

Positions	FY94	FY95	FY96	FY97	FY98	FY99
Positions	456	299	251	256	247	258

Fiscal Year

Source: City of Charlotte.

which represented a savings of $194,000 below the current budget, included all direct and variable costs associated with the performance of the contract; an allocation for capital costs, including depreciation and financing costs, for capital equipment and assets; and an allocation for semivariable and fixed costs that could be affected by the level of services provided by the city internally. To position themselves to win, they visited private plant sites, reduced personnel, reduced chemical and utility costs, increased training, increased automation, and included a provision for employee gainsharing incentives. All of these efforts resulted in significant cost-savings.

After careful consideration, CMCon-Op's proposal was selected. A Memorandum of Understanding (MOU) between the city and CMCon-Op formalized the RFP and proposal terms. It established the employee gainsharing program and required that the plant be operated and maintained according to the provisions set forth in the RFP and the CMCon-Op proposal.

In addition, the proposal requires that CMCon-Op maintain and report the financial and operational records necessary to determine that it is operating and maintaining the plant in accordance with the provisions of the RFP, the MOU, and the proposal. Reports are produced quarterly and audited by the city's Internal Audit division prior to being reviewed by the PCAC and Utility Advisory Committee. The plant has operated for $241,000 less than the contract amount during the first two-and-a-half years. That savings created $65,000 in gainsharing that has been distributed to employees.

In a process called optimization, the same principles used and lessons learned were applied to six additional plants and produced an immediate additional annual savings of $2.1 million and a staff reduction of 23 positions without layoffs. Total savings from these seven plants enabled Utilities to reduce the projected rate of cost increase for its 180,000 residential water/sewer customers from approximately five to seven percent to approximately three to five percent.

CASE STUDY—SOLID WASTE RESIDENTIAL COLLECTION

Prior to 1994, all solid waste residential collection was provided by city employees. In October 1994, the service was changed from manual backyard collection to fully automated curbside collection. The first 25 percent of residential collection was identified for competition in December 1994. The following month, the City Council voted to privatize that same quadrant. The resulting five-year contract with two possible one-year renewals was awarded to the private sector for $5.66 per household per month. The first year proposal was $70,000 less than the city's benchmark cost and resulted in a savings of $490,000 over the term of the contract and a reduction of 44 full-time positions.

Solid Waste competed for the second 25 percent, submitted the low bid, and was awarded the contract in June 1997. The city bid of $4.74 per household per month, as compared to the low private sector bid of $8.36, produced an annual savings of $542,000 below the previous budget for the work. Through the first nine months of the contract, employees performed at $72,000 below their bid and were awarded $36,000 in employee gainsharing.

Competition for the third 25 percent of residential service (approximately 45,000 residential units) was held recently with the city submitting a low bid of $6.28 per household per month. The city bid was $1,000,000 less than the budget, and significantly below the low private sector bid of $7.71 per household per month.

Proposals for the fourth and final 25 percent of the city were opened in October 1999 and are currently under review for award of contract. The city submitted the apparent low bid of $5.63 per household per month for the 45,000 residential units. The city bid was $1,900,000 a year less than the low private sector bid of $8.90 per household per month and $1,500,000 less than the current city budget for the service area.

CASE STUDY OF VEHICLE MAINTENANCE

The city fleet is one of the largest in the Southeast with a total of 3,600 units. The replacement value of the fleet is approximately $100 million. With the exception of Transit Buses and Aviation Department vehicles, the entire fleet was covered by the competition.

The city's Equipment Management Division (EMD) recently won a competition with private sector firms for the right to continue providing vehicle maintenance services to the city of Charlotte. EMD incorporated several private sector business strategies and practices in its winning bid, including performance-based pay, self-directed work teams, and profit sharing. Several lessons were learned from the competitive process, including the importance of organizing for competition, designing business-like cost structures, knowing your competition, and being proactive in approach to the work.

Public sector employees are not accustomed to competing for their jobs, while private sector competitors are skilled at competition and continuously seek opportunities to expand their business. In order to survive in this environment, employees and managers had to think private and seek to maximize the inherent advantages that existed as a nonprofit governmental agency.

The competitive process for vehicle maintenance services began with an issuance of the RFQ. Two private firms and the city's EMD were found to meet the qualifications. Two private firms were found to not meet the required qualifications which included a review of experience with large, diverse fleets and financial strength. The RFP was then drafted and after much review was issued.

Seven of the more important provisions of the RFP were as follows: (1) a three-year contract term with a possibility of two one-year renewals, (2) that fleet asset management services remain with the city, (3) no guaranteed monopoly of city customers, (4) contractor must use city's Fleet Management Information System, (5) contractor is under no obligation to hire existing city staff, (6) city's four shop facilities provided for $1 per year, and (7) financial incentives were established for exceeding performance standards in three areas along with liquidated damages for failure to meet standards.

The EMD bid team consisting of the division director, the vehicle maintenance manager, a mechanic, the division's business manager, and a member of the city HR staff hired a consultant to identify noncompetitive practices and to assist the bid team in proposal preparation. The bid team focused on adopting several private sector business practices that improved the EMD competitive position. They included the following practices: (1) fewer/higher paid staff reducing from a high of 90 to a bid of 67 with a fleet increase of 12 percent, (2) fewer supervisory and support staff with four positions eliminated, (3) requirement of Automotive Service Excellence

(ASE) certifications, (4) use of self-directed work teams to facilitate the reduction in supervisory and support staff, (5) increased overtime and training budgets, and (6) incentive pay and performance bonuses.

A second outside consultant was retained by the Evaluation Team to provide technical expertise. Proposals were evaluated in terms of the three-year net present value of the fixed bid for target services, transition costs, and an estimate of nontarget services costs based upon the rate structure contained in the bids and the historical experience of the city.

The EMD team submitted the lowest bid for the three terms at $24.1 million, followed by the private sector bids of $26.2 and $27.4 million, respectively. The city EMD team was subsequently awarded the contract through a MOU issued by the city manager.

The EMD team concluded that participating in a managed competition is a very informative process in that every aspect of the operation must be examined in detail for relevance, efficiency, effectiveness, and cost. Bidders must sharpen their understanding of the customers' business requirements and also take steps to understand competitors' strengths and weaknesses. Finally, bidders must develop new sets of skills in areas such as marketing, advanced customer service techniques, business planning, profit and loss analysis, team building, finance and accounting, contract monitoring, and incentive pay plans. To succeed in a competitive environment, public sector managers and employees who do not traditionally have these skill sets must obtain them quickly.

EMD learned eight specific lessons in the process of winning the competition. Most lessons learned relate to the themes detailed in the preceding paragraph and include the following: (1) we are not the shop, the garage, or maintenance; we are asset managers in charge of delivering essential mobility services to our customers; (2) a thorough and intimate understanding of all of cost factors is essential; (3) competition can come from many sources; (4) know the competition and how your organization compares; (5) agencies must organize for competition; (6) bidders must be customer-centered throughout the debate over competition; (7) be proactive, get out in front of the trend, and become experts in this field; and (8) involve employees early on and throughout the process.

CONCLUSION

In the city of Charlotte, progressive leaders have had to use a variety of management tools and techniques in the 1990s to meet service challenges and remain competitive, adjusting and tailoring these methods to meet their organization's unique needs. In practical terms, the hierarchical chain of command is dissolved and empowered KBEs are charged with running their enterprises like corporate CEOs. No longer department heads, each KBE now thinks in terms of "How do I run my business?"

Charlotte has used compensation and team training to develop a workforce that we believe is competitive, promotes collaborative problem solving, and has the capacity to rethink service delivery methods. The payoff is in the revitalized, results-oriented organizational culture that has emerged, and the citizens can see the payoff in the city's ability to maintain service levels without raising taxes.

Has it "worked?" Charlotte's workforce is providing quality services, and it is being done at a competitive cost. The results are encouraging, even compelling in some cases. The Utilities KB looked at how the private sector operated, changed their staffing configuration, used new supervisory techniques, and submitted a competitive bid for a water and wastewater plant that was 20 percent below the previous annual budget. The Solid Waste KB looked at the bottom line, examined costs, and changed the way they did business—the cost today is less than it was twenty years ago.

These changes have truly transformed "the way we do business." Simply put, the city is doing business in a new way.

12

A Bold, Innovative Approach to Privatization: Lessons Learned from Atlanta

Bill Campbell

The word "historic" is overused in our soundbite culture; however, the recent public-private partnership the city of Atlanta entered into is just that. The twenty-year contract with United Water Services makes history as Atlanta becomes the largest city in the United States to privatize its water system. This sweeping contract, which will provide the city with savings of up to 44 percent when fully implemented, is the result of a tumultuous twenty-month process to select one of five contractors for the $21.4 million per year agreement.

During the past two years, city officials from around the world have carefully watched Atlanta to see the process unfold and whether privatization delivers its promised benefits. Atlanta is, in effect, a living laboratory and case study for the largest urban privatization in America.

The two most compelling issues for every city in the nation during the next ten years will be crime—always number one—and infrastructure repair. As privatization of infrastructure and other local services becomes a viable option for more cities, officials will look for successful strategies to adapt to local circumstances. This chapter examines Atlanta's approach to privatization, including the operations assessment conducted; the process used to evaluate contractors and select the winning bidder; the innovative contract; and lessons learned throughout the process. But first, it is necessary to explore the factors that led the city to consider privatization.

BACKGROUND

Atlanta's population is slightly more than 400,000, an increase of approximately 10,000 from 1990. The metropolitan area is the 11th largest in the nation, with a population of nearly three million. Population growth in the Atlanta metro area since 1990 is among the fastest in the nation.

The budget for Atlanta's municipal government is approximately $2 billion. In spite of a rising population and increased demand for services, the city has been able to make government more efficient by reducing the workforce and by implementing the concept of Quality Service Improvement (QSI) at all levels of city government. Reinventing the government has helped improve the financial picture with increased revenues and a reduction of property taxes by 40 percent.

Atlanta's Department of Water provides water service to approximately 1.5 million people in the metropolitan area. Three treatment plants and a 2,400-mile distribution system service the region. In 1996, the year before the operations assessment program began, the Department of Water had a staffing level of 763 positions and an annual operating budget of approximately $49.5 million.

Responsibility for wastewater services is divided into two divisions of the Department of Public Works: (1) the Division of Wastewater Services operates and maintains three treatment plants and combined sewer overflows and (2) the Sewer Division maintains more than 2,000 miles of sanitary and combined sewers and serves a population of about 1.2 million. In 1996, annual operating costs for the Wastewater Services Division were $33.9 million and operating costs for the Sewer Division were $15.1 million. Total employment in the two divisions that year was 705.

After decades of neglect, it fell upon my administration to face the reality that hundreds of millions of dollars of investments were needed to comply with increasingly stringent mandates while maintaining a system that offers citizens the highest quality service. The city had been paying approximately $7.2 million annually in environmental fines for inappropriate discharges. During my administration, the city had already spent $1.3 billion to upgrade the water and sewer systems that included the following among other things:

- The Urban Watershed Initiative, in which the city cooperates with other stakeholders in the region to improve water quality in local streams
- The Light Construction and Debris Removal Program, a massive clean-up of 1,000 locations at creeks, streams, and drainage areas to improve the flow of water and prevent flooding
- The completion of two combined sewer overflow facilities, eliminating all fines previously imposed by the EPA
- The reduction of phosphorous discharges to the lowest levels in Atlanta's history

In spite of these investments, the city still needed an additional $1.2 billion to complete the job, making privatization an increasingly attractive option.

In March of 1996, the Georgia General Assembly passed Senate Bill 500 which imposed strict mandates on the city of Atlanta. To comply with the new regulations, the city had to expand and upgrade the three main wastewater treatment plants.

After analyzing various rate studies, city experts determined that an 81 percent increase would be necessary to pay for improvements to the wastewater treatment plants. If this were to happen, it would provide an unbearable financial burden on citizens and system users. Not surprisingly, news of the estimated rate increases brought strong opposition from the business community and many citizens.

Continued increases in rates were not an option for me either. Atlanta had the third lowest rates out of 17 surrounding counties, and I wanted to keep it that way. Given our city's large percentage of senior citizens and low-income residents, large rate increases would be unacceptable, not to mention immoral.

In February 1997, I announced that the city would explore privatization as an alternative to the massive rate increases. As part of an effort to keep city employees informed of all developments, I sent an open letter to all Water and Sewer Department employees regarding the problems and choices facing the city and raised the issue of privatization.

WHY PRIVATIZATION WORKS FOR ATLANTA

One of the things I heard while campaigning for mayor was a desire for a more efficient government. In order to achieve this goal, it is important to remain open to all management strategies. Privatization is one such strategy whose time has come. It will allow Atlanta to take advantage of the private sector's expertise while maintaining control of rates and refocusing our energies on other areas.

Privatization has often been posited as a cure for all the problems confronting government. I disagree. Privatization is a tool that should be applied only after careful analysis. During the past three years, with the guidance of technical experts, the city of Atlanta reached the following conclusion: Privatization of our water system was the right thing to do. In fact, more and more cities are currently exploring the option.

The EPA estimates that local governments will need nearly $350 billion in capital investment to maintain, upgrade, and expand the nation's water and wastewater systems during the next twenty years. Because of reduced levels of federal funding, the burden of raising these funds falls almost entirely on local governments. That is why cities must look to the private sector for innovative partnerships and capital needed to protect public health and the environment.

During the past twenty years, there has been substantial growth in public-private water partnerships. This is a result of growing investment requirements, shrinking local government financial resources, and regulatory compliance issues. As a recent survey by the U.S. Conference of Mayors clearly shows, these trends are continuing. According to the survey of 261 cities, 40 percent of officials responding said that they have some form of private sector participation in their water and wastewater systems. Of those that do not currently have public-private partnerships, 14 percent of water systems and 11 percent of wastewater systems are actively considering private sector involvement. There are several explanations for the surge in interest:

- *Finances.* Money remains the most important factor in the drive to privatize. In many cities around the United States, new plans have recently been put in place for needed upgrades to municipal water and wastewater systems. The big question is how to pay for these capital improvements, as well as rising operating and debt service costs, with the least impact on ratepayers. As municipal bond financing gets tighter for some cities, many are looking to receive "savings" up-front through private sector efficiencies so they can access cash for needed capital investment. Such concession fee arrangements have been adopted recently in Cranston, Rhode Island, and Danbury, Connecticut. Other cities are looking to private sector operators to make direct capital investments in municipal water systems.

- *Environmental Compliance.* Some municipalities have systems that are so old and outdated that they are out of compliance with state and federal regulations. Consent orders and fines are one motivation that can cause cities to seek assistance from the private sector.

- *Political Acceptance.* Leadership from the mayor's office continues to be a key factor in the growth of privatization. Cities need a clear, committed champion eager to demonstrate the benefits of this choice. From Indianapolis to Milwaukee to Chicago, privatization succeeds because of the leadership of dynamic municipal officials.

- *Start Small.* In spite of the benefits, many municipalities will never privatize operations of their water or wastewater systems; however, they may still need to buy equipment as well as engineering design and construction services from the private sector as they meet the requirements for plant reinvestment or growth. Many of these jobs are small and have typically gone to local engineering and equipment contractors, but consolidated equipment and service firms are now trying to establish themselves as turnkey suppliers. They believe that they will be in a better position than the traditional engineering and construction firms if the city does decide to privatize some services in the future.

No matter how much a city grows, there's one constant dynamic: water. Cities can grow without land because you can simply build up rather than out. Cities can even grow with bad zoning. Water, obviously, is indispensable.

The question that arose during consideration of the historic partnership agreement in Atlanta was, "How could the private sector deliver a level of savings that could help us avoid massive rate increases?" The answer is that the private sector does things smarter, faster, and cheaper. For example, contract operations in water and wastewater usually save 30 percent from consumables such as chemicals and electricity and 40 percent from both labor and maintenance improvements. Private firms can react quicker to changes in technology and adapt faster to the latest trends in management and computerization. They are more nimble because they face daily competition. If private firms are not able to effectively compete, they go out of business or are sold. If a public entity is not able to compete and faces financial difficulties, it either looks to raise taxes or reduce services. It comes down to incentives, competition, and choice—factors more common in the private sector.

As the reality of Atlanta's infrastructure problems and financial limitations set in, it became clear that we faced two options to pay for the necessary investments: (1) either continually raise customer rates or (2) find ways to save money. We chose privatization because we can do more with less and maintain our competitiveness. It would help generate the funds needed for nearly $1 billion in immediate capital improvements to the water and sewer systems without unduly increasing user rates. Privatization would also allow Atlanta to continue monitoring the management of its water system but without distracting it from other pressing management needs. The next step was to design a process to properly consider privatization and its ramifications.

PRIVATIZATION PROCESS

A city, or any government entity, doesn't just move swiftly into a privatization initiative. It requires extensive research, preparation, and analysis. The process we designed in Atlanta has been among the most scrutinized and carefully planned in history (Figure 12.1). In fact, it has been the most open process I have been associated with in my nearly 18 years in government.

As someone with a strong commitment to ethics, the process was as important to me as the final decision. A piece of legislation I helped pass during my 12 years on the City Council, the one of which I am most proud, is the comprehensive Ethics in Government package. It includes income disclosure requirements and conflict of interest rules governing all elected and appointed officials and employees. It is regarded as one of the toughest ethics laws of any municipality in the country. Because of the sensitivity of the privatization issue, I wanted to guarantee a process that guided the city toward a decision while maintaining the highest ethical standards.

The city of Atlanta developed a two-phase plan to address the various system challenges faced and to determine the best operational focus for reengineering and cost-saving measures. Phase I considered current operations, development and analysis of alternatives, and presentation of conclusions. Phase II focused on implementation and included development of

Figure 12.1
Analytical Approach Frames Evaluation

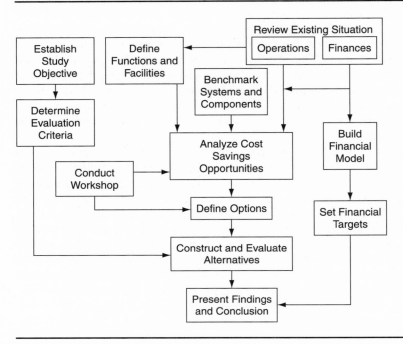

Sources: Brown and Caldwell; PricewaterhouseCoopers; Long Aldridge & Norman; Presentation at National Council for Public-Private Partnership (NCPPP) Conference, Atlanta, October 1998.

detailed schedules and plans, refinement of savings estimates, and initiation of a phased implementation.

There were several key factors that the city took into consideration in evaluating operations and cost-saving alternatives. Two conditions were put forward up-front: (1) that there would be no sale of assets and (2) that the city would maintain control over rates. These provisions were designed to protect the public interest and demonstrate the city's resolve to maintain control over the process. Other factors considered included degree of risk, track record, ease and speed of implementation, employee impacts, maintenance or improvements of service quality, and limitations of local and state statutes.

Other influences drove the direction and speed of city efforts as well. For example, the city faced fines for delays in combined sewer overflow construction. In addition, a large bond issue was needed to fund further water and sewer system improvements. Finally, the historic nature of privatizing the water system in one of the nation's largest cities would draw attention from the media as well as the state and federal governments. Media and public scrutiny could be positive for the city but could also increase pressure on city officials to make the right choices and conduct an open and fair process.

The independent technical consultants completed the Phase I assessment of the city's water, wastewater, and sewer systems in October 1997. Eight possible alternatives for cost-savings in operations were contained in the report, including outsourcing, privatization, and reengineering. The report highlighted ways for the city to improve performance, increase efficiency, and eliminate waste in business processes and operations. Reengineering would be applied to meet savings goals for functions or operations that were not proposed for private contract management. The path selected was a blend of the various alternatives that balanced all of our requirements with the overriding goal of cost-savings. We decided to contract out the entire water system for twenty years, as well as our largest water reclamation plant and reengineer the remainder of the wastewater treatment and sewer divisions.

The next step was to develop procurement and evaluation systems for the water contract. An aggressive schedule for water system contract management began with issuing the RFQ/RFP in late March 1998, with City Council approval slated for the following October. It included a three-step process for water system procurement. The city would select prequalified proponents who would submit technical and cost proposals in July. After the contractors submitted a best and final offer, city officials would select the top-ranked firm in late August.

Firms wishing to qualify had to have a minimum net worth of $100 million and demonstrate complete responsibility for operation and maintenance of a water system serving more than 250,000 persons. Candidates were also required to submit a $50,000 evaluation fee and have a $1 million proposal bond.

The technical and cost proposals were initially rated on a 100-point scoring system and judged by 12 teams. Teams involved in the evaluation process were chosen to examine the proposals on financial, legal, and technical grounds to ensure that they met the city's specifications. All five firms that submitted proposals were judged to be qualified for the best and final offer round of competition. In an effort to maintain an efficient and honest process, we conducted an open auction and provided first-round prices to local newspapers and technical bid summaries to each of the proposers.

The city included many important provisions in the RFQ/RFP. For example, one of the stipulations was that the winning proponent had to retain city employees for at least three years. Employee protection was judged by city officials to be a high priority—not only in terms of jobs, but benefits as well. At the end of the three-year period, the city pledged to give any employee displaced by privatization job placement priority within other city government agencies.

The RFQ/RFP also included incentives and penalties for water quality performance. With the city's history of noncompliance with environmental regulations and payment of millions of dollars in fines, it was vital to seek assurance that the contractor would provide performance guarantees and include provisions for penalties. Other key provisions in the RFQ/RFP included shared savings for new capital projects, utility pass-through costs, design/build options, and termination for convenience.

The best and final proposal stage included a 70-point scoring system for the competing plans. Each key area, possible points, and breakdowns are listed in Figure 12.2. A value index was also devised to determine greatest overall value to the city for the competing proposals. The value index bal-

Figure 12.2
Step Three: Best and Final Proposal Selection

■ **Quality of Technical Approach**   **20 points**
  • Operations and Management Plan, Staffing Plan, Innovative
    Technologies   10 points
  • Maintenance Management System and Customer Information
    System   5 points
  • Customer Relations; Interaction with Regulatory Agencies,
    the Public, and the City   5 points

■ **Quality of Management Team**   **20 points**
  • Organization and Staffing   10 points
  • General Manager and Key Staff Resources   10 points

■ **Equal Business Opportunity Plans**   **15 points**
  • Mentor-Protégé or JV Agreement   10 points
  • Subcontracting Plan and Supplier Plan   5 points

■ **Employee Relations and Transition Plan**   **10 points**
  • Plan for Smooth Transition for Affected Employees, Salary
    and Benefits Comparability   5 points
  • Employee Relations Plan, Programs for Advancement,
    Management and Skill Development, Standards of Termination
    Policy and Dispute Resolution   5 points

■ **Performance Capabilities**   **5 points**

■ **Total Possible Points**   **70 points**

Sources: Brown and Caldwell; PricewaterhouseCoopers; Long Aldridge & Norman; Presentation at National Council for Public-Private Partnership (NCPPP) Conference, Atlanta, October 1998.

ances technical and quality considerations with cost-savings potential. It was determined by dividing the best and final proposal technical score for each firm by the square of the best and final proposal first-year operation and management fee. By examining each proposal based on a value index, city officials were able to determine which plan generated the best overall value for the residents of Atlanta.

Atlanta has spent more than $2 million for the best technical, financial, and legal support during the privatization process. The city hired a team of financial and engineering consultants who helped plan, design, execute, review, and revise the technical aspects of the proposal process. A local law firm was also hired to provide legal advice. They partnered with another company that has handled more than 70 privatization projects nationwide. In addition, another firm was hired to provide oversight and to ensure integrity of the process. Working with them and monitoring all matters related to the technical, financial, and legal areas is a Washington, DC-based environmental law firm whose clients have included the EPA and many of the nation's largest cities and corporations. These are all nationally and, in some cases, internationally recognized firms.

The winning bid by United Water Services was nearly $2 million less than its closest competitor (Table 12.1). A key factor in the twenty-year proposal

Table 12.1
Comparing the Bids for Atlanta's Water System

	Annual Cost for 10-Year Contract	Annual Cost for 20-Year Contract	Technical Score* (out of 70)	Final Score** 10-and 20-Year Proposals
	(in millions of dollars)			
United Water	$23.3	$21.4	59.6	0.109
				0.130
Atlanta Water Alliance	$25.3	$23.2	60.4	0.093
				0.111
OMI Atlanta	$26.8	$25.9	62.8	0.087
				0.093
U.S. Filter	$24.0	$22.7	54.1	0.093
				0.104

*The technical scores reflect compliance with the city's minority participation requirements, performance on similar contracts, plans to transfer employees from a private to a public payroll, the quality of the company's management team, and its technical approach to running the water system.

**Final scores are achieved by taking the technical score and dividing it by the price squared (multiplied by itself).

Source: City of Atlanta.

was that the firm reduced its original price by nearly 21 percent, from $27 million to $21.4 million in its best and final proposal and increased minority participation from 15 to 35 percent. This was significant because minority participation accounted for about 15 percent of the criteria used by the city to determine the winner.

We strongly believe that the operations assessment and implementation steps undertaken by the city meet the highest industry standards; have been performed in the most professional manner; and will provide the city with a management plan that is technically, fiscally, and contractually sound. The $2 million spent on consultants is a large sum of money but was worthwhile to guarantee the integrity of the process.

CONTRACT HIGHLIGHTS

Because long-term contracts are a relatively recent phenomenon, Atlanta's agreement with the winning bidder was closely watched by industry and government observers for performance monitoring and implementation standards. A little noticed change in federal tax legislation in February 1997 allowed cities to enter into long-term privatization agreements for their water and wastewater systems, increasing from a maximum of five to a maximum of twenty years. This change allowed Atlanta to begin the privatization process and save ratepayers $400 million. The reason that the IRS changes are important is because the city, in essence, gets guaranteed funding of the savings. Thus, long-term contracting is one of the options many cities will consider. Every city will be forced to fix its water systems, not just because they are old and crumbling, but also because there are more stringent requirements from the EPA and state environmental regulatory agencies across the country and because cities serve more customers.

The contract was structured to accomplish the city's policy and financial goals, comply with all legal requirements, and achieve administrative goals. Among those in the last category are oversight by the city of contractor performance, clarity of provisions to avoid "agreements to agree," and contract administration that is both nonpersonnel and nonlawyer intensive.

Qualified contractors were invited to submit alternative proposals for ten-year and twenty-year contracts. The city was free to choose whichever contract best met its needs, with the winning proposal including a twenty-year term. In addition, the contract's fee structure included a basic operations and maintenance fee along with an annual Consumer Price Index (CPI) escalator. Provisions for pass-through costs and incentives for further cost-savings in the fixed fee structure were included.

Both parties agreed to adjustments to the contract in response to economic changes. Specific formulas were developed for base demand fluctuation, the effects of new capital projects and uncontrollable circumstances, commodity cost-savings, utility usage, and water quality adjustments.

The contract addressed employee issues by focusing on a smooth transition of existing employees from the public to private sector. It called for a three-year transition and required equal or better pay and reasonably comparable benefits. All finalists in the competition agreed in principle to a no-layoff policy for the 535 affected employees for the full duration of the contract. This concession by the firms voluntarily exceeded the three-year, attrition-only requirement in the city's draft agreement. The winning bidder is permitted, however, to reduce staffing during the planned three-year transition to optimum levels through early retirement incentives, drug and alcohol screening, cross-training, and transfers of skilled operators and managers within the firm's five regional business centers. United Water Services has transitioned more U.S.-based employees from the public to private sector in the past four years than has the entire water industry. The firm also has extensive experience with union workforces, with 50 percent of its operations represented by organized labor.

Capital repairs and replacements were another major category addressed. The capital repair section dealt with allocation of responsibility, normal versus material capital repairs, and replacements and incentive structures. Provisions regarding new capital projects include city review and approval rights, allocation of resulting cost-savings, and incentive structures.

Our private partner plans to invest heavily to improve operations during its first few years in Atlanta. United Water Services is already committed to spending up to $8 million over four years in automation, meter replacement, and other capital improvements to help produce early savings. Installation of computer systems by the firm will include a maintenance management system and billing and collection systems. This figure will be in addition to capital improvements funded by the city from its $29 million capital improvement program.

Technology also plays a key role in this successful public-private partnership. United Water Services will install a $4 million centralized control system that will link the separate systems now in place; remote robots will inspect and clean tanks; workers will use trenchless technologies for replacing buried pipes by digging holes in the ground every few feet instead of tearing up the whole street; they will apply the latest ultrasonic and infrared technologies to detect leaks; and technological improvements that addressed the Y2K compliance problem of the Department of Water's computer system.

Operational features were included in the contract to ensure proper regulatory compliance with permits and responsibility for fines. Monitoring performance was addressed through mechanisms for inspections by the city. Other important operational provisions included in the contract are billing and customer service, water quality maintenance and enhancement, inventory preservation, media/public relations, community involvement, and emergency planning and safety measures.

The proposed contract was amended two weeks before final offers were due to include a provision for termination of the service agreement without cause after a 90-day notice. This clause came about because of the insistence of the City Council and an influential business group. The insertion of the clause made it easier to support the twenty-year deal instead of the ten-year option. An effective termination clause reduces the risks of entering into a longer term agreement. As an added bonus, the city gains an additional $1.9 million in annual savings, the difference between the winning firm's first year fee for a ten-year and twenty-year contract.

To summarize the partnership agreement between the city of Atlanta and United Water Services, the company promised it could provide water services for $21.4 million annually compared to the city's cost for the same services of $49 million. During the twenty-year agreement, this amounts to savings of approximately $400 million for ratepayers. The city estimates that annual savings could approach as much as $30 million. Savings will be put into water and sewer system improvements that will enhance our competitiveness, protect the environment, and lead to further economic development opportunities.

An open and honest process ensured that the public interest was protected. In addition, by requiring that the company's headquarters be located in the Empowerment Zone and by ensuring no employees are laid off, the agreement demonstrates the city's ability to privatize services in a socially responsible manner and accomplish public policy goals and objectives in the process.

WASTEWATER CONTRACT

Recently, we have begun writing the specifications that will be used to solicit bids for the wastewater treatment plant privatization later in 1999. Consolidations and acquisitions among the companies in the emerging water industry will make the competition for the main wastewater plant even more fierce than last year's water contract. For the winning firm in the water competition, Atlanta is a worldwide reference, a kind of showcase. While the market for water used to be local, Atlanta and other recent privatizations in Buffalo, New York, Indianapolis, Seattle, and Milwaukee prove it is becoming increasingly national.

Two other city wastewater plants will continue to be operated by the city after the privatization of the largest one and a streamlining initiative in the rest of the wastewater system. According to one of the consultants, the privatization and streamlining of the city's wastewater operations should save Atlanta's water and sewer fund about $15 million per year, in addition to the $20 million the city saved from privatizing the water system. City officials are counting on the savings to help pay for a massive overhaul of its water and sewer system mandated by the state and a federal consent order.

LESSONS LEARNED

City officials in Atlanta have learned seven key lessons from the privatization agreement:

- *Lesson 1. Be bold; think big.* Officials must be innovative and prepared to face the challenges and criticism that will inevitably come in a comprehensive and massive proposal. While I do not believe privatization is the answer for all of the ills of government, when you have a separate enterprise fund for a water and sewer system, as most cities have, there's only one other way to find the funds needed to fix the system—raise rates. In fact, even with Atlanta's privatization agreement, the city still must raise water rates; however, as opposed to raising them 82 percent, we only have to raise rates on a blended scale of approximately 8 percent during the next four years—meaning massive savings for ratepayers. We were also able to examine the approach and find ways to lessen negative concerns. In summary, the first lesson is to be bold and make a quality decision instead of an easy one.

- *Lesson 2: Make the process open.* The city of Atlanta held 13 public hearings during the decision-making process. We researched, produced, and made public literally thousands of pages of documents. As mayor, I appointed a nine-member task force in August 1997. We held a privatization showcase for city employees, union members, and officials. I personally went to all city employees that will be affected and talked to them about the initiative. We brought in officials from other cities like Indianapolis, Indiana, Houston, Texas, and Charlotte, North Carolina, and vendors to share information about what they have done. We also allowed reporters to sit in on the process for the first time. In hindsight, this was a mistake. The resulting coverage was slanted and often inaccurate.

- *Lesson 3: Make the process fair and competitive.* The evaluation of the bidders must be comprehensive and must stand the test of scrutiny. All proponents must be given equal access to information. Our evaluation panel included 47 people. This is vitally important because assuming one or two could be influenced, you cannot influence 47 different people. We broadened it so that no one would be subject to any undo influence. Individual teams were assembled to review each aspect of the proposal based on the city statutory evaluation criteria and required scoring systems. The process was monitored independently by the consulting team to make sure that it was fair and competitive.

- *Lesson 4: Ensure absolute integrity and professionalism.* Our process was conducted with the highest degree of integrity. Since the beginning, we were advised by the consulting team of Brown and Caldwell; PricewaterhouseCoopers; and Harrington, George and Dunn—a team of respected engineering and financial consultants. They helped us learn early what the benchmarks and boundaries really were. Through intensive research and cost analysis we developed a benchmark for potential savings.

  In addition, we hired another group to provide oversight and advice. Now you may ask, "Why so many layers of oversight?" Again, it is to respond to questions about the process. We hired independent experts, lawyers, and consultants and an outside independent team to review the activities of all parties. The city paid more than $2 million to make certain that residents had the very best technical, legal, and financial advice available, and it worked.

- *Lesson 5: Get the best value for the city and ratepayers.* United Water Services was selected not only based on cost considerations, but also on a value index that considered factors such as experience of the company, track record on customer service, the commitment and level of minority participation, and the company's willingness to invest in the inner city by taking advantage of our Empowerment Zone designation. Three factors really made the proposal succeed. First and foremost was cost. The reason we got enormous cost-savings is because Atlanta is the first city to embark on a water system privatization of this magnitude. There is intense competition in the water industry for this type of large project. Every city must consider privatization at some point in the future, so timing was important. Whether you are an advocate of privatization or not, you cannot avoid the inevitable savings that will come as a result of the change in IRS regulations, especially when faced with the huge cost for infrastructure improvements.

Other things were important as well, including the two-step bidding process. The company that ultimately won the competition changed its minority participation from 15 percent to 35 percent from the first step to the second. That's important for Atlanta residents. The company more than doubled its minority participation from the first to second rounds. That is just one of the many benefits received.

The firm also made an innovative commitment on an important public policy issue by investing in Atlanta's Empowerment Zone, a 9.29 square-mile, largely impoverished area near the heart of the inner city. Atlanta is one of only six cities in the nation to have an Empowerment Zone. We realized that a creative public-private partnership holds promise for the people of Atlanta beyond rate savings. Working with United Water Services, we identified ways of using privatization as an economic development tool to revitalize Empowerment Zone neighborhoods. As part of its agreement with Atlanta, United Water Services made the following commitments concerning the Empowerment Zone:

- Require that 20 percent of its employees live in the area.
- Locate their national headquarters there.
- Provide $1,000 stipends for those who have purchased homes in the area.
- Provide $500 subsidies for those who rent there.
- Donate $100,000 a year in entrepreneurial funds for the development of small businesses in the area.
- Adopt a school and mentor children there.
- It was also stipulated that a $1 million research grant be given to one of our African-American colleges, Clark Atlanta University, to establish a Water Institute.

This is another example of getting the best value for your city and ratepayers.

Cities can combine the efficiencies and cost-savings of privatization with other good social public policy objectives through competitive bidding. This is harder to do when cities don't have an Empowerment Zone, but officials can certainly be creative.

- *Lesson 6: Make certain the contract protects the public interest.* Our contract provides for management that specifies clear outcomes and expectations. It provides for 24-hour, 7 days-a-week access and oversight by the city of Atlanta. Should the contractor fail to meet any deadlines, the company, not the city, pays the fines. The contract requires prior city approval for all improvements the company proposes. In addition, the city can terminate the contract at any time without cause, on fair terms, to both parties.
- *Lesson 7: Trust the process.* If Lessons 1–6 are followed, then a fair, open, honest process exists. A good system is in place. The most important lesson is that you must trust the process and stay with it because there will be bumps and bruises along the way. The privatization of one of its wastewater plants lies ahead for the city of Atlanta as well. We expect that process to be a little easier only because of our previous experience with the water privatization.

CONCLUSION

Reflecting on the scope of this historic agreement, it is important to review the many rich dividends it will yield for the citizens of Atlanta:

- At least $400 million in water and sewer rate savings
- Improved efficiency and customer service
- The highest quality drinking water
- Increased minority participation
- Jobs, training, and home ownership assistance for Empowerment Zone residents
- Funding for a world-class water research institute at one of our African-American colleges, Clark Atlanta University

We are proud to say that when faced with the challenge of bringing an aging and inadequate water system into the twenty-first century, we did not shirk from the responsibility by saying it can't be done. We said, "How can we do it?" Through vision, hard work, and commitment to excellence, we have strived to undertake a remarkable urban revitalization. We have forged innovative partnerships with the public and private sectors to empower communities and individuals with new tools and hope for the future.

Boldness has made Atlanta great, and only bold management strategies will enable our city government to meet the environmental challenges of the twenty-first century without overburdening residents. There simply is no viable alternative for many cities. It is a bold step Atlanta is taking with privatization but one we are doing with the public interest fully in mind.

Other cities across the United States will face similar challenges in the years ahead. Among the great challenges city officials will grapple with include rebuilding aging infrastructure systems. Atlanta's experience with privatization shows that officials can effect real change in their communities, save money, improve services, and still achieve important public policy goals. This is a historic innovation, not just for the city of Atlanta, but for cities worldwide. Atlanta will set the standard for delivery of city services into the next century. Already, we have received inquiries about how we were able to get such an incredible deal with such good provisions for our employees and great savings for ratepayers. It is our pleasure to share this information and help others reap similar benefits.

In short, we believe that this new partnership with United Water Services and the privatization of our water system will allow Atlanta to move even more progressively into the twenty-first century and beyond.

13

How Far Can Privatization Go?

John D. Donahue

Privatization in the United States has survived its awkward adolescence, and we can now begin to speculate on what it will look like when it fully matures. By some measures, of course, privatization is no newcomer at all but a venerable mainstay of American government. The private performance of public tasks is by no means novel. Indeed, it can be argued that private contracting is more typical over the whole sweep of America's history than the Progressive-era innovation of structured civil service.

However deep-rooted as a practice, privatization as a policy movement—an explicit, strategic effort to reshape how government operates—dates mostly from the 1980s. During the first half of its two-decade history as a theme of government reform, privatization was plagued by an unfortunate (if perhaps inevitable) quotient of clumsy ideological ardor. Some conservatives in and around the Reagan administration treated nongovernmental delivery as an instrument of their larger agenda to shrink government's reach. Some liberals responded in kind and resisted privatization reflexively and all but uniformly.

Today, privatization remains a matter of controversy, and properly so. The controversy has settled down into something calmer, less fervent, and more productive than the sturm und drang of a decade ago, however. A few on the left, to be sure, still decry almost any private involvement in the public's business. A few on the right still chant the mantra that free enterprise is always and everywhere superior to government bureaucracy. Except for the intellectually ossified and those with obvious vested interests, however, most commentators now approach the privatization issue as an honest debate—admitting distinctions, influenced by evidence—rather than as a clash of doctrinal absolutes. Unless either extreme seizes the political ascendancy, which seems improbable in the short run, the privatization debate promises to display more pragmatism than passion for some time to come.

In hopes of advancing that pragmatic debate, this chapter poses a basic question—How far can privatization go?—and attempts to map a few routes (some obvious, some less so) toward at least the beginnings of an answer.

HOW FAR HAS PRIVATIZATION GONE?

The volume of recent attention paid to privatization could invite the supposition that the government workforce is withering away. This is emphatically not the case. In the mid-1960s, there were approximately 65 public sector workers—military and civilian, at all levels of government combined—for every 1,000 Americans. This climbed to about 80 per 1,000 in the late 1970s. The public sector workforce remained at or above that benchmark until receding somewhat in the mid-1990s, dipping to approximately 75 per 1,000 in 1998.

One might object that this simply tracks the advance and halting retreat of big government and says little about how the public sector gets its work done. Yet the growth of overall public spending, as a fraction of the American economy, has been far more modest. The public sector accounted for about 25 percent of Gross Domestic Product (GDP) in 1962, climbed to 30 percent in 1975, and has remained within a percent or two of that level ever since (Figure 13.1).

It is hard to make a case that the public sector has been shedding workers, relative to the scale of its ambitions. Despite the rising importance of Social Security and other transfer programs, which spend major amounts of money with relatively few people and presumably serve to suppress government's staff-to-spending ratio, the public sector has been maintaining or even increasing the size of its payroll relative to the scale of its spending. Until the late 1970s, there were usually in the range of 600,000 public workers for every one percent of GDP moving through the public sector. This figure ranged from 474,000 in 1962 to 614,000 in 1974. Since 1978, there have been only two years in which this measure—thousand public workers per public percentage of GDP—fell below 600,000, and it exceeded 700,000 from 1996 through 1998.[1]

Certainly, these figures are at the highest level of aggregation, and it is perilous to conclude much at all from such coarse trends. There are perfectly reasonable grounds for arguing that the tasks performed by the public sector are inherently less subject to productivity improvements than other undertakings. If this proved systematically true, it would not be surprising that the public workforce would grow more quickly and shrink more slowly than the government share of GDP; however, the aggregate trends do undercut the notion that we have entered an era of headlong privatization.

Figure 13.1
Trends Since 1962 in Government Workers as Share of Population and Public Spending as Share of Gross Domestic Product

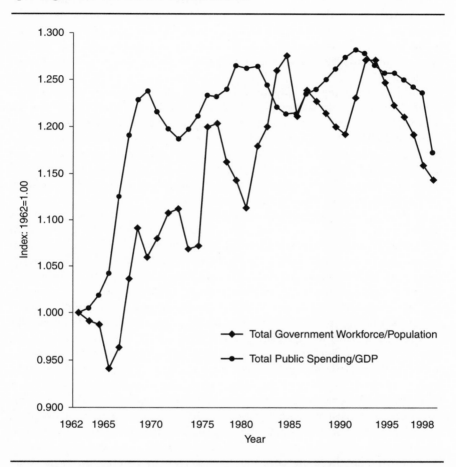

Source: Office of Management and Budget, Fiscal 2000 Budget, Historical Tables 15.3 and 17.5.

Indeed, it is remarkably difficult to determine how far privatization has gone—a seemingly straightforward prerequisite to speculating on its prospects and limits. While anecdotes and special-purpose statistical tallies can be invoked to demonstrate either a surge or a stall in the private performance of public functions, there is no clear-cut definition of privatization and no standard measuring stick. For present purposes, a rough definition might be publicly funded services that are not performed by public employees.

The best available gauge for the progress of privatization, by this admittedly rough definition, comes from the voluminous *National Income and Product Accounts* (NIPA) compiled and distributed by the Bureau of Economic Analysis in the U.S. Department of Commerce. These accounts disaggregate annual public spending along several dimensions. One dimension is the level of government—local and state versus federal. The federal category is subdivided into national defense and domestic versus international programs.

Within each category, spending is further separated into transfer payments like Social Security or (at the local and state level) general assistance, debt service, grants to other governments, and investment in structures and equipment. The remainder includes a large category somewhat confusingly labeled "consumption," which covers payments made to internal and external suppliers of goods and services. At a high level of aggregation (and with a correspondingly low level of precision), the answer to the question "How much privatization?" can be sought here.

In 1998 (the last year for which data are available), current expenditures for the entire U.S. public sector were about $2.5 trillion.[2] Roughly half of the total, however, consisted of transfer payments (dominated by Social Security) and net interest paid on public debt, rather than "public production." Since the question of public versus private delivery isn't very meaningful for transfer payments or debt service, a better baseline for calibrating the extent of privatization might be public spending minus federal transfers and interest.[3] As of 1998, about two-thirds of this baseline was devoted to paying for governmental services. The rest went mainly for goods purchases, intergovernmental grants, and consumption of capital.

A rough approximation of the current level of privatization may be sought in the allocation between salaries and benefits for government employees compared with payments to other suppliers of services. This approach is consistent with the gross employment data previously cited, which indicates the public payroll still predominates. In 1998, 53.9 percent of American public spending (other than federal transfers and interest) was devoted to the compensation of government employees, while only 12.3 percent was spent on "other services."

In fact, by this measure, privatization seems to have retreated a bit during the 1990s. As of 1991, the "other service" category had made up 13.3 percent of public sector operations. It claimed a slightly lower share in every other year of the decade through 1998. This trend against nongovernmental service delivery, however, largely reflects a falling federal share of public spending and, within the federal sector, a shift away from defense. While the share of outsourced defense services has been rising modestly during the 1990s, the share of defense within total public spending has declined. Excluding defense and looking only at federal nondefense and local and state spending, purchases of services from outside suppliers have risen slightly from about six percent of public spending in 1991 to about 6.5 percent in 1998.

In short, American government spends slightly less than $1 purchasing services from people and organizations other than public workers for every $4 spent on payroll. (Excluding defense spending, the ratio is about one-to-seven.) Thus, we are led to the most important generic question in policy analysis: Is this a big number or a small number?[4]

Not even the most avid privatization advocate would expect the government's workforce to wither away entirely, nor would even the most ardent defender of the civil service call for banning outside services. Yet, there remains a range of imaginable futures for the division of labor within American government. Private agents could stay at or fall below their current modest share of public operations, rise closer to parity with direct public delivery, or surge to claim a dominant position in the performance of publicly funded tasks. How might we determine which future we should anticipate and which we should prefer?

SHOULD THERE BE A BIAS FOR OR AGAINST PUBLIC EMPLOYMENT?

A fundamental question must be addressed early on: Should an inquiry over the proper extent of privatization concern only instrumental criteria, or are more basic issues at play in the choice between public and private supply? In other words, is the only relevant question whether public or private organizations can do a piece of work more cheaply, reliably, and conscientiously than the other? Or does the size of the public workforce have a value (positive or negative) beyond its capacity of public workers to do useful things for the citizenry at large?

Some conservatives believe that the public workforce should be shrunk to a minimum even if privatization fails to increase efficiency—indeed, even if it threatens efficiency—because of the inherent virtues in a small public sector. Little weight is given to that perspective here, primarily because the scale of the public sector is not directly at issue but, rather, the means by which it does its work. There are, no doubt, some conservatives who cherish the ideal of small government but who would change their minds and embrace an expansive state if it carried out most of its activities by contract rather than through employment, but there are probably not very many.

On the other side of the ideological spectrum, some see public employment as desirable in and of itself. Several values or predictions can be included in this view. Most basically, the public workforce can be seen as the emblem—not merely the instrument—of the common cause. A government institution may be taken to symbolize and christen shared undertakings with legitimacy in a way that a government contract cannot. In some cases, all or most people would probably endorse this sentiment—if the

institution under discussion happens to be an appeals court, for example—
and some people would probably endorse it all or most of the time.

The assertion that there is some bedrock desirability in having people on
the governmental payroll, however, is essentially a claim about the subjec-
tive perceptions of symbols: People simply feel better about having some
sorts of tasks carried out by public institutions rather than by profit-seeking
private institutions. Unless this perception is applied more generally and
shared more widely than I believe it to be, the fundamental value of public
employment will rarely be a deciding factor in choices about privatization.

Many progressives endorse a bias for public employment, not for such
intrinsic reasons—once their positions are examined closely—but from a
particular sort of instrumental logic. Public employment is a good thing, by
this logic, because it is an expeditious way to advance other common goals
en route to the delivery of public services. Such goals may include gender
and racial equity, safety and dignity on the job, family-friendly workplaces,
or generous wages and health and pension benefits. They may also include
the right of workers to bargain collectively, a right that has proven easier to
establish and preserve in the public than in the private sector. They may
even include employment itself.

While I have considerable sympathy with many such arguments, they are
impossible to endorse in any general way. Despite the admirable sentiments
that often inspire such briefs against privatization, they tend to be analyti-
cally flawed, tactically imprudent, or morally arbitrary.

The claim that direct public employment is essential to ward off mass
joblessness is most easily dispensed with, and would be so even if overall
unemployment were not "a happily minor policy problem." While there
have certainly been episodes in history when public employment reduced
economy-wide joblessness, to claim that this is the general case requires
invoking some complex and deeply vulnerable macroeconomic assumptions. Moreover, if employment itself (not the products of employment) is
the motive for a public endeavor, contracts can serve as well as the government payroll to boost the demand for labor. While there will be exceptions
(i.e., times and places in which public employment is the best or only way
to reduce joblessness), pointing to the specter of unemployment is usually a
weak tactic for the opponents of privatization.

Considerably more weighty is the argument that public employment is an
expeditious way to promote desiderata such as workplace fairness, safety,
security, dignity, and adequate levels of pay and benefits. One way to
accomplish such goals, of course, is to induce, require, or persuade private
sector employers to treat workers better than market signals, combined
with the dictates of conscience, would cause them to be treated. Another
way, however, is first to establish good employment standards for the public sector and then to have a lot of tasks assigned to government workers.

The second path may well seem like a more straightforward way to improve the lot of workers than the first. Yet this is a shakier basis than it might appear to be for insisting on public employment, instead of private contracts, as the instrument for getting the government's work done. To begin with, unless the ultimate goal is to have everything done by public employees—an approach that has been tried and found wanting in other contexts—this argument places a differential and ethically unwarranted weight on the treatment of one set of workers. Why should it matter if we believe custodians should be well-paid and provided with health benefits whether a custodian mops the floors at a high school or in an industrial park? Why should it matter if we believe lab technicians should be secure against racial discrimination or sexual harassment whether a technician works at a public hospital or a pharmaceutical company? Why should it matter if we believe a parent ought to be able to spend time with a newborn without risking his or her job whether that job is in the public or private sector?

A persistent privatization skeptic could respond with at least two kinds of arguments that it does matter. The first argument is based on the idea of the public payroll's demonstration effect. By this line of reasoning, governmental workplaces serve as laboratories and proving grounds for progressive employment practices. As limited workweeks, medical coverage, family leave, or job-sharing are introduced in the public sector and becomes refined and standardized, private employees may see that such conditions of employment are desirable to have, and private employers may see that they are feasible to offer. One by one, progressive employment practices may spread beyond the public sector vanguard into the private economy. This logic assumes, however, that public and private employers draw from the same pools of potential workers and face similar financial goals and constraints. Neither of these assumptions seems particularly sturdy, nor is it historically accurate that the public sector has pioneered every improvement in the conditions of employment. The "demonstration effect" argument for public employment is not negligible but neither does it seem to justify more than a minor nudge toward favoring direct public provision rather than contracting.[5]

The other justification is gloomier and might be termed the "enclave" argument for putting a differential moral weight on working conditions in the public sector. The net effects of intensifying market forces and workers' waning political influence render it unrealistic to expect good treatment for most private sector employees. Those who care about working conditions, accordingly, should beat a tactical retreat and concentrate their concerns on the public workforce. Insulation from market pressures and more favorable terrain for applying political leverage can make the public sector a defensible redoubt for working people's interests. This boils down to the precept that if one despairs of decent treatment for all workers, one can at least struggle to maintain a governmental oasis of decent treatment for some workers.

Yet in ethical terms, this argument seems painfully arbitrary; and in political terms, it is narrow and short-sighted. The enclave view of the public payroll invites progressives to divert their energies to preserving or expanding the governmental workforce, instead of struggling to improve employment standards in the bulk of American businesses. The objection applies even more strongly to the specific issue of labor organization. In 1998, slightly more than ten percent of the 98 million wage and salary workers in America's private sector were represented by unions. Even fewer were actual members of unions, but more than 40 percent of the 18 million government workers were represented by labor unions.[6] While the fraction of private workers covered by unions has declined by approximately 44 percent since 1983, union coverage in the public sector has been fairly stable and close to its peak in recent years.

Public sector labor organizations are probably the most consistent opponents of privatization, and it would be astonishing (and arguably in dereliction of their duties) were they to take any other stance. It is less clear, however, why sympathy with the labor movement in general requires endorsing a large public workforce. Boosting the size of the public sector is at best a dead end if one's goal is extending the benefits of labor organization; it could even undermine the effort. Few people, presumably, will dispute the prediction that many or most American workers will labor in the private sector for the foreseeable future. So even 100 percent unionization within government would represent a circumscribed triumph for the labor movement. If the gap between public and private sector unionization continues to widen, the labor movement risks losing the capacity and possibly even the will to organize as effectively outside government.

Concentrating on government workers exposes the labor movement to political fallout as well. As private workers see their counterparts in government enjoying a voice and a shield in the workplace that they lack themselves, they may resent supporting (in their roles as taxpayers) working conditions superior to their own. This seems likely to incubate broader alienation from both the labor movement and government.[7]

Even those who care deeply about the interests of workers in general, and who sympathize with the organized labor movement in particular, should work out the merits of privatization, function by function, with no thumb on the scale. Both a sense of decency and a rudimentary alertness to political reality should discourage proposals to slash the public workforce precipitously. This chapter looks to the long-run potential for privatization, however, and over the course of a decade or two even a sharp expansion of the private sector's role in delivering public services can be accommodated without undue disruption to current public workers.

MEDIUM-TERM INFLUENCES ON PRIVATIZATION'S PROSPECTS

Short-term predictions tend to be either dull or embarrassingly off base. The odds are long that the next several years will see expanded outsourcing of federal defense functions, limited action in other federal agencies, a mosaic of experimentation in the localities and states, and hotly controversial but mostly marginal initiatives in education privatization. Something may be brewing that will rapidly alter this picture, but if so, it will be a surprise. Long-term predictions, at the other extreme, tend to be safely self-indulgent daydreams. It is hard to say anything meaningful about what government will be like more than a quarter-century into the future, but the medium term (a decade or two out) affords some scope for informed speculation about what might affect privatization's prospects.

For those willing to grant that sympathy for current public workers is no fundamental bar to expanding privatization in the decades ahead (should that expansion turn out to be warranted on other grounds), what factors promise to affect the potential for delegating a larger portfolio of publicly financed tasks to private organizations?

To make explicit a fundamental precept, in so far as decisions hinge on simple economic efficiency, the private sector enjoys formidable advantages. Private organizations, whether for-profit or nonprofit, generally have more scope for specialization and managerial focus than public organizations. They can set the scale of their operations at whatever level is most expedient for operational efficiency, without regard to jurisdictional boundaries. They usually have far more flexibility in personnel matters and can present employees with more powerful and precise incentives than can most public organizations. For-profit private organizations have the additional distinction of a built-in and managerially pervasive sensitivity to costs.

In sum, it is no slur against governmental institutions, which are built to different specifications, with a different set of priorities, to say that private organizations are structurally more oriented to technical efficiency. Beyond this baseline distinction are American cultural and historical peculiarities that tilt the choice toward private delivery when other factors are balanced, or nearly so. In contrast to other nations—for example, Germany or the United Kingdom—government in the United States generally commands less public esteem and exerts less attraction on top-flight personnel than does business. Certainly, there are many exceptions, but, by and large, talent is more abundant in the private sector. Unless and until this durable American pattern begins to change, it makes sense to economize on scarce managerial and technical personnel in the public sector by turning to private alternatives for which there are no strong arguments to the contrary.

There often are strong arguments to the contrary, of course. A public task may be impossible to define in advance with sufficient precision to specify a private agent's responsibilities. Performance may be so elusive of evaluation that results-based reward and penalty schemes break down. Competition among alternative suppliers may be too weak—either from the start or, more often, once an incumbent has settled into a function—to discipline suppliers and ensure that taxpayers benefit from any private efficiency advantages.

Governmental decision makers may be too subject to influence by potential private suppliers (through the blunt instrument of corruption or the subtler persuaders of campaign contributions or aggressive marketing) for privatization to be consistent with accountability. For some functions, public opinion may simply balk at private supply. There will always be important parts of the public sector where privatization is impossible or imprudent, and aspiring reformers are well-advised to have other arrows in their quiver. Even if privatization is pushed to its limits, there will be ample scope for restructuring personnel systems, refining incentives, and promoting innovation within the public workforce.[8]

That said, there are at least five broad trends that seem likely to alter the limits of privatization over the next ten to twenty years.

Public Sector Reform

American public management is getting better. The progress is uneven, and there are abundant counterexamples, but relative to the recent past, public institutions are typically somewhat leaner, more flexible, and more focused. This is not the place to explore the extent and the sources of the improvement, nor do I wish to exaggerate the trend, yet reform campaigns at the local, state, and federal levels have had real effects during the past two decades.

Hierarchies have become less rigid. Innovation is more widely encouraged. Performance-based budgeting and management systems have become more common and more sophisticated. To a modest extent, a greater openness to privatization is part of this trend. More generally, however, improvements in the generic alternative to privatization (i.e., leaving a task in the hands of a public organization) will tend to reduce the fraction of governmental functions for which private performance is the superior choice. If recent efforts to reform public operations continue, this trend will serve on its own to limit the scope for privatization.

Easing Budgetary Pressures

The modern privatization movement emerged from the cauldron of fiscal austerity. Exploding deficits at the federal level and recession-induced budgetary shortfalls in the cities and states created fertile ground for proposals to perform the government's work more cheaply. Cost control has never been the only motive for privatization, but budget pressures have generally provided much of the political impetus for overcoming the inertia of the status quo and testing private alternatives. It is no accident that the military has far outpaced civilian agencies in experiments with privatization; the long period of post-war austerity has led defense managers to concentrate their shrinking staff resources on core functions. As this is written, these pressures have eased. The federal government is enjoying an unaccustomed budget surplus. Most local and state governments are similarly flush.

The relaxation of public sector austerity will probably serve to slacken the pace of privatization. The simplest reason is that public managers will be more reluctant to take on the political heavy lifting privatization often involves without the intense motivation of budget shortfalls. Beyond this obvious point, however, the loosening of fiscal constraints will push cost-minimization lower in the hierarchy of decision criteria, and to the extent that technical efficiency is a systematic advantage of private over public organizations, budgetary slack will tend to shift the game away from the private sector's strong suit.

This moderating influence on privatization's prospects, though, is both limited and contingent. It is limited because enlisting the private sector in government's mission can have virtues beyond reducing costs, and it is contingent because nobody knows whether the bright budget situation of the late 1990s will prove to be a change in the climate or just a break in the clouds. If the good times for governmental budgets continue to roll over the next two decades, then the private share of the public's business may not advance much beyond where it stands today. Such a durably rosy scenario, however, may not be the most likely version of the medium-term future.

The Comparative Cultural Legitimacy of Business and Government

Privatization surged into prominence during the recent nadir of public esteem for American government and the bureaucrats who populate it. Government has bounced back a bit since the 1980s in terms of the citizenry's perception of its competence and integrity, and one might expect that this would rob the privatization movement of some of its impetus.

It is not only government but a wide range of American institutions that enjoyed a modest increase in public confidence during the second half of the 1990s, according to several polls that track such views. The strong economy has softened the citizenry's grievances with institutions in general, and it is by no means obvious that government's comparative legitimacy has risen. As people become more comfortable with the notion of private businesses and nonprofit organizations taking on unconventional responsibilities, it is quite possible that this constraint on privatization will loosen over time. This is obviously a highly conjectural issue, but my expectation is that the private sector's edge on this dimension is more likely to grow than to shrink during the next twenty years.

Private Capacity to Compete with Government

A closely related issue is the readiness of the private sector to structure institutions that are able to take on traditionally governmental tasks. The richer the menu of alternatives outside government, the longer the list of functions that become imaginable candidates for privatization. While this is also a speculative point, contingent on many uncertain factors, it seems probable that recent trends towards the expansion of private capacity will continue.

Major firms, including large defense contractors and consulting companies, have enlarged and diversified their public sector service contracting units. Private nonprofit organizations continue to proliferate and expand their share of human services, education, and other areas. If this capacity continues to expand, it will shift calculations in area after area—both by inviting policymakers and the public to consider alternatives to conventional public service delivery and by bolstering the political constituency for outsourcing. Privatization may well benefit from momentum within the public sector, as familiarity with the idea breeds both more comfort and more facility with the relevant skills among government officials.

Information Technology

It has become drearily conventional to predict that the information revolution will change everything, no matter what the topic at hand, but in this specific case there does seem to be considerable reason to expect that improvements in IT will widen the potential for privatization. This is so for two reasons: (1) the private sector and especially private for-profit organizations appear to have some systematic advantages in exploiting each advance in IT and (2) improvements in gathering, processing, and disseminating data will themselves loosen some of the fundamental constraints on delegating tasks to nongovernmental agents.

Where government activities are closely analogous to business activities (i.e., where the work concerns delivering services, processing information, orchestrating transactions, and so on), the information revolution will have significant and mostly positive implications for the public sector. Costs will fall; productivity will increase; and process reinvention will accelerate. Today's "virtual one-stop" service centers linking multiple agencies through shopping mall kiosks, for example, or the IRS's exemplary web site, will turn out to be harbingers of a significant transformation. Government will continue to lag behind business in the adoption of IT advances, however, both because constraints on financial and human resources will retard innovation and because insulation from competitive pressures will tend to keep government behind the frontier of best practices.

The range of public functions suitable for delegation to private suppliers is generally constricted by the difficulty of specifying expectations, monitoring compliance with contractual terms, and measuring contractors' performance. IT improvements will ease contractual monitoring and evaluation and thus raise the proportion of public functions through which it is feasible to exploit the cost advantages of competitive private supply.

Moreover, the same characteristics that make a public function subject to major improvements from advanced IT—relatively clear-cut goals, a well-defined clientele, and insulation from other agendas—also render it a promising candidate for privatization. For governmental functions that are well-defined and charged with limited political voltage, the potential for privatization will generally outpace the potential for bureaucratic productivity improvements.

Both because public organizations will generally lag behind private organizations in the exploitation of new information technologies and because functions with high potential for public sector productivity gains will be privatized with disproportionate frequency, the average level of productivity in public agencies will increasingly diverge from the average level of productivity in private businesses. The information revolution, in other words, will subject the public sector to a more chronic and virulent form of Baumol's "cost disease." (The Princeton economist William Baumol has observed that some tasks are inherently, and for good reasons, resistant to productivity gains; the Minute Waltz cannot be performed in thirty seconds. Those performing such tasks come to look like laggards as other enterprises shed costs.) Unless the reasons for this gap become understood and accepted, it could further depress public esteem for government.

CONCLUSION

The net effects of the most likely trajectories for these broad trends will be to widen the potential for privatization during the next decade or two. The size of the direct public workforce is likely to decrease, relative to the public sector's overall role in the economy. This prediction could certainly prove wrong, and it begs many questions: Will we select wisely among candidates for privatization? Will government develop the relevant capacities in contracting, measurement, and monitoring? Will the potential for corruption, whether overt or subtle, be suppressed with sufficient relentlessness? Will we make serious efforts to buffer the transition for public workers subject to unaccustomed competition? Research currently underway explores some of these issues.

With respect to this chapter's broad question, "How far can privatization go?" my cautious expectation for the next twenty years is "Pretty far." If we are careful and pragmatic and respectful of government workers' irreplaceable roles in functions ill-suited to private delivery, this is not a bad thing.

NOTES

1. These trends discussed in these three paragraphs are calculated from Office of Management and Budget data taken from *The Budget of the United States, Fiscal Year 2000,* Historical Tables 15.3 and 17.5. All of the growth in public employment—indeed, more than all of the growth—has been in local and state government. Federal civilian employment was just fractionally higher in 1998 than it had been in 1962, and federal military employment was about 1.4 million lower. Meanwhile, local and state governments added 9.4 million people to their payrolls.

2. This figure and others in this section are drawn or calculated from NIPA data, *Survey of Current Business,* Section 3, various issues, Tables 3.1, 3.2, 3.3, and 3.7.

3. The data compilation used here does not net out local and state transfers, which would be somewhat preferable; however, this does not distort the trends in any major way.

4. The economist Thomas Schelling, author of *Micromotives and Macrobehavior* (1978) and *Choice and Consequence* (1983), and one of the founders of Harvard's Kennedy School of Government, has so characterized this question.

5. The strength of this argument depends on the relative size of the public workforce and is probably strongest in the middle range. If public employment is tiny, governmental employment practices would have little leverage over private practices. If public employment is large relative to private employment, a substantial fraction of workers who care greatly about benefits offered earliest in the public sector may have already opted for government work, rendering the extension into the private sector of progressive employment practices somewhat less urgent.

6. The specific figures are 10.4 percent of private workers and 42.5 percent of government workers. Data are from the Bureau of Labor Statistics on-line data collection made available online at <stats.bls.gov/news.release/union2.t03.htm>, accessed June 1999. Other figures in this paragraph are from *Statistical Abstract of the United States* 1998, Table No. 712, Labor Union Membership by Sector, 1983 to 1997.

7. A counterargument may be that unionized workers in the public sector stronghold are in a position to support the organization of their private sector brethren. This doesn't seem to be occurring to any major degree, however.

8. These issues are explored at more length in Donahue (1989), especially Chapter 5.

REFERENCE

Bureau of Economic Analysis. Various years. *National income and products accounts.* Washington, DC: U.S. Department of Commerce.

Index

Activity-Based Costing/Management
  (ABC/M), 10, 124, 126, 130
Activity-Based Management
  (ABM), 123
Activity-Based Costing (ABC), 1, 65,
  123, 125, 127–28, 154, 202–203,
  218, 224, 227
*Adarand Constructors, Inc. v. Pena, et
  al. (1995),* 150–51
Affirmative action, 148, 150
Agency capture, 20
Alabama, Birmingham, 120
Alliance for National Renewal, 51
Alternative Dispute Resolution
  (ADR), 32
America Works, 22
American Correctional Association,
  24–25
American Federation of Government
  Employees, 46
American Federation of State, County
  and Municipal Employees, 46, 196,
  205–206
Arizona, Phoenix, 102, 170, 182, 198,
  204–205, 226

Armament Retooling and
  Manufacturing Support (ARMS), 41
Asset sale, 18
Asset specificity, 66
Atlanta, GA, 7, 13, 109, 114, 143,
  181, 185, 193, 206–208, 237–52
Australia, 20, 24–25, 44, 49; University
  of Sydney, 44

Baumol, William, 265
Benchmarking, 25, 74, 126, 129–30,
  227–28
Black Enterprise Magazine, 148
Build-Operate-Transfer (BOT), 7, 19
Build-Own-Operate (BOO), 7, 19
Build-Transfer-Operate (BTO), 19
Business @ the Speed of Thought, 154

California, 48, 194; Garden Grove,
  175; Los Angeles County, 42, 44,
  145, 198; Marin County, 144;
  Proposition 13, 169; Riverside
  County, 38; San Diego, 46, 49; San
  Diego County, 202; San Jose, 132,
  145; Upland, 175

Campbell, Bill, 7, 13
Canada, 41, 49, 79, 227
Center for Advanced Purchasing
  Studies, 157, 159
Centre for Strategic Management, 196
Charlotte, NC, 12, 65, 169, 198–99,
  204, 208, 211–35
Chicago, IL, 7, 143, 144, 147, 150, 156,
  240; Chicago Board of Education,
  143; Chicago Public Schools, 142, 145;
  Chicago School Finance Authority,
  142; Coalition of the Chicago Board
  of Education Unions, 143
Chile, 50
Clark Atlanta University, 250–51
Clinton, William, 53, 177
Collective bargaining agreements, 132
Colorado, Denver, 170
Community involvement, 117
Compensation package, 195, 198
Competitive contracting, 102
Computerization, 14
Concession fees, 111
Concession payment, 119–20
Cone Corporation v. Hillsborough
  County (1990), 150
Conflict of interest, 114
Connecticut, 22, 24–25, 100; Danbury,
  120, 240; Manchester, 175; West
  Haven, 114
Conrail, 38
Construction financing, 121
Consumer Price Index (CPI), 118, 246
"Contestability" factor, 65, 72
Contestable Markets, 65
"Contract bundling," 162
Contract management, 18, 29, 33, 79
Contract monitoring, 80, 85, 136–37,
  234, 265
Contractor autonomy, 26
Contractor performance, 30
Cooke, David, 199–200
Coopers & Lybrand, 226
Coral Construction v. King County
  (1991), 150
Corporatization, 19
Cost-benefit studies, 8
Cost-plus, 29

Daley, Richard, 7
Delaware, Wilmington, 109
Dell Computer Corporation, 163
Dell, Michael, 163
Democratic Party, 2, 7, 37, 53, 81, 208
Denationalization, 38
Deprivatize, 9
Dershak, Kim, 31
Design-Build-Operate (DBO), 10, 112,
  114–16
Design/Bid/Build (DBB), 110
Design/Build (DB), 110, 112, 114–15
Design/Build/Finance/Operate
  (DBFO), 115
Discrimination, 114, 150
Dispute resolution, 32
Divesting, 38
Dole, Elizabeth, 161
Dougal, Carol, 149
Drake, Dr. W. Avon, 162
Drucker, Peter, 3

Economies of scale, 10, 69, 74,
  85–86, 102
Emery Worldwide Airlines, 47
Employee: compensation, 213;
  gainsharing, 204, 219, 231; morale,
  229; opposition, 12; protections, 12;
  resistance, 80, 224
Employee Stock Ownership Plan
  (ESOP), 19
England, 5, 44; London, 41, 44
Enterprise Development, 21
Entrepreneurial government, 9
Entrepreneurship, 85
Environmental Protection Agency
  (EPA), 73, 107, 112, 177, 183, 185,
  238, 239, 245, 246
Europe, 170
Executive Order 12803, 120

Faith-based programs, 52
Family-based programs, 52
Favoritism, 114
Federal Bureau of Prisons, 24
Federal construction grants
  program, 107
Fee-for-service, 29

Financing, 70
Fixed-payment contracts, 118
Florida, Coral Cables, 198
Follow-the-leader strategy, 61, 64
For-profit, 6, 19, 42, 50, 77, 95, 97, 149, 261, 264
Franchise, 19, 38, 174

Gates, Bill, 154
General Services Administration (GSA), 151
Geographic information systems (CISs), 79
Georgia, 38, 239. *See also* Atlanta, GA
Germany, 49, 261
Glass Ceiling Commission, 161
Goldsmith, Stephen, 7, 202
Goldwater, Barry, 52
Gore, Al, 2, 170
Government entrepreneurship, 85–86, 93, 97–100, 103, 205–206
Government mandates, 144, 146–47, 169, 185, 238
Government-Owned Enterprises (GOEs), 8, 46
Governmental Performance and Results Act (GPRA), 171
Graves, Earl G., Sr., 148
Great Britain, 20, 41, 49, 87; British Defense Ministry, 41; Royal Airforce, 41; Royal Mint, 41
Greece, 49
Gross Domestic Product (GDP), 254

Haines, Stephen, 196
"Hard" services, 6
Harvard University, 153, 161
Hewlett-Packard, 183, 201
"Hollow organization," 78
Holsworth, Dr. Robert D., 162
HUBZone Empowerment Contracting Program, 149

Illinois, 4, 146, 179, 193; Chicago; Cook County, 144, 146, 148, 157, 160; DuPage County, 142; Monmouth, 143, 181, 195, 206;

Northbrook, 175; Pekin, 183. *See also* Chicago, IL
Immigration and Naturalization Service (INS), 142
Incentives, 8, 21, 26, 72, 76, 110–111, 116, 118, 143, 149, 207, 216, 219, 231, 233–34, 241, 244, 246–47, 262
Indiana, 148, 206; Evansville, 185; Farmersburg, 206; Gary, 109; Indianapolis. *See also* Indianapolis, IN
Indianapolis, IN, 3, 7, 21–22, 24–25, 28, 31, 33, 49, 65, 102, 108, 114, 130, 169, 176, 182, 192, 198, 202, 204, 206–208, 226, 240, 248–49; Indianapolis Airport Authority, 28
Information management, 10
Information technology, 14, 78, 124–25, 247, 264–65
Initiative Management Reviews (IMRs), 33
Intel, 183
Intermunicipal cooperation, 87, 89, 93–94, 96, 99–100, 102
Internal markets, 19
Internal Revenue Service (IRS), 9, 111–12, 121, 173, 194, 198, 207–208, 246, 250, 264; Revenue Procedure 97–13, 9, 111, 120
International City/County Management Association (ICMA), 11, 22, 25, 87, 170, 204, 208

Jensen, Ronald W., 204–205
Johnson, Lyndon B., 147
Joint venture, 18–19, 32

Kelman, Steven, 153

Labor constituency, 2
Labor management, 101
Labor unions. *See* Unions
Lease-back, 112
Leasing, 38
Line item budgeting, 218
Living Wage Ordinance, 145–46, 155, 159, 163
Load-shedding, 38

"Loss sharing," 45
Louisiana, New Orleans, 114

Managed competition, 3, 11–12, 38,
   45, 75, 123, 130, 134, 136, 171,
   182, 187–88, 191, 200, 203–204,
   206, 208–209, 211, 216–17
Management contracts, 19, 197
Management information systems, 32
Massachusetts, 81, 142, 169, 196;
   Boston, 145; Cambridge, 175;
   Devens, 109; Fall River, 114;
   Gardner, 109; Taunton, 109;
   Worcester, 175
MasterCard, 141, 157–58
Media, 243, 247, 249
Mexico, 49
Michel, Harriet, 148
Michigan, 38, 40, 169; Ann Arbor,
   196; Detroit, 143; Ypsilanti, 146
Microsoft, 141
Military, 263
Milwaukee, WI, 23, 109, 114, 181,
   205–207, 240, 248
Minimum wage, 145
Minnesota: Minneapolis, 28;
   Minneapolis Public Schools, 28
Minorities, 144, 148, 224, 246,
   250–51
Minorities and women, 142–43, 150,
   155, 160–61
Minority Business Enterprises
   (MBE), 148
Minority Business Enterprises/Women
   Business Enterprises (MBE/WBE),
   150, 155, 157–63
Monopoly, 2, 46, 75, 86, 102,
   217–18, 233
Moore, Mark H., 161
Municipal financing, 121
*Municipal Service Delivery: Thinking
   Through the Privatization
   Option,* 152

National Aeronautics and Space
   Administration (NASA), 41
National Commission on Employment
   Policy (NCEP), 193

National Income and Product Accounts
   (NIPA), 256
National League of Cities (NLC),
   170, 172
National Minority Supplier Development
   Council (NMSDC), 148–49
National Performance Review, 2, 170
Negotiating, 201
Nevada: Las Vegas, 32; Reno, 128, 130
New Hampshire, 38
New Jersey: Bergen County, 143–44;
   Jersey City, 24, 27, 38; New
   Brunswick, 119
New York, NY, 40, 49, 88, 97,
   100, 206
New York State, 9, 22, 38, 86–88, 94,
   100, 102, 147; Berlin, 97; Buffalo,
   197, 248; Chautauqua County, 98;
   Gardiner, 96; Genesee County, 95,
   101; Hammond, 97; Livingston
   County, 96; New York City; *See*
   New York, NY; Ossian, 98; Oswego
   County, 98; Pendleton, 94; Penfield,
   96; Putnam County, 97, 100;
   Rochester, 96, 101; Schroon, 95;
   Ulster County, 95; York, 98
New Zealand, 20, 49
Nondiscrimination, 148
Nongovernmental Organizations
   (NGOs), 51, 63, 75
Nonprofit, 6, 19–20, 42, 50, 63, 77,
   90, 95–97, 206, 261, 263–64
North Carolina: Charlotte; *See*
   Charlotte, NC; Mecklenburg
   County, 230

Ohio, 198; Cleveland, 143, 198;
   Franklin, 109, 114; Huber
   Heights, 114
Oklahoma, 26; Oklahoma City,
   108, 113
OMB Circular A-76, 65, 152
"Opportunity cost," 158
Outcome measures, 137
Outcome systems, 33
Output-based models, 33
Output/outcome, 21
Outsourcing, 19, 38, 41, 59, 106

Pakistan, 40
Pataki, George, 38
Pay-for-performance, 126
Payments-in-lieu-of-taxes (PILOT), 120
Penalties, 29, 183, 185, 244, 262
Pennsylvania, Philadelphia, 7, 169, 176–177, 193, 208
Performance: evaluation, 183, 188, 262; guarantees, 114, 185, 244; management, 128; measurement, 22–25, 73, 137, 201, 215, 265; monitoring, 183, 186, 188, 246–47
Performance-based: budgeting, 262; contracting, 18, 21, 26, 29, 80, 201; pay, 101, 233; strategies, 7, 115
Personal Responsibility and Work Opportunity Reconciliation Act of 1996 (PRWORA), 145–46
Political, 90, 93, 142, 152, 170, 177, 179, 188, 191, 199–200, 223, 240, 254, 259–60, 263–65
Political cycles, 60
Political resistance, 78
Politics, 71, 73, 78, 114, 208
Pony express, 2
Privatization Watch, 152
Process reengineering, 127, 129–30
Program Planning Budgeting Systems, 1
Public sector reform, 13
Public-private associations, 62
Public-private competition, 17, 199, 201–202, 223–24, 226
Public-private partnership, 5, 17, 20–21, 32, 38, 47, 97, 108–109, 112, 114, 122, 170–71, 207, 247
Puerto Rico, 49
Purchaser-provider split, 20, 25

Quality Assurance Plan (QAP), 30
Quality Service Improvement (QSI), 238

Ratner, Hedy, 149
Reagan, Ronald, 5, 52, 169, 253
Real-estate investment trusts (REITs), 49
Reason Foundation, 199, 225
Reason Public Policy Institute, 152

"Reduce cost" rationale, 61
Reinventing Government, 2
Rendell, Ed, 7
Republican Party, 2, 7, 37, 52, 81, 208
Restructuring, 98, 100, 102
Reverse privatization, 88, 93, 95, 99–103
Rhode Island, Cranston, 109, 120–21, 240
Richmond v. J.A. Croson (1989), 150, 162
"Rightsizing," 212
Risk, 46, 71, 86, 112, 114, 118, 178, 207, 242, 247
Risk management, 80
Roosevelt, Franklin, 53

Sale-leaseback arrangement, 19
Service contracting, 74, 222
Small Business Administration (SBA), 149, 151, 160–62
Small disadvantaged businesses, 160–61
Social insurance, 8, 49
Social mandates, 10–11, 141, 151–52, 158–59, 161, 163
Social Security, 50, 254, 256
"Soft" services, 6
Spin-off strategies, 3
St. Lawrence Seaway, 41
Start-up costs, 70
State-owned enterprises (SOEs), 47
Switzerland, 49

Task complexity, 66
Tax Reform Act of 1986, 110–11
Telecommunications, 14
Tennessee Valley Authority (TVA), 142
Termination-for-convenience, 116–17
Texas: Austin, 176; Houston, 108, 176, 249
Thatcher, Margaret, 5, 41
The Mercer Group, 175, 204, 208
The Wall Street Journal, 153, 161
Top-down approach, 52
Total Quality Management (TQM), 1, 87

U.S. Army, 41
U.S. Coast Guard, 38
U.S. Conference of Mayors, 109,
    170, 240
U.S. Congress, 42
U.S. Department of
    Commerce(DoC), 256
U.S. Department of Defense (DoD), 41,
    42, 44, 193, 201
U.S. Department of Energy (DoE), 201
U.S. Department of Housing and
    Urban Development (HUD),
    141, 194
U.S. Department of Labor (DoL), 147,
    193, 195
U.S. General Accounting Office (GAO),
    43, 78, 175, 193, 196, 202
U.S. General Services Administration
    (GSA), 44
U.S. Hispanic Chamber of
    Commerce, 148
U.S. Marines, 40
U.S. Naval Academy, 40
U.S. Postal Service (USPS), 8, 47
U.S. State Department (DoS), 40
Unemployment, 142–43
Unions, 88, 101, 127, 142, 145, 171,
    181, 192, 195, 197, 205–207,
    249, 260
Unionization, 78, 90
United Kingdom, 261

United States, 20, 37, 41, 42, 44, 47,
    49, 50, 52, 87, 121, 169, 170, 175,
    227, 253, 261

Vinroot, Richard, 213
Virginia, 202; Richmond, 38
Virginia Commonwealth
    University, 162
Volunteers, 20, 51
Vouchers, 20, 38, 51, 75

Wages and benefits, 194, 247, 258
Washington, 148; Seattle, 114, 248
Webb, Wellington, 170
Weld, William, 81
Welfare reform, 145
Wisconsin: Milwaukee; See
    Milwaukee, WI
Women Business Enterprises
    (WBE), 148
Women's Business Development
    Center, 149
Women's Business Enterprise National
    Council (WBENC), 149
Workflow analysis, 203
Workforce reduction, 228
Workforce transition, 199
World Bank, 26

Zero-Based Budgeting, 1

About the Editors
and Contributors

BRIDGET M. ANDERSON is the partner in charge of the KPMG Costing Analysis and Management Services product. Ms. Anderson is also responsible for coordinating KPMG's Midwest Advisory Services to Public Sector entities and is located in the Chicago office. Anderson has more than eighteen years experience in serving government and other organizations such as Chicago Public Schools, city of Indianapolis, state of Indiana, U.S. Treasury, U.S. Customs, Milwaukee Metropolitan Sewerage District, city of San Jose, state of Iowa, Marion County, and the Health and Hospital Corporation of Marion County. Anderson has assisted governments in a variety of areas including: development and implementation of Activity Based Costing Systems, managed competition, bid preparation assistance, RFP development, competition strategy, performance measurement and performance budgeting. Ms. Anderson is a member of the American Institute of Certified Public Accountants, Illinois and Indiana CPA Societies and Government Finance Officers Association.

BILL CAMPBELL became Atlanta's 57th mayor, as well as its third African-American Mayor, in 1993. He was re-elected to a second term in 1997 and his vision of a new Atlanta has driven the city's revitalization. Prior to becoming mayor, Campbell served as a prosecutor for the U.S. Department of Justice Anti-trust Division. In 1981, he was elected to the Atlantic City Council and served three consecutive terms. He has served on three national commissions: the FAA's National Civil Aviation Review Commission, the FCC's State and Local Advisory Committee on

Telecommunications, and the Fannie Mae National Advisory Council. He also chaired the U.S. Conference of Mayor's Transportation and Communications Committee. *Newsweek* named him one of the *25 Most Dynamic Mayors in America.*

CHRISTI CLARK is co-founder and Executive Vice President of Master-Plan Consulting Group, a firm that specializes in consulting services for corporate leaders and public officials who wish to maximize the performance potential of their organizations. She worked for more than 20 years in key leadership positions for a Fortune 200 corporation based in Houston, Texas. Clark has been a featured panelist at national conferences like the National Solid Waste Management Association and the Solid Waste Association of North America. She is a published author and public speaker and is currently completing an International Masters in Management Degree through Purdue University.

JOHN D. DONAHUE is the Raymond Vernon Lecturer in Public Policy at Harvard University's John F. Kennedy School of Government, where he directs the Visions of Governance in the twenty-first Century research project and serves as faculty chair for the David T. Kearns Program on Business and Education. His writings include *Making Washington Work: Tales of Innovation in the Federal Government* (Brookings Institution Press, 1999); *Hazardous Crosscurrents: Confronting Inequality in an Era of Devolution* (Century Foundation, 1999); *Disunited States* (Basic Books, 1997); and *The Privatization Decision: Public Ends, Private Means* (Basic Books, 1989 and 1991). He held senior policy posts in the U.S. Department of Labor from 1993 to 1995.

DOUGLAS HERBST is currently president of the National Council for Public-Private Partnerships, a non profit organization founded in 1985, and has more than 15 years experience in the structuring of privatization (public-private partnerships). He was a pioneer in developing the privatization concept for the water and wastewater industry and has a wealth of experience in both the public and private sectors. Herbst has published numerous articles in industry publications including *American City & County, The Privatization Review, Public Works Financing, Government West and Empire State Report.* He is also a member of the Design/Build Institute of America (DBIA) as well as a member of the Board of Directors for the Texas Chapter of the DBIA.

WADE HUDSON is an economic policy analyst at RPPI, specializing in government performance, privatization, and urban redevelopment. He has written extensively on privatization trends and practices. His current projects include RPPI's "Competitive Cities Project" which analyzes how efficiently the nation's largest cities deliver services and identifies "best practices" in service delivery and municipal management.

ROBIN A. JOHNSON is Director of the Illinois Center for Competitive Government, a partnership between the Illinois Department of Commerce and Community Affairs and the Illinois Institute for Rural Affairs at Western Illinois University. The Center conducts research into cutting-edge management practices of local governments. He has co-authored several reports on privatization and had articles published in *Illinois Municipal Review, Public Works, Government Finance Review, Privatization Watch* and *American Small Business Association Today.* Johnson is also an Alderman in Monmouth, IL (pop. 9,500) and is a member of the Executive Committee of the National Council for Public-Private Partnerships.

JAMES L. MERCER is the president and founder of The Mercer Group, Inc., a management consulting firm. He has more than 27 years experience in management consulting and has been designated a Certified Management Consultant by the Institute of Management Consultants. Mr. Mercer's firm publishes the periodic *The Mercer Group Privatization Survey,* which is an authoritative source of information on the state and local government privatization market. He has also consulted with many governmental and private clients on issues of privatization. Mercer has published five books and more than 250 articles on various aspects of management.

ADRIAN MOORE directs Reason Public Policy Institute's (RPPI) Privatization Center where he is responsible for research on privatization, reinventing government, and economic policy. He also publishes the monthly newsletter *Privatization Watch* and the *Annual Privatization Report.* Moore is co-author of *Curb Rights: A Foundation for Free Enterprise in Urban Transit,* published in 1997 by the Brookings Institution Press. Also, he has written many articles on privatization for such publications as *The American Enterprise, The Independent Review, Economic Affairs,* and *Regulation,* and writes regular columns on privatization and government reform for *Privatization International* and *Intellectual Ammunition.*

JOHN O'LOONEY is a Public Service Associate at the Carl Vinson Institute of Government at the University of Georgia. He provides technical assistance in the areas of program evaluation and performance measurement, strategic planning, database development, operation and service delivery reengineering, and sustainability planning. O'Looney is a trained mediator and has published extensively in the areas of human service and information systems design, contract management, conflict resolution, economic development, and land-use policies. He is the author of five books: *Economic Development and Environmental Control, Redesigning the Work of Human Services, Outsourcing and State and Local Government Services, Beyond Maps: GIS and Local Government Decision Making,* and *Emergency 911 Systems.*

E. S. SAVAS is professor at the School of Public Affairs of Baruch College of the City University of New York and founder/director of the Privatization Research Organization at the University. Formerly First Deputy City Administrator of New York and Assistant Secretary of the U.S. Department of Housing and Urban Development, appointed by President Reagan.

Professor Savas is one of the pioneers in privatization, having first advanced the concept in 1969 as a New York City official. The author of nine books and 110 articles, his book, *Privatization: the Key to Better Government,* was published in 13 foreign editions. His most recent book, *Privatization and Public-Private Partnerships,* was published by Chatham House in 2000.

DAVID SEADER is a Principal Consultant in the Privatization and Restructuring of Utilities Group of PricewaterhouseCoopers LLP. He has more than 25 years of professional consulting experience, including capital project planning, development, and financing in energy, environmental management and infrastructure projects, and privatization, as well as other public private programs and partnerships. Seader is also co-founder and director of the National Council for Public-Private Partnerships and founding editor of *The Privatization Review.* He is also a Certified Cogeneration Professional, a member of the American Planning Association, a member of the Association of Energy Engineers, and a Director of the Cogeneration Institute. Seader has served on the faculty of architecture at Columbia University and taught at the City University of New York.

ED SIZER began his career with the city of Charlotte in 1966. Prior to becoming Charlotte's contracts administrator for managed competition and privatization contracts in 1993, he served as General Services and Parks and Recreation Director. In his present role, Mr. Sizer works with city business units in developing potential areas for competition or privatization, developing requests for qualifications and proposals, determining costs, preparing bids and establishing budgetary and performance monitoring systems. He also works to ensure contract service delivery standards are met, develops reporting systems on savings generated, tracks overall contracting activities, and serves as staff to Charlotte's Privatization/Competition Advisory Committee. Mr. Sizer has previously written for the American Public Works Association and International City/County Management Association.

MARGARET M. "PEG" SWANTON is a principal with Tactics, Inc., a management consulting firm with a track record of helping governments and businesses operate more effectively. She has nearly twenty years of professional experience designing business processes that work efficiently, giving management the tools for decision making, and incorporating strong controls—making fraud difficult to commit and easy to detect. Tactics, Inc., a certified Women Owned Business (WBE), is located in Chicago's Loop.

NORMAN WALZER is professor of economics and directs the Illinois Institute for Rural Affairs at Western Illinois University. He has worked with many state and local government agencies and commissions. Walzer has co-authored or edited twelve books and more than 250 articles, reports, and other professional publications on a variety of issues relating to local public finance, economic development and governmental organization. His articles have been published in the *Review of Economics and Statistics,*

Land Economics, National Tax Journal, Industrial Labor Relations Review, and *Finances Publiques,* among others. His most recent book, *Public-Private Partnerships for Local Economic Development,* was published by Praeger in 1998.

MILDRED WARNER is an assistant professor in the Department of City and Regional Planning at Cornell University where her work focuses primarily on the role of local government in community development. Current work focuses on the financial impact of federal and state devolution on local government capacity for investment. She works closely with public sector unions and associations of local elected officials at the state and national levels to build collaborative approaches to service delivery improvements. Previously Warner founded and served for nine years as the Associate Director of the Community and Rural Development Institute at Cornell which linked academic, practitioner and policy maker interests. She has published recently in the *Journal of Planning Education and Research, Rural Sociology,* and *Rural Development Perspectives.*